Voice & Speaking Skills

FOR

DUMMIES®

by Judy Apps

WILEY

A John Wiley and Sons, Ltd, Publication

Voice & Speaking Skills For Dummies®

Published by
John Wiley & Sons, Ltd
The Atrium
Southern Gate
Chichester
West Sussex
PO19 8SQ
England

Email (for orders and customer service enquires): cs-books@wiley.co.uk

Visit our home page on www.wiley.com

For general information on our other products and services, please contact our Customer Care Department within the U.S. at 877-762-2974, outside the U.S. at 317-572-3993, or fax 317-572-4002.

For technical support, please visit www.wiley.com/techsupport.

Wiley also publishes its books in a variety of electronic formats and by print-on-demand. Some content that appears in standard print versions of this book may not be included in e-books or in print-on-demand. If this book refers to media such as a CD or DVD that is not included in the version you purchased, you may download this material at http://booksupport.wiley.com. For more information about Wiley products, visit www.wiley.com.

British Library Cataloguing in Publication Data: A catalogue record for this book is available from the British Library

ISBN: 978-1-119-94512-3 (pbk); 978-1-119-94381-5 (ebk); 978-1-119-94382-2 (ebk); 978-1-119-94383-9 (ebk)

Printed and bound in Great Britain by TJ International Ltd, Padstow

10 9 8 7 6 5 4 3 2 1

WILEY

MIX
Paper from
responsible sources
FSC
www.fsc.org
FSC® C013056

About the Author

Judy Apps is an international voice specialist, coach, author and inspirational conference speaker. She has spent many years unravelling the secrets of how great leaders inspire and for 20 years has coached people from all walks of life – from leaders in major international corporations to executives, politicians, media people and all who want to understand the voice better and communicate with more influence. Judy is a Professional Certified Coach with the International Coaching Federation and a fully qualified NLP Trainer and member of the NLP University Global Trainers' and Consultants' Network. Her popular 'Voice of Influence' open programmes in London include workshops on coaching, voice and influence, leadership and communication, and NLP.

Judy is the author of two books: *Voice of Influence – How to get people to love to listen to you,* a fascinating mind-body approach to finding your authentic voice and expressing yourself with integrity, presence and passion; and *Butterflies and Sweaty Palms – 25 Sure-Fire Ways to Speak and Present with Confidence* – invaluable reading for anyone who's ever faced the fear of public speaking.

Judy is passionate about voice, knowing that by changing your voice you grow in confidence and miracles begin to happen in your life. She combines a thorough vocal knowledge with a whole mind-body approach that's fascinating and highly effective. Her energy and humour are infectious, and her dynamic techniques and highly intuitive way of connecting with people's inner potential have enabled hundreds of people to achieve great leaps in their speaking, charisma and, above all, personal confidence.

Dedication

To those who speak with a voice of truth – we surely need more of them!

Author's Acknowledgements

I would like to thank Kerry Laundon at Wiley for her initial belief in the importance and topicality of a book on voice and in commissioning me to write the book. My grateful thanks too to Rachael Chilvers and Brian Kramer for supporting me through the writing, and to all the production team at Wiley. They are a fantastic lot, all highly focused on producing a book that's the best it possibly can be.

Where does a book come from? So many threads came together to create this one. Long ago, I remember breaking out from the conformity of traditional singing lessons one afternoon and experimenting freely with new ideas with a colleague – very fruitful, thank you Carl! I remember listening to an eloquent speaker with a rich voice at a conference on another occasion and suddenly realising that his opulent voice was boring me – reflecting on that brought important new insights, so thanks, whoever you were. I remember the excitement of beginning to explore mind-body connections through bio-energetics – thank you Alexander Lowen. Such precious threads are too plentiful to enumerate. They include many of my coachees through both their successes and failures. They certainly include many wise voices from the exciting world of books.

Many thanks to the people who shared their voice wisdom with me: Jessica, Mario, Gus and Peter. Many thanks too to those who gave me important insights about communication. They include Robert, Ian, Judy, Stephen, Suzi, Deepak and Jan. Also to friends and colleagues who have given me much in this enterprise. Thank you Kate, Elizabeth, Kit, Jenny, Jackee, Phil, Celia, Gale, Arielle, Richard, Neil, John, Stewart, Alison and Jane.

I would like to thank my friends and family who have been there for me and encouraged me while I've been focused on writing. Special thanks to John who has the sensitivity to be there at every turn with whatever is needed, and to Chris and Rosie who always cheer me on. Also Keith, Di, Sue and John who ask for regular updates! Thanks to my father, who taught me early on to be curious and think for myself.

Publisher's Acknowledgements

We're proud of this book; please send us your comments through our Dummies online registration form located at www.dummies.com/register/.

Some of the people who helped bring this book to market include the following:

Commissioning, Editorial and Vertical Websites

Project Editor: Rachael Chilvers

Commissioning Editor: Kerry Laundon

Development Editor: Brian Kramer

Assistant Editor: Ben Kemble

Technical Reviewer: Cath Baxter, Head of Voice, Mountview Academy of Theatre Arts, London

Proofreader: Kim Vernon

Production Manager: Daniel Mersey

Publisher: David Palmer

Cover Photo: © iStock / selimaksan

Cartoons: Rich Tennant (www.the5thwave.com)

Audio Recording and Production: Heavy Entertainment

Composition Services

Project Coordinator: Kristie Rees

Layout and Graphics: Carrie A. Cesavice, Jennifer Creasey, Joyce Haughey

Proofreaders: Melissa Cossell, Susan Moritz

Indexer: Estalita Slivoskey

Publishing and Editorial for Consumer Dummies

Kathleen Nebenhaus, Vice President and Executive Publisher

Kristin Ferguson-Wagstaffe, Product Development Director

Ensley Eikenburg, Associate Publisher, Travel

Kelly Regan, Editorial Director, Travel

Publishing for Technology Dummies

Andy Cummings, Vice President and Publisher

Composition Services

Debbie Stailey, Director of Composition Services

Contents at a Glance

Table of Contents

Introduction

Your voice is so much part of who you are! You can't leave home without it, and every time you open your mouth it's *your* voice that comes out. You're probably already well aware of this fact because you picked up this book. What if you opened your mouth and people hung on your every word? What if people understood you better – and even appreciated you when you spoke? If you like these ideas, read on!

I've worked with literally hundreds of people in one-to-one consultations and in workshops, and had the pleasure of witnessing again and again the positive life changes that come when you successfully develop your voice. Some people come to me in such fear and trepidation, they can scarcely walk through the door; others consult me to prepare for important international presentations or media interviews. In each case, voice improvement is accompanied by a new inner confidence. They *find their voice* in every sense. That will happen for you too.

When your voice is strong and expressive, doors open for you. Most professions welcome people who sound good and can speak well. People form remarkably fixed and strong opinions based on your voice. I'm sure that you've heard remarks from time to time like, 'she sounds intelligent' or 'he sounds friendly'. Promotion often depends on your voice. Relationships blossom or founder on it.

But you also probably know several people who are unaware of just how much their voices are liabilities. You'd like to spend more time with them, but their voices! Maybe you find a certain man negative when his moaning tone is really what puts you off. Or you find that woman too sharp because of her clipped tones. Or the sheer decibels and shrieking pitch of certain people have you running for cover!

Research and personal experience confirms that body language has a strong impact. Your voice is equally powerful and maybe even more so. The tone of a voice affects others physically with its vibrations. A loud unpleasant voice can feel like an assault on your very person. But equally, the impact can be below the level of consciousness, influencing your view of a person without your realising why.

When you discover how to speak well, you find that people treat you differently, and that you attract different connections. Finding your voice is a journey that takes you beyond the world of sound. As you read through these chapters or work with a voice coach, you find that the ability to speak your mind authentically builds your confidence and allows you to know yourself better. In finding your unique voice, you discover your way of being in the world. You realise that you have something to say. What starts as a quest for a good voice, becomes the discovery of the person you were born to be. You become more at ease in your own skin, and more able to connect successfully with other people. This is a great recipe for success.

So, dip into this book; have a look around. Playing with the instrument that is your voice is a fun thing to do, and the results are sure to be awe inspiring. You can start at any place in the book . . . or if you prefer, just turn the page.

About This Book

This book explores how to use your voice more effectively and influentially in every context. Plenty of books on public speaking exist, but they concentrate mostly on tips for creating presentations. This book gives you the practical help to use your voice powerfully in intimate one-to-one conversations, presentations before enormous audiences and everything in between.

The basics of a great voice are the same whether you wish to connect well with one other person or are booked to speak to an audience of thousands. What I want for you is the ability to use your voice freely and authentically with interest and variety, so that it serves you well on all occasions.

This book is for anyone who wishes to improve their voice – you don't need any previous know-how. You already have all you need, and that's your vocal instrument. That said, if you're an actor or professional speaker you can still find plenty of useful nuggets here to enhance your performance and bring added range and subtlety to your sound.

The journey to acquiring a great voice includes many helpful techniques, but you mainly need to think about *getting out of your own way* to enable your natural full and powerful voice to ring out.

I include audio tracks so that you can hear exactly what I'm describing and understand what you're aiming for as you practise the exercises.

Conventions Used in This Book

You'll recognise the terms in this book; I don't use any medical or other jargon to put you off. I use *italic* text for titles of films and books and for when I get excited and want to emphasise something for your attention. The key concepts in a list and the headings for numbered steps are in **bold**. Web and email addresses are in `monofont`. And that's about it!

What You're Not to Read

The great thing about *For Dummies* books is that you don't have to wade through loads of uninteresting information to get to what you need. By using the Table of Contents, you can easily turn to the pages that are going to be most useful to you and take it from there.

After years of working with clients, I can't resist giving you background information or related stories of interest from time to time; these fascinating but not-essential items are marked so that you can skip them whenever you want. They include:

✔ **Text in sidebars:** The sidebars are shaded boxes that appear here and there. They often contain historical information, background or personal stories.

✔ **The Copyright page:** Unless you're determined to read from cover to cover, you can skip this page of legal language and reprint information!

Foolish Assumptions

I've yet to meet you personally, so I've made a few assumptions about you in writing this book. I'm assuming:

✔ That you have a voice!

✔ That you genuinely want to do something about improving your voice and speaking skills.

✔ That you're willing to have a go.

✔ That you'll approach the exercises with a light heart in a spirit of curiosity and experimentation.

✔ That you're willing to be pleasantly surprised by your efforts.

I wonder if that's foolish . . . I'm thinking not!

How This Book is Organised

I organised *Voice and Speaking Skills For Dummies* in six parts. Each part covers a range of subjects to help you find out about voice, with exercises for you to practise. Each part is divided into chapters, which contain all the information you need to build your skill to a high level. The Table of Contents gives you all the headings to find your way around. The Index is also helpful if you don't see a particular topic in the Table of Contents.

Part I: Introducing the Human Voice

In this part I lay the foundations for exploring voice and speaking skills. You find out about voice coaching, explore the characteristics of successful voices and discover what to listen out for in your own voice and others' voices. You get the opportunity to really listen to your own voice and decide how you want to develop.

Part II: Beginning with Voice Basics

Here you embark upon the all-important foundation of a good voice – how to breathe well while staying open and relaxed. You discover how your whole body has a part to play in producing the sound. With these skills, you can practise freeing your voice and improving its sound. Get ready to have fun playing with vowels and consonants that bring your language alive. You also discover how to speak with clarity so that nobody *ever* misunderstands you again. Here's your opportunity to get good at tongue twisters as well if you wish!

Part III: Playing Your Instrument Well

Now the fun starts! You're able to turn your volume up and down, surprise people with a loud voice, seduce them with a soft voice – and everything in between. Discover how to sustain a slow authoritative pace or energise your listeners with a faster pace. I introduce you to *resonance,* the professional speaker's dream secret for sounding confident, excited, firm, statesmanlike or passionate. As you gain control of your instrument, you discover that you're beginning to move beyond technique to sound authentic and at ease.

Part IV: Beating the Voice Gremlins

In this part, I name and shame the gremlins that have beset your voice in the past! You discover how to overcome whatever blocks you from speaking well, including fear and other emotions, and you expose your various subterfuges. I guide you through the tricky topic of accents and show you how you can have your cake and eat it – in other words, keep your accent but have others listen and clearly understood you. I offer help for stuttering and hesitation, including information on the latest thinking around tackling the stop reflex and becoming fluent.

Part V: Engaging with a Broader Public

This section is the one to consult if you have to give a presentation or speech, so you can both engage your audience and enter the state of mind where you're at your best. I show you how to lead and influence with your voice and how to walk your talk – or rather talk your walk! If you use your voice a lot in your work, this part is for you. You find reassuring advice on keeping your voice in good condition as well as useful material on how to use your voice effectively in different professions.

Part VI: The Part of Tens

These short fun chapters are a famous part of every *Dummies* book. Here you find top tips for sounding as if you mean business, inspirational ideas for increasing your charisma, and invaluable hints for looking after your voice. I also share my ten favourite examples – at the moment! – of great voices for you to enjoy. See whether you agree with my selection.

Icons Used in This Book

Throughout the book you find the following icons to guide you to the important bits and focus your attention:

This icon offers you the opportunity to try certain techniques and ways of speaking and get them 'in the muscle'. Voice work is highly practical. You'll get the most out of it by 'having a go' at exercises with a curious but not too serious frame of mind. You don't have to get things right first time!

The icon highlights particular speakers or speeches that you can find on the Internet. Listen to a particular voice or type of voice and then spend time reflecting on the sound you hear and noticing the response it attracts.

This icon indicates exercises that have an accompanying audio track where you can hear me demonstrating how to approach them. Appendix B lists the audio tracks.

Anecdotes are examples of real-life experiences that I include to help you understand better. The stories are all based on real people with names changed to protect the innocent. Occasionally, I've combined the stories of more than one client to make a point clearer.

This icon reminds you to watch out for points that you're sure to find especially valuable. Note these bits with special care.

This icon indicates handy practical tips that help you get the best out of the vocal exercises and voice work in general.

Where to Go from Here

Jump into any part of the book you wish. I wrote it so that you can start at any point and then dip in and out as suits you. If you don't know where to start, Part I gets you going with an overview of all the voice essentials, and then you can broaden out from there. See what grabs your interest. Rely on the Table of Contents to guide you around.

Voice change happens most easily if you don't make heavy weather of it. So try out any of the suggestions in this book in a spirit of curiosity and play and you'll get the most out of it, just as people do in my workshops. Enjoy the book and have fun with your voice!

Part I

Introducing the Human Voice

In this part . . .

You find out what a huge difference your voice makes to your impact when you speak to people, and you realise why so many prominent figures have decided to work on their voice. You explore the many different exciting possibilities of voice, and discover what voice coaching can do for you. I lay the groundwork for developing your voice to become an excellent speaker, and you get to know your own voice to be ready for an exciting voyage of discovery.

Chapter 1

Having a Great Voice

*W*hen you imagine a great voice, what springs to mind? A beautifully touching scene in a romantic film? A charismatic leader addressing an enraptured audience? A business leader skilfully persuading the board? A parent reading a bed-time story to a child? What a difference having an inspiring voice makes in all these scenarios!

Maybe you picked up this book because you don't like your voice. Many people feel this way for different reasons. Perhaps you dislike your accent or your tone, your lack of volume or the fact that speaking causes you physical problems. Maybe you're curious because currently you take your voice for granted and assume that you're stuck with what you've got, even if you don't particularly like the way you sound. Maybe you know in your heart of hearts that you can speak confidently and effectively – if you just had some advice from a seasoned professional?

Well, you've come to the right place! Your voice matters. It has a big impact on other people. Each time you open your mouth, you can have a profound influence on your success in personal relationships and in your career. Developing your voice is one of the most useful things you can do to improve your prospects in many different arenas. And you *can* change your voice.

In this chapter, you discover what a radical difference developing your voice makes – in terms of your impact, relationships, job opportunities and more. You find out what voice characteristics constitute a great voice and look at how you can acquire those characteristics for yourself.

Your voice as your calling card

Your voice tells people a lot about you – more even than how you look or what you wear. People hear your voice and make immediate assumptions and snap judgements about you.

Do any of the following statements sound familiar?

✔ 'He doesn't sound like leadership material to me.'

✔ 'I'm sure that she liked it – she sounded really pleased.'

✔ 'He despises me; you can just hear it in the way he talks to me.'

✔ 'She doesn't sound authoritative enough to convince people.'

Are people coming to the right conclusions about you when they hear you? If not, it's enormously worthwhile to do something about it. Although many activities in this book are, on the surface, about technique, most have a deeper purpose – bringing your sound and your meaning together in order to have the greatest impact possible.

Trumpeting the Voice

Everyone has a voice, and your voice is your golden opportunity. Your voice is the strongest communication tool you have – *if* it's working for you as you intend.

When I say *voice,* I'm talking actual sounds, not the words you may say. Think about voices you've heard. Just the sheer tone of a voice can irritate you to death, melt your whole being or make your soul soar – you don't even need to understand the speaker's language to feel his or her meaning in your very depths!

The effect of a voice can be devastating. The post office worker who took the fateful warning call before the Birmingham pub bombings in 1974 can still clearly remember the voice of the man at the other end of the phone almost four decades later. 'The way he spoke it was as if he had a grudge against me personally,' he says. 'There was hatred.'

On the other hand, ask someone to describe the person they love, and many times you hear, 'I just love to listen to him,' or 'She has the most beautiful voice.' Something about the voice reaches the innermost recesses of your being and works its magic.

I often refer to the voice as an instrument, but really, having a voice is more like having a whole orchestra, the possibilities are so varied. So if your voice sounds permanently like a strident cornet or a squeaky flute, you're missing out on the other instruments of your voice orchestra – all those other possibilities of expression that can affect people in different ways.

Exploring the power of your voice

Your impressions of others are bound up with how they sound. People's voices impress deeply. They're a living part of who they are and give clues to their character, values, attitudes and current state of mind.

Like everyone else, your tone of voice has the power to lift people up or put them down.

- ✔ As a manager, you can intimidate others with your voice – or make them appreciate your support.

- ✔ As a caregiver, you can frighten or stress other people – or give them such peace of mind that they feel better just being near you.

- ✔ As a leader, you can energise your troops so that they follow you into battle – or so demotivate them that they want to get rid of you.

- ✔ As a teacher or parent, you can give children the confidence to achieve their highest potential – or you can strip them of all belief and self-respect.

- ✔ As a coach, you can use your voice to call others to action, to encourage reflective thinking or to open the way to feeling and emotion – or your voice can sound oppressive and sap others of confidence.

The poet Henry Longfellow said, 'The human voice is the organ of the soul.' Sometimes the living sound of a voice stays with you long after the person speaks. With your voice you have the glorious potential to persuade, to influence and inspire; to woo someone, to affect people deeply or to make their hearts rejoice.

Reaping the rewards of a great voice

I contend that sound matters today more than ever. People who speak easily and well seem to get more opportunities in life. Their words flow and people warm to them. You don't often find a corporate chief executive or senior politician today with an inadequate voice. The rapid political rise of Barack Obama, David Cameron and other prominent politicians started and flourished with brilliant speeches. Look at the popularity of interviewers with the gift of the gab, like Jonathan Ross or Ellen DeGeneres. Note the respect given to anchors who are interesting to listen to, such as Walter Cronkite and Diane Sawyer.

No one can avoid the spoken word. More talking than ever goes on in the workplace – team meetings, conference calls and presentations; offices are arranged open plan for all-day constant communication. Jobs are more vocally demanding. This is the age of the sound bite. You need to sound good.

Former United States Secretary of State Colin Powell, who came from a humble background in the Bronx, claims in his autobiography that working on public speaking early on in his career made all the difference to his success in public life. He committed to becoming a persuasive public speaker and developing his abilities to connect with people and speak from the heart. He was noticed for promotion because he spoke well. His life story shows you not only that effective public speaking brings success, but also that not all great speakers are born. You can make the effort to discover how to do it well.

Powell is by no means the first person whose rise to high office was facilitated by his skill in public speaking. It has been a constant pattern through the centuries. Even 2000 years ago, Cicero, though not from the leading class, rose to the exalted rank of consul of the Roman Empire through the power of his speeches (see Chapter 8). From that time to this, eloquence continues to be an important factor in political success.

Just for curiosity, invent an image of Sir Winston Churchill giving his war-time speeches in a tight little head voice. Absurd, isn't it? The voice *does* matter.

The voice is an integral part of the whole message. In every great speech, the voice brings the message alive and gives it its grandeur. When you speak to someone professionally in a confident voice, they take you seriously. When someone says, 'I love you' in a heartfelt voice, the sound can make the stars shine brighter.

Making small changes for big impact

You may understand that a voice can have a big impact on people but doubt that changing or improving *yours* is possible. You've lived with your voice for a long time, and now it may feel as comfortable as an old shoe. Your family and friends may all speak in the same way. Perhaps by now your voice feels so much part of who you are that you can't imagine how to change it.

Let me encourage you here. You only have to make minor changes to how you speak in order to enjoy big rewards. For example, if your voice sounds just a little bit stronger, other people begin to see you as a stronger person, and then you feel stronger in yourself and begin to act stronger – before you know it, people are treating you with more respect than before. The same cycle plays out when your voice sounds a little more positive, empathetic, caring or genuine. Slight changes bring big results in terms of the impact you have on others – and also therefore on your self-confidence and esteem.

Whatever voice changes you need (or don't need) to make, you can't really ignore your voice because it has the tendency to give you away even when you're trying to create a different impression. For instance, you may want to sound pleased, but the edge in your voice suggests otherwise. Or you seek to impress people with your decisiveness, but your weak tone suggests instead lack of authority.

Take the plunge to discover the power of your authentic voice. The following sections are a voice journey during which I show you how to bring out the innate power of your voice and how to connect with people so that they hear your passion, your empathy, your energy and intellect.

Enjoying the Advantages of Speaking Well

When your voice expresses fully the nuances of what you want to say, then you achieve real communication with others, and all your interactions become easier and more enjoyable. When that happens, other people begin to view you differently, and all manner of possibilities open themselves to you.

I take you through some of the principal advantages of speaking well in the following sections.

Being understood clearly

You may be surprised at the additional clout you have when people can understand you easily.

Mumbling is a sure way to give people the impression that you don't want to be there! It's as if you're saying, 'I sort of want you to hear what I'm saying; no I don't want you to hear after all, or maybe I do; no, no, I don't!'

When you can articulate clearly, people listen to you without strain, and beyond that, they engage with you. Chapter 6 gives you lots of advice and exercises for making your speech clearer and easier to listen to.

Being a pleasure to listen to

It's a wonderful compliment when people tell you that they can listen to you for hours because they love your voice. Getting your message across to an audience is so much easier when they're enjoying the experience!

The key to sounding good begins with breathing well, and Chapter 4 takes you through the whole process of effective breathing for speaking. A good breath allows the sound to *resonate* through your body, giving your tone depth and colour. Go to Chapter 9 for more about resonance and its importance for adding variety and engaging your listeners.

Tension is always the enemy of a good sound. When you're stressed or nervous, your voice usually tightens up and sounds thinner and tinnier. You almost certainly find that you sound best when you're at ease, feeling happy and content, in the comfortable companionship of friends for instance.

Ask a few friends how you sound when you're having a relaxing time compared with when you're more tense. Find out what specific differences they notice in your voice.

Feeling more confident

When I work with people who are nervous, they sometimes tell me that if they gained in confidence they believe they would speak better. That's probably so – and the reverse is also true. If you improve your speaking skills, you gain added confidence straightaway. Speaking well to an audience and receiving a positive response is a great confidence-booster.

Discover how to relax your body when you speak – doing so gives you a freer and stronger voice. I cover relaxation in Chapter 5. Additionally, slowing your pace increases your gravitas and gives you more thinking time too.

Until you try adjusting your tone or pace, you probably don't realise just how people's reaction to you changes when you speak differently. Your adjustments create a circle: the better they react, the more confident you feel and the more powerfully you present – which creates an even better reaction, which in turn makes you feel even more confident which . . . you get the idea!

Conveying authority

Your voice can influence people in many different ways. When you speak with a steadier and lower-pitched voice, you sound authoritative and people pay you more attention and respect. A high squeaky voice just doesn't convey a strong image. When you know how to speak comfortably in a deeper voice, the simple change in your tone can achieve amazing differences in people's perception of you.

Achieving the change is just a matter of adjusting your volume and speed, and pitching your tone of voice lower. Chapter 7 contains helpful advice on how to speak more strongly and steadily, and Chapter 9 shows you how to speak in deeper tones without forcing your voice. In Chapter 17, I give you a whole chapter of ready hints and tips for sounding more authoritative.

Influencing others

Voice coaching techniques can enable you to come across clearly and create a powerful impact. But real influence is subtler and takes you to another level, where you discover how to make a close connection with people through your voice. Through connection people are attracted to follow your lead, and then you begin to influence them more deeply. Chapter 15 shows you how to tune in more accurately to your listeners and create closer rapport.

Influence also depends on the strength of your intent – your internal energy and sense of purpose – which I explore in Chapter 10. Strong intent allows you to influence people with a quiet voice just as much as with a loud one. This inner energy is one of the secrets of influential people that you can readily acquire yourself.

Technique tends to lead speakers to acquire proficient skills that make them sound the same as each other. Influential speakers who use powerful connection and intent sound different from each other – and much more interesting!

Listen to public speakers you admire. Notice how different they are from each other. Each one is authentic in their own way. That's real influence at work.

Inspiring others

Sometimes when I ask coaching clients what they want from our sessions, their faces light up and they tell me they want people hanging on their every word. Sound has the potential to do this.

You have the possibility of inducing positive states in people by the sound of your voice. One person's voice makes you feel warm and comforted; another arouses enthusiasm; a third induces a state of calm. This skill isn't the same as having a voice with a beautiful tone, like a charismatic film star. Of course, a beautiful voice may well put you in a good frame of mind. But more often, inspiration is about using your voice so that your audience catches your emotion and becomes fired up by it, rather than just having a beautiful tone as such.

Dare to express genuine feeling in your voice, and your audience catches the energy of your emotion and is moved by what you say. In Chapter 9, I show you how to use body resonance to express your feelings in sound. You also find useful material in Chapter 18, which gives you hints on how to speak with charisma.

Entertaining people

In public-speaking courses, laughter is rarely mentioned. I did hear a trainer once who announced in a highly serious voice that the only way to begin a presentation successfully was to start with a well-prepared joke to break the ice. But a single pre-prepared joke is not really the point – and right at the start they often fall flat.

Speaking is about entertaining people – or at least keeping their attention – *whatever* you're speaking about. The key is your attitude. You want to give your audience an interesting and pleasurable experience rather than a boring one, even if you're talking about serious or technical topics.

Make entertainment one of your speaking aims. Doing so makes you think in terms of *your listeners'* experience of your presentation or speech rather than focusing on how well or badly you're presenting. As you prepare a presentation, ask yourself the following:

- ✔ What is going to make this presentation interesting for my audience?
- ✔ How can I introduce moments of lightness in this speech?
- ✔ How can I give my audience a good time?

A liberal sprinkling of the following helps:

- ✔ **Variety:** Keep people awake and interested by including a range of subject matter, pace, volume, tone and more.
- ✔ **Spontaneity:** Don't be afraid to make an off-the-cuff comment and to react genuinely to questions. Dare to be real.
- ✔ **Humour:** You don't need to memorise jokes or do clever characters. Just be ready to see the funny side of something (staying appropriate of course!). Some speakers are so buttoned-up and stiff that they don't even respond to the obvious. Much humour just happens if you allow it to.
- ✔ **Enjoyment:** Have a good time – don't bore *yourself*! Then other people will enjoy your presentation too.
- ✔ **Stories:** Use anecdotes, and relevant examples from your own experience to liven your presentation. Turn to Chapter 14 for lots of effective ways to incorporate metaphors and stories into your speaking.

See the audience as friends, not people there to catch you out. Whether your subject is serious or light-hearted, your audience wants to have an enjoyable time, so your job is to help them do that.

Connecting better

Your voice has enormous potential to create *rapport* with other people. Through your voice you can tune in to others, show them that you understand their points of view, reassure them, care for them, encourage them and attract them into your world.

- ✔ With warmth in your voice, you can promote relationships.
- ✔ With firmness in your voice, people heed your words.

✔ With excitement in your voice, they catch your mood.

✔ With calm in your voice, the atmosphere changes and becomes quieter.

The skill to express the emotional energy within you – your warmth, firmness and so on – in the sound of your voice can transform your work as a teacher, coach, trainer, business leader or parent. And it can fundamentally change personal relationships in every part of your life.

When you remember a heated or emotional exchange with someone, you probably remember the words that were said. But the impact of the words was due to the *way* in which they were said rather than the words themselves. You can say 'that's outrageous!' with worldly cynicism, with laughter in your voice or with passionate venom – the expression is what carries the energy of the comment, giving it the power to sooth or wound.

Chapter 9 takes you through ways to vary your voice with different tones. Take note of the 'heart voice' in Chapter 9, which shows you how to express genuine personal connection in your voice. You may also find Chapter 15 useful for discovering how to tune in to other people subtly with your voice.

Finding Out about Voice Coaching

The most obvious way to develop your voice is through voice coaching, and I am your personal voice coach throughout this book.

A voice coach may also be called a voice trainer or teacher, and all three terms are sometimes used for singing coaching. The old word for spoken voice coaching was 'elocution', which focused on getting students to pronounce words clearly and 'correctly' by reciting poetry with 'correct' pronunciation.

Voice coaching today is different. Instead of spending most effort on accent and articulation, a voice coach today focuses on liberating your natural voice (see the following section) in order to give you power and fluency. Politicians and those in public life have used voice coaches for this purpose for many decades. The practice used to be a well-kept secret. Voice coaching seemed unusual and even a bit shameful. Indeed, King George VI's voice coaching has caught the public's attention now because of the successful film, *The King's Speech*, but at the time the establishment hid from the public the fact that the King was being coached. (See Chapter 13 for more on King George and his coach Lionel Logue.)

Voice coaching has become respectable and remarkably common. Many people in the public eye – Princess Diana and David Beckham, as just two examples – received voice coaching. Numerous politicians from John Kennedy and Hillary Clinton to Margaret Thatcher and John Major have worked with voice coaches too. Politicians regularly have coaching to create the impact they need in conference speeches and on other important occasions.

Discovering your natural voice

There's voice coaching and voice coaching! You can learn from a coach or a book how to speak loudly and strongly and even have people admire your voice after your efforts, but that is not what gives your voice a powerful impact on people. The way to an influential voice is through discovering and developing your *natural voice* – the voice you were born to have before you developed the habits of constricting and contorting your voice in various ways through life's ups and downs.

Your voice is unique, and as you develop your voice, you need to maintain the qualities that make it a true expression of you. Discovering your natural voice is about finding the accurate audible expression of your inner intention, including its thinking, feeling and unique energy. If you want to achieve a natural, authentic voice, your mind, emotion and body need to all work in harmony, and this harmonisation is what a voice coach can help you to do.

Facing the challenge

Unlike the simple elocution task of just pronouncing your words properly, voice coaching is all-encompassing and, sometimes, emotional work. Voice sounds remain stored in your sub-conscious, and at times, speaking can stir up emotional – even painful – memories. At the same time, recovering freedom in your voice changes your whole feeling about yourself, in a positive way that is wonderfully liberating.

John, a middle-aged retail manager, came to me for voice coaching with a constricted, buttoned-up voice and expressed his desire to speak freely and expressively. In our sessions, the very first time he relaxed enough to produce a freer voice, he suddenly became tearful. He told me that the experience of speaking more freely, though pleasurable in itself, had awakened a memory of life at home when he was young. He remembered that every time he got excited and burst out with a spontaneous loud comment, his father would tell him that he was tedious and stupid. So he learned not to speak with joy or enthusiasm. This realisation of the origin of his vocal difficulties was an important turning point for him in his voice coaching, and he went on to develop a rich and expressive speaking voice. 'It's not only my voice that's changed; I'm a changed man in every way!', he said to me with satisfaction.

The journey of working on your voice is a highly practical one, and its main ingredients (which I explore in various chapters) include:

- ✔ Discovering good breath control to make your voice expressive and resilient (Chapter 4)
- ✔ Releasing the tensions that can block the breath (Chapter 5)
- ✔ Making your speech clear and distinct (Chapter 6)

- Investing mental energy in speaking loudly as well as quietly (Chapter 7)
- Adding emphasis and strong cadence (Chapter 8)
- Discovering the music of speech (Chapter 8)
- Exploring the possibilities of your whole instrument (Chapter 9)
- Expressing your feeling and passion in speaking (Chapter 9)
- Allowing your inner self to speak through your voice (Chapter 10)

You can discover much to improve your voice through the chapters of this book, and if you practise without straining or forcing you can make excellent progress with your voice on your own. If you decide to contact a voice coach, see the Appendix for tips and resources.

Thinking About What You Want to Develop in Your Own Voice

Before jumping into a series of voice coaching sessions – or even the rest of this book – think about what you want to develop in your voice.

Run through in your head all the times and places where you speak. (Yes, this task may produce quite a list!) Think about where you feel you lack something or are in need of something extra. Your responses may be entirely obvious to you, but often they're not. You don't have to come up with anything precise at this point; you may just get a slight sense on occasions that your voice is letting you down in some way. For example:

- Do you say something and then find that no one seems to have heard you, or do you suspect that people switch off when you talk sometimes?
- Do you get the feeling that people dislike your accent or tone, even when they don't go to the extent of teasing you or commenting upon it?
- Do you feel confident speaking in one part of your life but lack confidence in another? For example, you're happy to explain a system to a colleague at work but get tongue-tied talking one-to-one on a social occasion? Or vice versa?
- Do you sometimes say something only to have people take it the wrong way so you feel misunderstood?
- Does your voice let you down physically from time to time, even mildly? For example, you get too much phlegm or find you want to clear your throat.
- Do you find it hard to get your words out sometimes?

Jot down your thoughts. Your answers to the preceding questions give you clues as to how to proceed with developing your voice. Whatever your particular issues, working on the basics of good voice production helps you at the outset. The basics consist of breathing well (Chapter 4), freeing up your body (Chapter 5) and speaking clearly (Chapter 6).

After you consider the basics, think about the particular occasions when you want your voice to work better for you. The following are requests I hear most often from clients.

Getting people to listen to you

Nothing is as frustrating as not being listened to – particularly if you've something worth saying. Apart from being audible enough and clear enough, some people just attract listeners. Try doing what they do:

- **Speak slowly enough to be heard and understood.** Are you rushing to get your words out so they tumble over each other? Have a look at Chapter 7 for techniques to sustain a more measured pace.

- **Increase interest with variety and emphasis.** If you mumble or speak in a monotone, go to Chapter 8 where I explain how to add emphasis and impact to your speech. Chapter 11 offers a helping hand if you tend to mumble.

- **Speak in an adult voice.** If your voice sounds rather high and young, work on allowing your voice to resonate lower in your body. Chapter 9 shows you how.

- **Break into conversations firmly.** If you find that people speak over you, use a contrasting tone of voice to introduce what you say.

- **Have confidence that you'll be heard.** This sentence sounds like a Catch 22 – if you knew you'd be heard, you'd be confident! Having confidence is about your intention and attitude. Find out more about it in Chapter 10.

The skill of getting others to listen to you is vital in the workplace, for addressing a meeting, presenting to the board, making a sales pitch, bidding for a tender and countless other occasions. If this skill is relevant for you, check out Chapter 14 on developing your public voice and Chapter 16 on developing a professional voice.

Working with your accent

If you dislike your accent or hesitate to open your mouth because you worry about your accent, take heart – you don't have to entirely change your natural way of speaking to get the results you want.

At the beginning, your accent may seem to you to be the most glaring negative factor in how you speak, but it usually turns out not to be. An accent itself is seldom entirely to blame; rather, the problem is more often just some aspect of the way that you speak that you can change without too much difficulty. For example, if when speaking in your natural accent your voice sounds high or thin, or throaty or harsh, you can deal with those aspects of your voice production, rather than 'correcting' how you pronounce every little word and phrase.

Saying what you mean and meaning what you say

Well, of course you *intend* to say what you mean! Yet sometimes people get you wrong. They fail to take you seriously, or think that you're angry when you're not. Or they call you patronising when that is farthest from your mind. More than likely, they're picking up something in your tone of voice.

One of the most valuable ways you can develop your voice is to ensure that people understand not just your words but the intention behind your words. Get your words and intention to line up and you can avoid an awful lot of misunderstanding!

Feeling nervous or self-conscious affects your voice, and you may sound squeaky, or you may mumble and trip over you words. Your voice also comes out 'wrong' when you're too eager to please and put in too much effort. Some people make earnest efforts not to show emotion when they speak or play an artificial role, and as a result sound like drones or automatons. In Chapter 11, I give you strategies for overcoming some of these 'gremlins' of speaking and show you how to find the true power of your voice through being more authentic.

Developing a robust, healthy voice

Your voice is so important to you, you must develop it in a way that promotes its well-being. That doesn't mean you have to wrap your voice in cotton wool. Your voice is fairly tough. Babies don't lose their voices – even after hours of loud vocal exercise!

Singers and actors look after their voice, and if you're in any sort of talking profession you need to take special care. Chapter 16 gives particular indicators for you if you work in a talking profession. If, on a regular basis, your voice breaks, your throat hurts, your jaw aches or you lose your voice entirely, you're doing something wrong and need to do something about it! Chapter 19 offers you tips for looking after your voice and the Appendix has lists of professionals and organisations to contact if you have serious problems.

Becoming fluent

Most people aspire to be able to speak fluently and easily whenever the occasion arises. If you feel that you aren't fluent, the reasons can be physical or mental – or both.

Physically, lack of fluency is often connected with poor breathing. Shortness of breath can cause you to rush and mumble, tail off, hesitate, stutter and even sound confused. Good breathing makes a *huge* difference. Simply slow down and follow through with your breath (see Chapter 4).

Fluency is one of the first things affected by your mental state. As soon as you feel you're going to make a mistake or can't think what you're going to say, you find that you can't start to say anything at all! If this situation sounds familiar, my first suggestion is still, 'breathe!', but other remedies are worth considering. Slow down and take your time. With a bit more space, your mind is able to order itself. Secondly, use plenty of emphasis as you speak. Emphasis enables you to focus on the important words and remember where you're heading in a sentence. I give you a few ideas about what to do if you get tongue-tied in Chapter 11.

If you call yourself a stutterer, fluency may seem out of reach. Help is at hand in Chapter 13! I draw on some of the latest research into stuttering to give you successful strategies for attaining fluency.

Identifying Good Voices

Developing your voice involves technique, but technique alone doesn't give a voice its impact and magic.

What *does* a great voice consist of? I give you ten examples of great voices in Chapter 20, and they all have special qualities that go well beyond technique. In my view, a great voice is vibrant and alive and sounds genuine. It connects with an audience and creates a bond between speaker and listener. This kind of voice has a sense of purpose behind it. All these qualities contribute to a great voice and I explore each of them in the following sections.

The alive voice

An excellent voice vibrates with an ever-changing sense of being alive. A voice can be strong, loud and even impressive without being great. A great voice communicates through constantly varying nuances of expression – a slight emphasis here, a light tone there, firm certainty here, a suggestion of hesitation there – and in this way expresses a whole range of feelings and thoughts. The alive voice convinces, inspires, comforts, amazes, reassures and influences in turn.

The effect of a voice that's alive is that listeners feel they're listening to a person, not a voice.

At a high pressure event, Amanda had to report on a new research project in which she'd been involved. She stuck closely to her prepared speech with its accompanying slides, speaking in a dull formal voice, actually reading much of the text off her slides. Suddenly, the projector broke down. After a minute or so of confusion (and inner panic), Amanda, in her desperation, had an idea. She said in quite a different informal voice. 'Well, that's the formal part of the proceedings, and now I'd like to tell you a bit more about my own experience in our new area of research.' She then talked about her project in a conversational tone that drew her audience in. The topic was genuinely interesting for her, and her voice expressed it. Her audience found the presentation – and her – fascinating. Amanda had discovered something she'd never forget – if you want to connect with your audience, nothing compares with bringing your live humanity to the party.

The authentic voice

When you listen to great voices of the past, the quality of authenticity is one that always shines out. A great voice never fakes it. Listen to Nelson Mandela at his trial in 1962, or the novelist Toni Morrison's Nobel lecture in 1993.

Every time you pretend to be something you're not, your voice takes on a quality that at some level sounds inauthentic. If you're open, at ease and free, your voice reflects that. Then when you mean something, the sound of your voice expresses it.

Authenticity is a physical and mental thing. Your body needs to be relaxed enough for sound to resonate freely, but your mind also needs to be bold enough to allow you to be yourself. Being authentic can make you feel vulnerable, but the effect is for you to sound more powerful. In Chapter 17, you find useful tips for becoming more authentic as a speaker.

The connecting voice

Communicating with your voice is all about making a connection. You may think that giving a great presentation is about speaking powerfully and impressing people, and that's fine and good. But if you listen to the greatest speakers of past and present, you find that they have the additional skill of being able to tune in to an audience and create a link.

To connect with others, you need more strings to your bow:

✔ **Meet your audience where they're at.** Get a sense of their culture, sense their mood and through language, voice and energy meet them in their space. Have the flexibility to change your approach to appeal to your audience.

✔ **Don't hide behind formal language and style.** Instead, use current colloquial language and speak directly to people.

✔ **Speak to your audience personally**. Talk to them as if you're speaking one-to-one with each person in your audience. Tell personal stories and anecdotes that give the audience glimpses of who you are.

✔ **Be the real thing.** Let your voice be honest, open and true.

In Chapter 15, I explain how to tune in to your listeners and create strong connections.

Making connection is the key to successful personal conversations and intimate relationships, and your voice plays a big part. When you can express empathy, caring and love in your voice, connecting with others becomes natural and easy.

The voice that has something to say

A voice empty of meaning isn't worth much. A great voice has a sense of purpose and something to communicate. Listen to Ben Zander talking about music and passion, or Shukla Bose talking about schools for slum children. As a speaker, even in a one-to-one conversation, you have a gift to give the other person in your speech. When your voice works beautifully, it conveys the full message you want to share, and your listeners receive what you have to offer.

Think in terms of your intention when you speak. To uncover your intention, ask yourself:

✔ What do I want – for me and the other person?

✔ What am I trying to say?

✔ What's important about what I want to communicate?

✔ What is my gift in this conversation?

Starting Out

You aren't starting from scratch when you set out to develop your voice. You've probably had a lot of speaking practice before you ever pick up this book – a lifetime!

Collecting voices

Keep a sound archive of voices you love. Search You Tube for clips from television and film and create a folder of your favourites. (*iPod and iTunes For Dummies* by Tony Bove will show you how if you aren't technical.) Enjoy researching and finding wonderful voices. Make notes for yourself of what you like about each speaker. The more you listen to voices you like, the easier it becomes to replicate what you hear. After all, we all learned to speak in the first place by listening to our parents or carers – this method is tried and tested!

As you practise listening to other speakers, your listening skills improve. You start to hear more subtle differences in people's voices. Think of the whole process as a wonderful detective game. When you're convinced by someone, listen for a firm chest sound in their voice. Listen to how the voice drops lower for words spoken with emotion. Listen to the lightness in the voice when the person is happy or excited. These variations in sound give you the potential to express yourself powerfully and authentically.

Include live speakers in your research too. When you hear someone you admire, watch out for the response of others to their delivery. Notice what gets a good response from the audience. Build up an awareness of what works and what doesn't. Try out the different voices you hear, talk as if you are that person, and take on for yourself the characteristics that you like.

So, before you go any further, take stock of where you are, and get to know what your own voice sounds like. You find much more about this topic in Chapter 3. Then you can look at what needs to change for you to sound the way you want. Keep in mind how you would like to be able to speak. I suggest one excellent way for getting to know what you like and honing your listening in the sidebar 'Collecting voices'.

All right, it's true: you'll meet the odd hiccup from time to time, those old gremlins of fear and anxiety, or feelings of helplessness or hopelessness. Part IV tackles voice gremlins – those personal blocks that get in the way of speaking to your full potential. I include accents in this part as they often present themselves as gremlins. Probably the most challenging of the gremlins is stuttering, and you find some of the exciting latest resources for gaining fluency in Chapter 13.

If at times the task of developing your voice seems daunting, trust that you will get to that place you want to get to. And you will.

Choosing your method

Voice work is an activity of the body as well as the mind. In fact, it works best if you get quite physical when you're practising sounds. Although your vocal folds, your mouth and tongue and even your thinking all appear to happen above your shoulders, your voice's power comes from your main body below – from a robust breathing system, strong stance, and the energy felt in your body that gives power to the sound of your words (see Chapters 4 and 5).

Whether working with a coach or trying the various activities in this book, you can start your voice work at various points:

- ✔ Delving into the nuts and bolts of breathing, relaxation and articulation.
- ✔ Creating the flexibility to produce a free and expressive voice.
- ✔ Building the strength of your intention to speak and communicate, which gives your sound energy.

You can also start your vocal journey, from the point of simply enjoying language. Listen out for the music and rhythm of language that brings speech alive. Try out different rhythms and emphasis; speak loudly, softly, slow and fast just for the joy of it.

Finding yourself in your voice

The examples of great voices in Chapter 20 include actors, politicians, broadcasters and activists, men and women – and each one sounds unique. In developing your voice, you must find *your* voice, the voice that best expresses you. I explain how to find your unique voice in Chapter 10.

Speaking to your full potential is more than just getting people to listen to you. When you find your authentic voice, you're also finding your identity. You gain in confidence in every way, and know more surely who you are. Finding your voice is a great adventure, and I hope you enjoy it!

Chapter 2

Exploring the Amazing Human Voice

The human voice is powerful. Throughout history, voices have moved people and swayed opinions. Although words are important, they aren't essential. The voice's power is in the sound. I'm sure that even before language, when prehistoric man shouted 'Aaahhh!' from a mountaintop, his tribe down below could tell from the sound whether it meant, 'I've caught supper' or 'I've been attacked by a sabre-toothed tiger!' – and responded by stoking the fire or rushing to the rescue.

Before the printed word, the voice alone carried a group's history via spoken stories. Each telling of a story was a new telling; the different tones and variations played major parts in creating the story's impact. People listened intently and were moved by the sound of words. Words *were* sounds. Even after the introduction of the printed word, the great speeches were what caught the public imagination.

In the following sections, I take a quick tour of the highs and lows (sometimes literally) of powerful voices. Along the way, I break through some unhelpful assumptions about voices, including your own, and set you on the path to developing your unique, powerful voice.

Discovering the Power of Voices

Talk is the currency in today's world. People are talking more today than ever before. Just think about it. You chat on mobiles and Skype; you contact help-lines and call centres; you have access to YouTube, DVDs, film and TV; you listen to 24-hour news, chat shows, discussion groups and interviews on every subject under the sun.

Even with the rise of email and other forms of electronic messaging, business is conducted vocally. Managers spend more time in meetings than ever before. They talk to colleagues across the globe through video conferencing and webinars. Speaking is essential when approaching potential customers, launching products and making bids.

Politics today is about personality and sound bites. You listen to politicians in action on radio and TV. You expect these leaders to be articulate champions in interviews, debates and on the podium. People say that the issues are paramount, but most choose leaders based on how they look and sound. Memorable phrases and media gaffs alike are taken up and repeated endlessly. A leader's televised speeches hold more sway than his or her party's programme of reforms.

Voices that changed history

At pivotal moments, words spoken with emotional power literally have changed the course of history. The voices of the following moments were all different, their moods and energy quite different, but they all shared the ability to hold audiences enraptured and transform opinion.

- When Queen Elizabeth I spoke to the English Army in 1588, the troops were galvanised to great deeds and came through victorious over the Spanish Armada. Her famous words have come down in history: 'I have but the body of a weak and feeble woman; but I have the heart of a king.' In her day, she had to speak directly to the troops without amplification in the open air so her voice had to have the power to carry.

- President Abraham Lincoln's Gettysburg address is an unforgettable landmark in American history. At just two minutes long, this speech made Lincoln's listeners feel part of something greater than themselves and exhorted them to ensure the survival of America's democracy so that, in the famous words, 'government of the people, by the people, for the people, shall not perish from the earth'.

- Nelson Mandela addressed the court from the dock at his trial in 1964. He said of his ideal of democracy and equal opportunity, 'It is an ideal for which I am prepared to die.' His uncompromising and dignified courage gave hope to millions. His is the slow, emphatic and well-reasoned voice of a lawyer, yet the passion in his sound is electrifying.

- Barack Obama's 2008 campaign speeches drew audiences into his passion and focus in a way that almost seemed to surprise the nation. In that campaign, his voice, with its powerful mix of preacher, politician and friend, brought him more than 65 million followers.

In Chapter 20, I shine the spotlight on ten great voices of today and the recent past. Go also to Ted Talks at www.ted.com for riveting talks by inspirational people from around the world.

Spend a few minutes listening to YouTube clips of politicians – past leaders, current candidates, famous political creatures, whatever you fancy. However, don't look at the images or pay attention to the messages as each clip plays. Cover your computer monitor, turn away your chair or close your eyes and listen to the voices. What impression does each voice give you. What is it that you like in each voice? What do you dislike?

A powerful voice doesn't require a mighty sound. A simple authentic voice can be powerful, and have a great impact in private moments. You probably remember the exact tone of voice in which someone said to you, 'I love you'.

Voices have the potential to move people deeply. It's not the words themselves; they can sometimes be ordinary. It's not the volume either; that can be quite soft. It's the intensity and emotional truth. An amazing voice isn't only something that has to be worked at from the outside; it happens from the inside too.

Hearing All the Sounds that Make Up Your Voice

The 21st century world is noisy, with many different ways to speak. Your voice differs from others' voices in several major ways and for several noteworthy reasons:

- ✔ **Your language, especially your first language, influences how you speak.** More than 6,700 distinct languages are spoken in the world, and each one uses the voice in subtly different ways. Compare the deep sounds of Finnish with the 'nightingale' voices of some Japanese speakers; the strong emphasis of German with the singing rhythms of Italian. Hear the subtly differing pitches of Vietnamese and the guttural sounds of some middle-eastern languages.

- ✔ **You probably retain at least a shadow of your childhood accent in your voice today.** English is the official language of about 341 million people in more than 50 countries. However, its accents range from the commanding tones of the UK establishment to the questioning cadences of Sydney; from the confident fast talk of New Yorkers to the sing-song rhythms of Indo-Caribbean people. Even within today's interconnected world, accents abound. Travel within 100 miles of London, and you come across the notably different accents of London Cockney, Surrey Received Pronunciation and slower rural Hampshire and Dorset with its faintly American drawl. Accents throughout the southern US are similarly rich and varied within a relatively small geographic area. Chapter 12 digs deeper into accents.

Accent refers to the distinct different pronunciations of words, the varied rhythms and ups and downs of pitch in different parts of the world. When people refer to *dialect*, they include accent but go beyond it to incorporate different grammatical usage and even vocabulary. Many dialect words are so wonderfully descriptive, they've slipped into general usage. But others remain impossible to understand: 'Haud yer wheesht!' says someone from Scotland for example – 'Be quiet!'

Listen to someone who has always lived in the country and then to someone who lives in a city. For example, compare the voices in *Sex and the City* with those in *Emmerdale*. What differences do you hear? Country dwellers tend to have slower, more musical voices while city dwellers often speak more sharply and quickly. In fact, city people probably have more in common vocally with cosmopolitan speakers across the Atlantic than with their nearer country neighbours!

- **Your profession and previous jobs most likely affect your speed, pitch, enunciation, tone and other vocal qualities.** Think of the smooth flow of the barrister, the fast patter of the fish market auctioneer, the prayerful intoning of certain Christian priests, the rapid chatter of young students and the smooth spiel of the sales presenter.

- **Your voice changes with age.** Listen to the uninhibited high calls of children in the playground, the flat tones of uncommunicative teenagers, the sharp quips of young adults, the stentorian tones of middle-aged officials, the frail murmurs and 'pipes and whistles' of old age.

- **Your health affects the way you sound.** If you lack energy, your voice sounds less robust. If your breathing is affected by illness, people can often hear it in your voice. If you're bouncing with health, your voice sounds vibrant.

How you approach voice development depends on your starting point and what you want to achieve (see Chapter 1 for more on goals). Working on your voice is an exciting project, one that can lead you to discover more about how you make sounds and more about who you really are. Whatever your goals, the journey starts with getting curious about people's voices – and, of course, your own.

Listen to the voices of two different friends the next time you're on the phone. Pay less attention to *what* they say – and more attention to *how* they say things. What information can you pick up from just their voices? To what extent can you hear where they come from? If you didn't know them already, would you be able to guess from their voices what they do for their living? Do they sound their age – or would you guess they were younger or older?

Dispelling Voice Myths

The qualities of voices are important and much discussed in the current world. Yet oddly in everyday life, most people act as if they can't do much about their own voice. Voices don't change – or can they? Before I get down to the practical nuts and bolts of speaking, I need to clear up some all-too-common misconceptions about voices.

Myth 1: You're stuck with your voice

Most people still think that the voice they have currently is the voice they were born with and that they can't do much about it. Perhaps you think this too.

Whether you hate your voice, love it or struggle with it in some way, many people believe that they can't use their voices differently – or that doing so is incredibly difficult. Furthermore, you may feel too that your voice is in some way *you,* and that changing your voice is a bit radical, like losing your identity.

Leaders and celebrities have long worked on their voices, and voice coaching is gaining in popularity over a wide spectrum.

In the early days of her leadership of the UK's Conservative party, Margaret Thatcher's voice in Parliament was piercing and shrill. Her advisers were keen for her to change it. She worked hard at her delivery with a voice coach and eventually acquired the deep breathy tones that characterised her television interviews. However, she was sometimes ridiculed in the media for it and the general opinion was that the new voice was artificial or pasted on somehow. However, her deeper tones gave her increased gravitas, and did increase the respect of the general public. Listen to the 'Downing Street Years' clips on YouTube, starting with the beginning of episode 1 from 1971, and then flipping quickly to episode 4. What a difference!

Today more and more people are developing their voices, sometimes significantly, sometimes more subtly. They're changing regional accents, class accents, pitch and tone and appreciating the different response they get as a consequence.

You *can* change your voice – and when you change your voice, you get a better reaction from other people and a more positive feeling about yourself.

Myth 2: Your voice is out of your control

This myth links to the preceding one. If you believe that your voice is something you're born with, you may also believe that your voice is out of your hands when things go wrong. You realise how important your voice is – and know how difficult life becomes when you lose it – but your voice does what it does regardless of your actions.

Changes in your voice, including negative changes, are most likely due to human factors:

- ✔ If you sing karaoke in a crowded pub and then stand on a freezing train station for hours without a scarf, you may lose your voice!
- ✔ If you produce your voice badly, you put a strain on your vocal cords and may eventually damage them permanently.
- ✔ If you never rest your voice, it never gets a chance to recover and becomes more prone to damage.
- ✔ Your diet may also affect your voice. Certainly, smoking and drinking to excess don't improve its tone!

Chapter 19 has more ideas about looking after your voice.

You can do *plenty* about your voice. You can develop your voice just as you can build up your muscles or develop your dance moves. The entire process is about being interested, picking up the skills and practising them. Your original speaking was learned, so you can definitely learn how to talk differently – and *better* – now!

Myth 3: Words matter more than voice

Many people continue to believe that only the words matter, and that how you say them is of secondary importance. In today's world of dynamic omnipresent audio and video, you encounter an enormous amount of communication in print – including emails, text messages, the Internet, newspapers, magazines, books and articles – which encourages people to think that communication is only about words.

When you prepare a speech – even just a short introduction at a meeting or dinner party – your first instinct is usually to write down on paper the words (or an outline of the words) you intend to say, and then as a second phase, work out *how* you're going to say them. Within today's heavily scripted, public-relations driven environment, the printed speech is the thing. The press often receives printouts of political speeches or corporate announcements before anyone actually delivers them, which enables the press to report bizarrely that 'the Prime Minister *will* announce today that . . . ' But the influence of the printed word is nothing compared with the influence of an inspirational speaker. *How* you deliver those words makes all the difference – and can even change emphasis and meaning without altering a word.

Ray is an executive working for an international insurance company who had put immense effort into getting the words just right for an upcoming conference speech. By the time he came to me for coaching, he'd honed the text of his remarks and was pretty confident that his presentation was inspiring and his message upbeat. Then he read the speech to me. What a let down! His flat tone was so boring that I failed utterly to keep my mind on what he was saying. Inspiring words turned into lacklustre delivery; an upbeat message became a depressing experience for listeners. My reaction while listening to him showed him that communication is more than the words you choose. Ray worked with me on finding what really mattered about his message, and communicating his energy and passion to his audience. His delivery was transformed and on the important day his presentation provoked an enthusiastic response.

If you convey an upbeat message in a downbeat way, the impression is downbeat. Delivery always wins out over words. See Chapter 9 for more ways to awaken the enthusiasm in your voice.

You can tell that many people think in terms of the written word if you ever see a written speech with annotations. Speakers often include visual reminders to 'express' their written words in particular ways. They add exclamation marks, write in bold, italics, different sizes and colours, or even add instructions and performance markings in the margins. A few reminders can clearly be helpful, but with too many it's as if the speech starts as written words and has to have the expression put on top. Certainly, a teleprompter instruction 'Pause and smile here' is more likely in the heat of the moment to produce an awkward grimace than a genuine warm smile! You can find more about preparing and reading from scripts in Chapter 14.

The trouble with the written word is that until you say the words aloud and your audience hears *how* you say them, you don't fully understand their impact.

When you listen to others, the meaning of what they say isn't the same as the words they use. The sound is what conveys the sense most accurately. In *Through the Looking Glass* by Lewis Carroll, Humpty Dumpty asserts: 'When I use a word . . . it means just what I choose it to mean – neither more nor less.' To this I say, 'Of course it does, Mr Dumpty.' Interestingly, without knowing my *tone of voice*, you can't tell whether I agree or disagree. If I say it with a high-pitched energetic voice, I may be expressing genuine enthusiasm. If I say it in a slow drawl without a rise in tone, I'm probably expressing sarcasm. Try saying the phrase a few different ways yourself right now. Notice how changing your tone of voice can actually change the meaning of the phrase from one sense to its very opposite. Obviously, getting your tone to match your meaning is important; I cover the topic in more detail in Chapter 10.

The many meanings of 'love'

You can consult a dictionary to check the meaning of words and usually feel pretty confident that the definition you find is correct. But dictionary definitions are based on actual usage, and that can change from situation to situation. It all depends how you *say* the word.

Before the first English language dictionary in the 17th century cast the meanings of words in stone (well, print), there was more fluidity about the meanings of words. In everyday usage, people accepted that the precise meaning of words depended on inflection and tone as well as visual clues from expression and body language.

Take the word 'love' for instance: a wife and a husband love each other; teenagers love their school mates ('loads' according to Facebook); people love dogs; they love oysters; they love working out; they love their religion; they love arguments or troublemaking; they love truth and dignity. Love absolutely abounds, but the meaning of the word is heavily dependent on context. If you shout, 'I love you' and take another person by the shoulders and shake him or her, the meaning is certainly not the same as if you whisper gently 'I love you' as you gaze adoringly into your beloved's eyes.

It's not what you say – it's how you say it. Or even more specifically, it's not what you say – it's how you make your listener feel!

When Sarah's new boss asked her to come into the office at the weekend to clear the backlog of work, she quipped to him, 'What a great way to spend a Saturday!' She relied on his sense of humour to catch the irony in her tone. His response however indicated that the satire was lost on him. 'I'm glad you think that way,' he said earnestly, completely missing the nuance, 'I think it's really important to get ahead of the competition, don't you? I'm thinking of starting a Saturday rota for the team. Great to know you'll be behind me.'

Misunderstandings based on tone can occur particularly easily in cross-cultural exchanges where two parties interpret certain vocal qualities differently. British straight-faced jokes are often misunderstood by foreigners, who expect a different tone for humour. Indian tonal inflection can sound dogmatic to western listeners when no domineering attitude is intended. Find out more about cross-cultural concerns in Chapter 11.

Myth 4: Only looks really count

Think of this myth as the flipside of the preceding one. You may live in a world full of sound, but appearance is the real star of the show. In terms of time, money and attention, appearance wins out every time:

- ✔ The fashion industry churns out clothes for every occasion, while the jewellery industry adds all those 'essential' details.

✔ The beauty industry promotes make-up, creams and lotions, while hair-stylists, beauticians, manicurists, and myriad other specialists tend to every part of your body.

✔ The personal training and plastic surgery industries tend to every part that may not be keeping up – from kickboxing to Botox and beyond – all in the effort to look good.

Look at your own experience. Are you more concerned about what you look like than about what you sound like? Take a mental inventory of how much money, time and attention you spend on your appearance every year.

✔ Think about how much you spend on clothes as well as grooming, make-up, haircuts, style magazines, facials, manicure, plastic surgery.

✔ Consider how many hours you spend going shopping or trawling the Internet, looking after your clothes, having your hair cut, your nails done, your legs waxed, brushing your hair and just looking at yourself in the mirror.

✔ Ponder what you do before leaving the house in the morning. Do you look at yourself in the mirror and check your appearance? Do you examine your complexion, your hair and your outfit?

Now think about your investment of money, time and attention in your voice. Do you spend any money or time to improve your voice? Do you check out your voice before leaving the house? Don't be surprised if these questions sound odd. Nearly everyone focuses more on appearance!

And yet, the all-consuming importance of appearance is a myth. Yes, when you meet someone for the first time, you do tend to pay conscious attention to appearance and general presentation. And yes, in *sounding out* others initially, you probably only pick up their accents or notice if a voice is especially beautiful or particularly unpleasant. But your deeper, subconscious reactions to others' voices are massive and powerful. You may not consciously give what you hear from another person your complete attention, but you're making meaning from people's sound all the time, as I explore in the following section.

Digging Deeper into How You React to Voices

Spend a few minutes in a space with other people, just listening for a moment to the array of different voices around you. What pitches, speeds, and rhythms do you hear? Can you tell anything about people's energy level or moods?

While listening to others' voices, have you ever:

✔ Cringed when a high-pitched shrieking voice assaulted your ears?

✔ Squeezed your lips together in irritation when someone made a request of you using a hard-edged dominating tone?

✔ Been moved to tears when someone stated their feelings simply or honestly?

✔ Become galvanised to do something based on a friend's confident tone?

✔ Had an initially positive estimation of someone quickly shatter when he or she started to speak?

✔ Felt disconnected when a person's voice clashed with his or her appearance? Perhaps you met someone slim and petite with an overpowering voice, or someone who looked fighting fit with a thin and strangulated voice. How did you feel talking to that person?

Other people's voices affect you – profoundly and usually to a much greater degree than you realise.

Experiencing sound's physical power

Sound has a physical impact on you. If you've ever stood on a train station when a fast train shot through, you'll recall the thunderous roar of the engine and the vibration you felt in your body. Sound moves you. You can't separate sound and vibration.

In the same way, when people speak, the timbre of their voice – their particular vibration – enters your ears and creates sympathetic vibration inside your body as well, creating a pleasant or unpleasant effect. You can't avoid the resonance inside yourself. You can't shut yourself off from sound as easily as you can shut your eyes against something you don't want to see. If the vibration is unpleasant, you have a negative reaction to the person; if the vibration is pleasant you feel positively towards the individual. Sound touches you, deep within your body. Sound *is* feeling in a literal way. So when you react spontaneously to a voice, *feeling* informs your reaction.

Responding to sound's vibrations

Because voice sounds vibrate inside you, voices can move you. (The word *emotion* is a reminder that feelings include a sense of motion or vibration.)

You may warm to a voice or get turned on by a voice. You may respect, believe or trust a voice; and equally mistrust, fear or disbelieve a voice.

✔ Listen to the American actor James Earl Jones. Many clips are available online. Rich and deep tones resonate from his huge frame. People who've worked with the actor report that his sound seems to come from deep within him, right from the heart. They report that they hear his voice deep within themselves too. Yet for all its power, Jones's voice also has the potential for laughter. His voice is 'a voice that can melt butter' in the words of one commentator.

✔ For contrast, listen to the actor Vincent Price. Well known for his scary voice, he played dozens of villains and creepy characters throughout his career. Listening to his meaningful emphases and chilling lighter tones literally makes people's hair stand on end.

A practical joker, Price once attended a showing of one of his horror films and sat directly behind an unsuspecting couple. When the part came up where he spoke with his scary voice in the film, he spoke from behind the couple in that very voice. Talk about inner vibration; they leapt out of their seats!

With such a strong largely unconscious reaction to people's voices, it isn't surprising that it plays an important part in our response to celebrities.

ANECDOTE

Hearing before seeing can be confusing!

I'd already spoken to my colleague David on the phone many times before I met him. He had a hesitant, light and rather nasal voice. I pictured him as young and thin with a slightly nervous air. I looked forward to mentoring and encouraging him in his trip down south to my office.

He arrived at the station along with two other male colleagues. One was quite slight and dressed formally with short smoothed-back hair, one was portly and elderly, and the other man had the broad shoulders and look of an American footballer.

The elderly man spoke first – in a gruff voice, so that wasn't my colleague. The smartly dressed man then introduced himself in confident aristocratic tones – different again. And then the 'American footballer' spoke and I recognised the thin nasal tones immediately. The shock of the mismatch meant that I was scarcely able compose my features to welcome them to London!

Of course, confusion may happen the other way around too. You meet people whose looks give you a weak impression and the force of their delivery when they open their mouth makes you step back in shock. Just one more indicator of the power of sound to influence your views of people!

Think of three or four celebrities – for example Margaret Thatcher, Barack Obama and Catherine, The Duchess of Cambridge (Prince William's wife). Imagine each celebrity speaking with someone else's voice. Imagine Margaret Thatcher speaking with the squeaky voice of the airhead Bubble in *Absolutely Fabulous*. How about Barack Obama speaking in public with the small high voice of David Beckham? Now try Catherine, Duchess of Cambridge with the raucous voice of the cockney journalist, Janet Street Porter. Some people report that the examples feel so wrong that they're impossible to imagine. Certainly, after doing this exercise, you'll find it hard to maintain that tone of voice doesn't make a difference. The voice is such a mark of the person that a change of voice seems to alter fundamentally their identity. With a changed voice, they come across as a different person.

Perhaps people respond unconsciously to *your* voice. How might people regard you differently if you developed your voice and sounded different? Would they take you more seriously? Warm to you more? Prepare to change people's assumptions about you!

Making meaning from voice sounds

When you have a physical reaction to someone's voice, you instantly make meaning from your reaction. For example:

- ✔ If people have robust voices, you tend to consider them confident.

- ✔ If they have deep voices, you're more disposed to take them seriously.

- ✔ If they speak quite fast and energetically, you consider them quick-witted.

- ✔ If adults speaks with very high pitch, you're likely to consider them silly or naïve.

- ✔ If they speak driving the voice hard into the nose, you think of them as insensitive or boorish.

- ✔ If you hear hesitation in the sound, you assume you're speaking to an unconfident person.

People interpret voices in a myriad of different ways, and most of this happens in an instant without you giving it conscious awareness.

Your voice is amazing because of what you can do with it in terms of sound, not only because of the words you choose. Take the time to familiarise yourself with the ways that people typically react to different vocal qualities and develop your ability to use your voice effectively!

Chapter 3

Getting to Know Your Own Voice

A man calls for a taxi. 'I want to go to the station,' he says. 'Fine,' replies the taxi driver. 'I'll pick you up. Where are you now?' 'Er . . . I don't know. But I want to go to the station!' Every journey goes from here to there, and you can't start unless you know where you're coming from. So where are you now vocally? What's your voice like at present?

You may think that the answer is obvious, but it's not because being sure exactly how your own voice sounds is difficult. You are, literally, too physically close to the actual sound you produce, and your hearing is influenced by your fears and expectations.

Many people hate their voices but can't really explain why. They say, 'I just have a feeling' or 'It's the way people ignore me' or 'People look at me oddly when I open my mouth'. Some jump to conclusions because of their views about accent or class. Some have no idea at all what they sound like. Others, the majority probably, latch onto one specific aspect that they dislike. They think that their voices are too high, too quiet or too dull.

Most people assume that each person has one particular voice. The truth is that most people have more than one voice. You change it according to circumstances – who you're speaking to, your perception of status and how you're feeling, physically and emotionally, at any given moment. The subject of your voice is a complex one. So, what clues *can* you gather about how you really sound? Read on – and gain new familiarity with your voice.

Hearing What You Sound Like

I can hear someone protest, 'I don't even *want* to know what I sound like; I just know my voice is awful!' Don't worry. Most people don't rate their voices highly and fear to discover that the reality is worse than they thought.

Rest assured that the activities in this chapter are only a preliminary exploration, to give you information on the best next steps for you.

Listening to a recording

If you've ever played back your personal answer message on your phone or mobile, you know that listening to yourself in a recording can be a weird sensation. Your voice sounds sort of familiar, only it's not. It probably sounds higher than you're expecting, has an unattractive tinny quality and comes across as mechanical – or at least not very human.

The technology that's recording and replaying your voice is creating all three effects. You do indeed sound higher, more tinny and more machine-like. But much of that is the fault of the recording machine.

To gain genuine feedback from listening to a recording of yourself, you need to grit your teeth, ignore your first impression and listen carefully for those characteristics that don't depend so much on the quality of the recording. Ask yourself:

- ✔ Am I unclear?
- ✔ Am I rushing?
- ✔ Is my voice all on the same volume and pitch level?
- ✔ Do I suddenly boom out loudly on isolated words?
- ✔ Do I stop and start hesitantly?

If your responses to these questions get you feeling anxious or despairing, stay calm! This book has chapters that deal with each of the preceding issues.

Listening from inside

The main shock of hearing a recording of yourself is that the experience is so different from listening inside when you speak. The bad news is that the sound you hear through your ears when you speak is scarcely more reliable than listening to a recording – you don't hear the voice that other people hear. When you speak, the sound you hear bouncing off the resonant surfaces of bones in your head and chest seems much louder and more resonant inside your head than the sound that other people hear. In addition, you feel satisfying vibrations as the sound reverberates around inside your skull. No wonder your voice sounds richer and fuller inside you!

However, you can get a better idea of what others hear with the following technique:

1. **Cup one hand behind your ear, and gently bend your ear forward.**

2. **Hold your other hand gently rounded in front of your face, about a hand's width away from your mouth.**

   Point the fingers of the hand in front of your mouth towards the hand cupped behind your ear, so that the two hands are almost touching.

3. **Speak normally into the rounded hand in front of your face.**

   Adjust the front hand until the sound seems to emanate from outside you.

   The voice you hear sounds quite similar to what other people hear when you speak. Almost certainly, the sound is higher and thinner than the sound you hear inside your head – don't worry though; everyone has a similar experience.

Getting feedback

You can also ask a friend or trusted colleague to give you feedback on your voice. Tell the other person that you're seeking a balanced opinion, both positive and negative. Explain that you want to hear a *physical* description of the characteristics of your voice, rather than an emotive personal opinion that describes the kind of person they think you are.

When you ask other people for feedback, they may label you or describe your voice in emotive terms such as, 'You sound rather patronising' or 'You sound timid.' If so, after recovering from this blow below the belt, follow up with a question. Ask your friend what exactly he or she hears *in the sound* that gives rise to that opinion. For example, is your sound hard-edged or do you raise the tone at the end of a sentence? That's the kind of information that is going to be useful to you.

Be open to the feedback! Harold, a participant on a course I was leading, didn't agree with feedback from others that his voice was soft. Indeed, he was so adamant that his voice was loud that he brought a decibel counter to the second day of the course to prove his point. We tested various voices, and only after he saw how low his count was on the dial compared with others was he willing to admit that maybe he did speak rather quietly. Harold was a good example of someone who trusted the sounds in his head more than feedback from recordings or from other people. He *felt* that he sounded loud and put his trust in his inner feeling, refusing himself permission to speak louder, even though people were always asking him to speak up! (If Harold's experience sounds familiar, turn to Chapter 7 where I tackle the topic of volume in detail.)

Informal observations are as useful as formal feedback as you gather information. Start noticing others' reaction to your voice. Remind yourself to be casual and impartial – you can easily jump to conclusions or become defensive about what you discover. Pretend that you're a scientist observing a subject and take note of all that you can about the effect of your voice. For example:

- Do people often ask you to repeat what you say or not notice that you have spoken?

- Do you see people leaning forward to hear – or maybe backing away?!

Mentally log your observations and ask yourself what you may do differently to have a different impact on your listeners.

Recognising your unique sound

Your voice is yours alone. You don't sound quite like anyone else. Your voice is an amalgam of many different factors, resulting in your unique sound and manner of speaking.

- **At the simplest level, your voice quality depends on the shape of your body.** A violin doesn't sound like a cello because it's violin-sized. Twins sound similar partly because they have similar bone structure, particularly of their skulls. But every violin is still different from other violins, and even twins develop differences in their voices as they mature. See Chapter 9 for more on the ways your body and skull affect your sound.

- **You sound the way you do because of how you hold yourself.** If you stand stiffly like a sergeant major, you sound different from someone who slouches as if down on their luck. See Chapter 5 for the more on how your posture affects your voice.

- **Your sound depends on how you hear others and use your ears.** Listening is key to finding out how to speak in the first place and then affects your ability to modulate your sound as you mature.

- **Your sound depends on *how* you play your vocal instrument – and that is influenced by your thinking and feeling.** Your sound is affected by the kind of person you think you are, as well as the kind of person you wish you were and the kind of person you fear you may be.

    If you suspect that you're a boring person, you tend to produce a boring voice. If you aspire to be confident, you try to inject that into your voice. As your confidence waxes and wanes, your voice changes in quality. Similarly, your voice reflects whether you're more of a slow, deep thinker or quick, spontaneous one. Chapter 10 explores this mind-body connection in greater detail.

✔ **Your voice depends on what sounds you prefer.** Your attempts to sound the way you want to are bound up with your sense of identity and how you see yourself fitting in with respect to class, education, cultural environment and so on. See Chapter 12 for more about regional and class accents.

✔ **Your voice is who you *allow* yourself to be.** Which aspects of your personality come out in your voice and which remain hidden? The whole palate of expression is available to you, but you may neglect certain voice tones, such as the intimate voice, the silly voice, the ecstatic voice or tones of sadness or anger. See Chapter 11.

Some voice teachers say that changing the way you sound is difficult and that you're on the whole stuck with what you've got. Not so! Your voice isn't like your fingerprint, totally distinctive and unchanging through your life. Changing your voice may be a challenge if you approach the task purely physically, through tuition and exercises. But lessons and practice only get you so far because your voice represents so much more than the physical. When you change emotionally, intellectually and spiritually, your voice changes naturally. Finding yourself, you find your voice.

Gathering Insights into Your Voice

You may worry that your accent or way of speaking gives away too much information about where you were born, raised or educated. (I address the issue of accents head-on in Chapter 12.)

Actually, your voice gives away even more information about you than that! Your voice is absolutely full of clues about your physical size, race, birthplace, social class, age and probably your occupation too. It's a barometer of your state of health and well-being. It reveals whether you're stressed, tired or drunk. It suggests your state of mind, your level of confidence and your ability to connect. Who needs complicated psychological instruments to test people? Your voice reveals all this even as you toss off a brief comment, 'Going to rain, d'you think?'

I read of an experiment where two violinists, one a well-trained famous player and the other an fine amateur, took turns to play both an ordinary violin and a Stradivarius behind a screen. Afterwards, musical experts assessed the sounds. You may guess that the instruments would make the biggest difference, but this wasn't the case. The biggest difference in sound came from the players themselves. The famous player made a wonderful sound on both instruments.

You can relate the story to your voice. Your instrument is predetermined; your vocal cords are of a particular length; your physical make-up is what it is – but the way you use your voice is what really makes the difference.

Whatever your physical make-up, the way you play your instrument tells the story of who you are including:

- How relaxed and supple you are.
- How much and in what ways you utilise your voice.
- How you respond to people and how much you desire to connect with them.
- How you've responded to your life up to now: whether you've sailed through life or struggled every inch of the way.
- How you see yourself in the world, especially how much you play a role or how much you feel at ease in your own shoes.

Picking up the traces

Your voice is sticky. It picks up attributes as you go through life. If you go to school in one part of the country and move as an adult to another, your accent usually reveals traces of its original accent. If, as a child you make close friends with a child with a different way of speaking, your own voice picks up nuances of theirs – not only their language and their accent but also their intonation, rhythm and expressive idiosyncrasies. Your voice is influenced particularly by people you admire and choose as role models.

You may think that, with this 'stickiness', at least members of a single family all speak the same way but voices within families aren't always similar. I was surprised when I first met the children of a colleague who is a university professor and speaks in patrician tones. His son spoke with a strong regional accent picked up from other children at his school. You wouldn't know that parent and child were even related!

Some people have particularly 'sticky' voices and react instantly to whatever they hear. They speak to children like children themselves, to older people in quivery voices or to foreigners in foreign accents. If they're part of a group where one person is speaking in a broad southern drawl, these people find themselves doing the same, even though the rest of the group may be cringing in embarrassment to hear what sounds like a theatrical act.

I was at Bill's house when the electrician arrived. Bill is a city lawyer who specialises in complex international finance cases. He is a convincing public speaker whose deep tones speak of authority and confidence. However, the moment Bill greeted the electrician, I realised that the person I knew had departed. 'Hi, Terry, mate,' he quipped in a high-pitched voice. 'A'right, mate? Yeh, it's the ole socket, Terry, playing up something awful. Only put in last year, I ask you?! Yeh, can't trust 'em can you, mate?' It was an extraordinary performance. He was picking up traces of the electrician's way of speaking and converting this type of speech into an exaggerated stereotype of electricians worldwide. When I mentioned his new accent afterwards, he had no idea that his voice had changed at all!

When you become more aware of your voice, you can moderate this tendency to mimic and save yourself from embarrassment. However, the ability to match someone else's accent and way of speaking, when honed and polished, comes in useful as a means to create a closer connection with others. I cover creating connections with your voice in more detail in Chapter 15.

Sounding out your life story

Your voice is affected by your earlier emotional experiences in all sorts of ways:

- ✔ **If you're hurt emotionally and conceal feeling deep within you,** you often bury the warmth in your voice.

- ✔ **If your childhood response to bad treatment was to grit your teeth rather than exploding with anger,** that clenching may make your voice hard today.

- ✔ **If you always got what you wanted by flattering grown-ups around you,** your voice may acquire an ingratiating lightness that becomes part of its regular make-up.

- ✔ **If you were always timid and reserved,** your voice is likely to lack forward energy and get stuck in your throat, scarcely reaching your listener.

- ✔ **If you were regularly put down and criticised when you were young,** your voice probably no longer has access to its high enthusiastic tones even when you feel excited.

Everything you've done and felt in your life shapes the way that you breathe, arrange your skeleton and use your muscles. You get used to particular patterns in using the muscles of face, mouth and throat and mould your physical body around these habits of sound, strengthening certain muscles and weakening others in the process.

The interconnectedness of body and emotion is the reason that people can hear the life you've led in the sounds of your voice, both in your actual sounds and in all the possibilities of sound and feeling that are now excluded. Your voice shows especially the defences you built up against emotional trauma. See the sidebar 'Bioenergetics' for more on the effects of emotional stress on the body. For many, people the range of possibility in their voices tends to shrink as they mature. The cry of abandonment in the baby, the scream of anger in the toddler and the shout of joy in the infant are given up for the more 'civilised' repertoire of the adult. If that has happened to you, recovering these lost possibilities of expression can open the way to a voice that has a much fuller range and depth. (See Chapter 10 for more on uncovering your full voice.)

Bioenergetics

In his now-classic book *Bioenergetics* (Penguin, 1995), American psychotherapist Alexander Lowen gives a fascinating account of the long-term effects of emotional stress on the body and offers bioenergetics as a healing therapy. Based on the work of Austrian-American psychiatrist and psychoanalyst Wilhelm Reich, bioenergetics helps people to regain their energy through releasing muscular tensions in the body. It demonstrates the close connection between mind and body and shows how stifled emotions can lock or suppress parts of your body. For example, if you're constantly fearful, you narrow and tighten your shoulders, or if you're inhibited by constant criticism, you lock your neck and jaw. These changes in your body become set and inhibit you from expressing certain energies, such as tenderness, aggression or joy.

The therapy helps people to release muscular tensions, such as those connected to headaches or back pain, and thus relieve the body, release the linked emotions and restore the natural energy and sense of well-being.

Bioenergetics is particularly relevant to the voice because every block in your body is mirrored in your voice. As body blocks are often the result of stifled emotions, you can't always release them by physical exercises alone, particularly if they're the results of childhood trauma. Taking into account the findings of bioenergetics and other related research, the best voice development works on two fronts, physical and emotional. For example, if you want to cultivate dynamic enthusiastic tones in your voice, you can both develop your head register physically (where enthusiasm usually resonates), and discover the dynamic feeling of enthusiasm (which releases somatic tension) in your body with the help of body-mind techniques such as bioenergetics.

Revealing Your Different Voices

I sometimes ask clients in workshops, 'Which of you think that your voice changes in different circumstances?' A few people typically raise their hands. 'Now, which of you think that your voice is more or less the same on most occasions?' Many more raise their hands.

I then lead the following three-stage exercise that you can try as well with a friend or two – or just by imagining you're in a room full of people. Listen in to Track 2 on the audio file.

1. **Recall a time you felt shy or intimidated.**

   Have you ever played the party game 'In the manner of' where you perform an activity, say ballet dancing, in the manner of a particular character, like a heavyweight wrestler? That's the game here. If you seldom feel timid, then imagine that you are; if you often feel timid, then you'll find it easy! Walk around the room and greet others 'in the manner of' a timid person.

2. **After a while, break off from that activity. Then imagine that you're at a business networking event.**

   Greet others formally and confidently, and introduce people to each other in business mode.

3. **Finally, imagine that you suddenly bump into a special close friend whom you haven't seen for years.**

   Greet this person excitedly with pleasure and amazement, shrieking with delight if you want.

4. **Compare the experience and energy of each scenario.**

In the first part, when I lead this activity, the noise level is low and stays at the same low pitch. In the second part, the sound of talking is much louder and also raised a notch in pitch. In the last part, the noise level is extremely high with the voice pitches rising to the stratosphere. This high volume happens with every group, even though each group has participants who are fairly restrained or shy. People are surprised at how different they sound in different circumstances.

Your pitch and tone most likely change from day to day and from minute to minute, according to your mood and your reaction to events. Even without meaning to, your voice leaks what is really going on for you. You speak differently to parents and friends, to siblings or children, to your boss or your colleagues. Moreover, people can usually tell the difference when you say 'I'm fine' on a good day and 'I'm fine' on a bad day.

I had a manager once who spoke regularly to her staff in sharp domineering tones. I couldn't believe my ears the first time I heard her speak to *her* boss. She sounded like a seductress!

Some people's voices scarcely change at all. They neither absorb others' ways of speaking nor react vocally to different circumstances and people. You may be one of them. If you want to be expressive with your voice, you need to be able to vary it at will.

Being able to change your voice for different circumstances is one of the best ways to connect better with others. When you greet people and your voice rises with pleasure, they *know* that you're pleased to see them. When you sympathise with a sad friend and your voice takes on a gentle quality, they trust that you feel genuine empathy for them. At work or at home, speaking with more variety in your voice brings you increased understanding and better relationships.

Shifting pitch

People complain more about the pitch of their own voice than about any other aspect. Usually they think their voices are too high, though some people believe their voices are too 'growly' and down in the back of their throats.

Although people have differing opinions about pitch, most listeners favour lower voices. In the early days of the BBC, female announcers were unthinkable because the people in charge (men) believed that a woman's voice lacked authority and that the nation wouldn't want to listen to high tones. Perhaps partly for this reason, for decades women in business and public life have aimed for lower voices, sometimes to their detriment.

You can lower your voice in various ways – notably by pushing down, which can harm your voice, or by using more pharyngeal resonance (resonance down in your throat), which sounds artificial. Margaret Thatcher employed the latter for media interviews. However, the best way to lower your pitch is to use lower body resonance, which I cover in Chapter 9.

If your voice sounds unnaturally high, the most likely reason is tension. As soon as you get nervous, your voice pitch goes up. Feeling constantly stressed also makes you tight and thins your voice. When you're able to relax, your voice tone settles down at a lower pitch.

If you speak higher than is natural, your voice can often sound thinner or unpleasantly nasal. If you push too deep, your voice probably sounds strained or you frequently feel the urge to clear your throat.

Finding your natural pitch

Aim for your natural pitch. That is the pitch that is most easy on the ear for your listeners and kindest to your voice. This pitch also gives you the most resonance and impact. Finding your natural pitch is especially relevant for women. If you force your voice low, you may reach a pitch associated with 'authority' and 'gravitas', but you sacrifice the variation and subtlety of your voice and probably end up boring your listeners rather than displaying authority.

For most people, the pitch that is easiest for your voice is the one you use naturally for *non-verbal encouragers*. These are sounds you make when you're listening to others and want them to know that you're actively engaged in what they're saying. They include 'uh-huh', 'mm' and other encouraging noises.

Say 'mm' in a humdrum effortless way as if you're agreeing with someone. Then speak a few words at the same pitch. For example, 'Mm, mm, yes, it was an excellent event, wasn't it?' Now try with 'uh-huh'. Say it on its own first. Then add a comment, 'Uh-huh, that sounds like a good solution.'

Natural pitch in children

Sometimes people tell me that they're 'tone deaf' and 'have no ear' for music. I believe that they get this idea because their natural pitch wasn't honoured when they were children. When you speak, your pitch varies only by a few tones, and when children are young their singing range is also limited to a fairly narrow range of 5 or 6 notes – the range of most nursery rhymes (think of 'Twinkle, Twinkle, Little Star' for example). If, as a child, your voice was naturally deeper than the norm, your pitch range lay below the notes of the songs, and you were unable to reach notes that were easy for other children to sing. If the teacher had played the tune in a lower key, *you* would be have been able to sing accurately and other children would have had the problem. But the teacher, in ignorance, called you a 'growler' and ordered you to stop singing and mouth the words silently. From that time onward, believing that you had the disability 'tone deafness', you grew up fulfilling the prophesy.

I want to reassure you that, unless you're deaf, any vocal problems you're experiencing now probably have nothing to do with your listening skills or musicality. And if you're stuck with the belief that you're tone deaf, you can probably, with a bit of the right help, discover how to sing in tune!

'Uh-huh' is particularly interesting because it contains two pitches – a higher 'uh' and a lower 'huh'. These two sounds give you a useful rule of thumb for your normal pitch range. In order to sound interesting and natural, vary your pitch so that it mostly fluctuates between these levels. Confirm that you're working with your ideal pitch by placing your hand on your breast bone and speaking at your natural pitch. You should feel vibrations there.

You can also find your pitch by humming energetically, feeling the vibration in your nose and around your mouth. Then speak with the same feeling and at the same pitch.

Taking Stock

What is the best way forward for you in developing your voice? Right now is a good opportunity for you to take stock and look at your current voice as well as decide what you want to sound like and how you're going to go about developing your voice.

You know how to speak of course. You've had years of practice! But like an amateur golfer who turns up to play every week and never has the time to examine his game, you carry on using your voice day in, day out and have probably picked up bad habits. Time for some coaching!

While you can't pick up another voice as easily as choosing a new golf club, you can play the instrument you've got in different – and better – ways.

The following sections help you begin to assess your voice and plan the direction you want to aim for.

Evaluating your voice

Take stock and ask yourself some questions about your voice. Table 3-1 contains numerous statements – many of them negative or critical – that you may have said or thought about yourself. Read through each statement and determine whether you agree or disagree.

Table 3-1	Where Are You Now?		
Statement	**Agree**	**Not Sure**	**Disagree**
People often don't hear me.			
I've been told I mumble (even if by my half-deaf granny).			
People sometimes ask me not to shout.			
I hate my voice.			
I feel ignored when I speak.			
I think that I sound boring.			
I get tongue-tied when the pressure's on.			
I tend to stutter.			
My voice gets tired quickly.			
I think that I sound childish.			
I'm told I growl.			
I think that I sound nasal.			
I've no idea what I sound like.			
I just sound feeble.			
My voice is shrill or piercing.			
People mistake my gender when I speak.			
My voice gets stuck in my throat.			
I always feel I can't get a word in edgeways.			
I sound common, like someone from the sticks.			
I rush my words when I speak.			
I constantly say 'er' and 'um'.			

Assessing how your voice fits you

In my twenties, I was thrilled to win a scholarship to study singing at the Music Conservatorio in Rome. It seemed the perfect place: the country with the most beautiful sounding language and a city that loved beauty. I was in love with everything there. A Italian told me with pride, 'It's all *bella figura* – beautiful form – here.' One day, after I had sung the beginning of a Verdi aria, my singing maestro shocked me by exploding, 'Stop trying to sound *beautiful!* It's not your job to sound *beautiful!'* Seeing my appalled face, he explained more gently, 'Singing is not about sounding beautiful. In the opera you hear characters who are good and evil, comic or ridiculous; they all have their different tones. The voice has to be *expressive,* that is all. That *is* the beauty of voice – that it *speaks* to us.'

I didn't fully understand what he was saying until later. I just wanted to sound like renowned divas Joan Sutherland or Maria Callas. But, in fact, my role models were themselves singers who first and foremost expressed themselves.

Whether speaking or singing, your voice needs to express what you want to say, and it needs to express *you.* Begin figuring out who you are with the following:

1. **Draw a line vertically down the centre of a sheet of paper and write down some of your best personal qualities on the left side.**

   Don't qualify what you write with, 'Well, *some* people say that I'm . . .' or 'I suppose that on a good day I'm *sometimes* . . . '. Just do this exercise quickly and freely without censoring yourself.

   Write down at least 20 personal qualities on the page. Include a quality that is secret, that you know to be part of yourself but that no one knows about. List one quality that is so obvious that you haven't even thought to say it yet!

   I may write: happy, generous, thoughtful, loyal, friendly. But choose words that describe you.

2. **On the right side of the paper, write down the physical qualities of your current voice, as far as you can judge at present.**

   I may write for instance: deep, husky, softish, slow. But choose words that describe *your* voice.

3. **Compare your two lists.**

   Do they relate to each other? For example, if you wrote 'spontaneous' in your first list and 'tight' in your second, or 'tough' in your first and 'sweet' in your second, then clearly you have a mismatch. Of course, you exhibit different qualities at different times, but if you notice major differences between the two lists you may be experiencing some disconnection between your life and your voice.

4. **Reflect for a moment on how the qualities in your first list can manifest themselves vocally.**

   What is a kind voice, a dynamic voice, a focused voice, a loyal voice? How does each of these voices sound? What changes can you make in how you stand, move and breathe that may help produce these various voices? For example, when I use the personal quality 'generous' as a word to describe my voice, I think of a full rich voice with warmth in it. When I use the personal quality 'happy' for my voice, I think of light higher-pitched sounds and energy in the voice.

5. **Try out different tones of voice to match your personal qualities.**

   Have fun with this part. Be inventive. Think of as many ways as you can to bring your best personal qualities into the sound of your voice.

Preparing for Your Journey

I'm sure that you want to begin developing your new voice skills quickly and easily, so this section offers a few of my favourite hints and tips to get you going.

Developing your voice isn't a merely intellectual endeavour. Your body has to respond as well, and oddly your body is not always willing to obey instructions. If you're someone who blushes, you already know that telling yourself not to has no effect whatsoever; the same goes if you're trying to steady your trembling hands during a nervous moment. So what *is* useful? Some of the approaches used in sports coaching can help you develop your voice as well. Have a look at *Neuro-linguistic Programming For Dummies* by Romilla Ready and Kate Burton (Wiley) for other ideas.

Keep the following in mind as you begin to develop a stronger, more authentic voice:

- ✔ **Voice work is mental, emotional and physical.** Treat these approaches as equal partners, never relying on just a single approach.

- ✔ **Try things out in practice.** Don't just read the descriptions of the exercises in this book; you get most out of them when you try them out.

- ✔ **Be curious.** Whatever results you get, avoid becoming critical of yourself. Be fascinated instead. Tell yourself, 'That's interesting! I wonder how that happened?'

- ✔ **If things don't work for a while, get curious, but don't despair.** Development is always uneven; sometimes you have a sudden spurt; then you reach a plateau for a while. You'll get there!

- ✔ **And above all, approach the whole subject of working on your voice in a spirit of play.** If you have fun, you gain new skills fast and effectively.

How babies discover speech

If a manual 'learning to talk for babies' existed, it would be the longest manual in the world. Acquiring language is exceedingly complex. Hundreds of muscles are involved in the shortest utterance. Your vocal cords vibrate millions of times a day. Your vocal equipment is moulded in your first years almost like water wearing away a stone with millions of small impulses from your ears, your thoughts and feelings and your relationship with other people.

Every healthy baby starts with the full vocal equipment. Anna Karpf in her wonderful book *The Human Voice* (Bloomsbury, 2006), explains how the babble of babies tends to include the same sounds whatever country they come from, and then – little by little – they attune to their own language and their vocal apparatus focuses increasingly on certain sounds while losing the ability to make others. They gain the ability to talk by listening. Indeed, babies are stupendous listeners. Even tiny babies move to the rhythm of their mother's voice and soon prefer her voice to any other sound. Moreover, they're incredibly sensitive to tone of voice; long before they learn language, they can 'read' sounds around them, distinguishing their mother's voice from other female voices, and reacting strongly to particular emotional tones in her voice.

Beginning with the nuts and bolts

Considering that your voice is such a vital instrument for you in almost every part of your life, the fact that vocal training is rarely taught in school is amazing. Okay, you do work on some aspects of communication at school. You find out about vocabulary and possibly grammar or elocution, but you don't explore the mysteries of voice tone as part of a traditional academic curriculum. These lessons you have to pick up for yourself.

I first met my Dutch friend Marian's baby when she was only a couple of months old, and on that first meeting I heard mother and baby have a conversation. Marian said something in a playful tone to baby Eleanor, and she responded with a gurgle. Marian said something else in the same tone; answer – a different gurgle. Then Marian introduced a different up and down of the voice and Eleanor followed her lead. It was the most beautiful dialogue, and I was amazed that it could happen with a baby so young.

Listening and trying out new things is still the best way to develop your voice. What you did as a baby is still relevant now. Making rapid progress is mostly about getting rid of unhelpful 'adult' gremlins such as judgement, self-criticism, self-doubt and impatience. (More about tackling these in Chapter 11.)

At the same time, being adult, you can put in some useful practice, as you would when taking up a new musical instrument. 'Slow is the new fast,' one music teacher said to me. If you take things gently and slowly at the beginning you find your acquisition of skills speeds up as you go along. Many projects, from getting fit to mastering a sport or even slimming work best according to this principle.

Getting in the right frame of mind

Your beliefs make all the difference when you're exploring and developing your voice. If you believe that you can't do something, that belief influences your ability to do it. When I stopped believing that children can be tone deaf and believed instead that every child is born to sing (see the sidebar 'Natural pitch in children'), I was able to teach them how to sing.

Play is very important. I use the word 'play' frequently in this book because play is about make-believe. In make-believe, children act *as if* something is true. They 'put on' a belief. This process can work for you too. As you try the voice practices in this book, ask yourself some of these 'as if' questions:

- ✔ If I could do this practice really well, what would that be like?

- ✔ If it's this time next year and I can now do this practice brilliantly, what does that feel like?

- ✔ Who can do this activity really well? If I step into the shoes of that person, what is the experience of doing this activity like now? What do I know now that I didn't know when standing in my own shoes?

- ✔ If this practice were really easy, what would that be like?

- ✔ If I were just playing with this practice for fun, how would my experience be different?

Putting yourself in the driver's seat

Some people embark on a sport as a purely physical exercise at first, and passion comes later. Some mathematicians and scientists learn their subjects as techniques at first and discover that they're also about imagination later. Many of the greatest artists, sportsmen, mathematicians and scientists don't do that. They *start* with passion, which provides the driving force for all further activity. Einstein was a dreamer before he became a fully-fledged scientist. David Beckham was passionate about football before he reached the top of his game.

Speaking well relies on technique, but you improve quickest and best if you're driven by passion. Passion produces amazing shortcuts. For example, you can work on a thousand elements of technique to produce a warm rounded voice, while one second of genuine heart warmth from you can produce the same sound.

The main driver for improvement is your desire to communicate. Your breathing and vocal apparatus come into play in answer to your energy to express something inside you. So, although you can speak better by working from the outside-in and focusing on technique, you make bigger, better, quicker and more enjoyable gains from the impulse to expression arising from deep inside you.

The voice journey can be an emotional one. But the joy of expressing yourself authentically repays itself a thousand times.

Part II
Beginning with Voice Basics

The 5th Wave
By Rich Tennant

"You should always clear your throat, relax your vocal cords, and take a deep breath before saying something as stupid as that."

In this part . . .

Here you discover that the key to a great voice is something you already do all day, every day – and that's breathing. You find out how to take a full breath and allow the sound to flow by taking things easy and relaxing your body. Then you have a great time putting life into the sounds with long vowels and sparkling consonants. You realise that people are understanding you easily because you are clear.

Chapter 4

Discovering How to Breathe Well

I want to give you some good news: you're the owner of a fine wind instrument – for that's what your voice is. Your vocal apparatus doesn't look particularly like a wind instrument because the moving parts are hidden inside you, but your voice works much like a trumpet or a clarinet. The first step towards having a great voice is to know the basics of blowing your instrument, and that takes air in the form of breathing.

Making a Sound: How Your Voice Works

Your mouth and throat are complex and multi-purpose, involved in eating as well as in speaking, singing, shouting, crying or laughing. But the basic sound-making process is straightforward, and it all starts with air.

Demystifying your breath: It's just hot air

The part of your voice that creates sound is really small. Your vocal folds (also called *vocal cords*) are a couple of bands of muscle stretched horizontally across the larynx in your neck. They're tiny – approximately one to two-and-a-half centimetres long – and shorter in women than in men. These muscles vibrate to produce your voice.

You produce sound when air passes across these folds and creates a vibration, like the wind whistling through trees. That's all your voice is – just warm, vibrating air. I say 'just'; your vocal folds are very active, vibrating at least 100 times per second, sometimes much more. Your vocal folds need to be free from tension in order to vibrate freely. If your throat is tight, your vocal folds can't vibrate naturally and experience tremendous physical stress. Freedom of your vocal folds is crucial if you want to make good sound, and that means that you need to relax. In Chapter 5, I share ways to relax your voice and body so you can produce the best sound possible.

Amplifying the sound

Instruments always have some means of amplifying the sound. A bell rings clearly because the sound echoes around inside its concave form. A clarinet is bell-shaped at the end to augment the sound. The old gramophone had its sound trumpet. (Remember pictures of 'His Master's Voice' with the dog listening to a wind-up gramophone?)

Your tiny vocal folds certainly need a bit of help to ramp up the sound they produce, and that's where your body comes in. When you speak freely, your voice resounds in your head and echoes in your chest and other parts of your body. Your voice's volume is amplified many times. Your whole body is involved in amplifying sound, from head to toe, like the body of a guitar or a double bass. *That's* how you create a great voice.

The greatest difference between people with wonderful voices and people with weak voices is in how they use their breath and resonating spaces.

When Maria Callas, one of the greatest sopranos in history, was studying her craft, she used to watch her pet canary to see how it breathed. She was captivated by the way the bird used its whole body and energy to create its wonderful song, and she imitated this technique in creating her own sounds. You can see a similar whole-body engagement if you watch a baby cry, a dog bark or a chimpanzee make sounds to protect its territory. In the following section, you discover how to engage your whole body too.

Getting Started with Breathing

I don't imagine you normally worry much about air when you speak. If you're like most people when they talk, you merely think and out come the words – or possibly even just the last bit! Developing the ability to speak well is about rediscovering air.

You're something of a breath expert. Think about it. What authority in any other subject has pursued his field of expertise since the day he was born?

But you have. From the moment you uttered your first cry, you've been breathing. When you were born, that first wonderful breath and that first cry were free and full.

Breathing is everything when you speak. Specifically, breathing:

- ✔ Gives your words power
- ✔ Brings life to what you say
- ✔ Sustains the sounds you make
- ✔ Creates interest and makes people want to listen to you
- ✔ Provides the basis of emotional intensity in your voice
- ✔ Provides subtlety and shades of meaning
- ✔ Serves as the life blood of your inspiration when you communicate

Breathing has quite a lot going for it! Taking the time to get your breathing working well before you utter a single sound makes all the difference to your progress as a speaker.

Fortunately, you already know how to breathe. Chances are that you breathe really well when you're asleep. However, in the stresses and tensions of living, your breathing may have become shallow or restricted. The following section helps you reconnect with your breathing.

Becoming aware of your breathing

If you aspire to having a great voice, you simply need to rediscover your breathing by bringing it to your conscious attention for a while. The following activity brings your breath into focus. I run through it on Track 3.

1. **Sit or lie calmly for a while in a quiet place.**

   You can sit on an upright chair or lie flat on a bed or on the floor. If you're lying down, put a small cushion under your head. If you're sitting, don't slump; instead find a position that is comfortable. Take a few moments to settle into the peace and quiet.

2. **Observe the wave of your natural breathing with a sense of idle curiosity.**

   Consider what is actually happening as you breathe in and out. You're not trying to change anything at this stage. No judging! You just want to note what happens. Ask yourself:

   - What parts of my body am I most aware of?

   - Which parts of my body gently move as the air moves in and out?

Are you aware of the upper chest? Does your belly move? What about the ribs – are they involved? Is there movement in your back? Do you sense the air entering your nose? Does your throat make itself felt?

3. **Mentally scan your whole body and pay attention to the areas that are taking part in your breathing.**

    Just be aware, that is all. Continue for a couple of minutes or for as long as you remain curious.

Observing your breathing without trying to control it is a great practice for your voice. While you work through the various activities in this chapter and book, you will be thinking consciously about breathing, but breathing is a natural reflex and therefore consciously trying to impose firm control over your breathing doesn't improve it in the long run. The most useful thing you can do to improve the ease and capacity of your breathing is to remove tensions; then your natural reflexes are able to do their work.

Thinking low

When you breathe correctly for speaking, many different parts of your body are involved in the process in an easy co-ordinated way. However, when you're just starting to pay greater attention to your breathing, you may be tempted to over-emphasise any instruction to use a particular part of the body. When you do, the breathing process gets distorted and you end up more constricted than before. If for example I say, 'Take in a really big breath!' or 'Push your ribs out!', you may put so much effort into those actions that other, more subtle, but important parts of breathing are lost.

That said, I can offer one instruction that you're likely to find particularly useful. As you focus on your breathing, *think low – in a friendly, curious way.* Pay attention to your abdomen and all the lower part of your body. This invites the muscles that are most useful for supporting the voice to come into play, and at the same time leaves the area around your vocal folds free from getting involved in the breathing process.

Repeat the breathing awareness practice in the preceding section, preferably lying down, although you can also do it in a chair. Breathe gently in and out through your nose for a few moments, and turn your attention to different aspects of your breathing. I walk you through this exercise in Track 4:

1. **Turn your attention to your belly.**

    If you like, place your hands lightly on that area. For a few breaths, pay attention to how you can allow your belly to rise gently with the in-breath and fall again with the out-breath.

Feel how this soft part of your body goes comfortably up and down with the breathing, moving your hands up on the in-breath and down on the out-breath.

2. **Imagine that your belly is a balloon and let it gently expand and then go back to its original position again.**

   Repeat breathing in and out in this manner several times. Keep everything simple and easy. You're breathing beautifully – this is how you need to breathe when you speak.

3. **Continue to breathe in through your nose and begin to breathe out through your mouth in a sigh – a sigh of comfort and pleasure.**

   Think of an evening when you arrive home after a busy day, and you sink down in the sofa, put your feet up and sigh. Aahh, this is goo-ood!

   Breath in, and out again, with a contented sigh, making an audible 'Aahh …'.

   Repeat a few times. Feel how each out-breath naturally becomes fuller and longer and in the process causes a fuller, deeper in-breath. Don't force it. Just observe how it happens naturally.

   If you feel dizzy at any point, just pause for a few moments until the dizziness passes. Feeling dizzy is quite natural, especially if you're not used to breathing deeply. You'll soon get used to the breathing practice and will no longer experience dizziness.

Breathing for speaking is the same as for living, only instead of the in-breath and the out-breath being much the same length, your out-breath needs to be longer because sound is produced only when you're breathing out. You make this longer out-breath naturally when you sigh.

Engaging your diaphragm

Books about voice often make the process of breathing sound complicated. As I describe in the preceding sections, breathing is actually not difficult. (Of course, I do have more to say on the subject in this and following sections.)

When you speak in normal conversations, you're often speaking to someone close to you and don't usually talk in long, extended sentences. Your need for air is not very great. But if you want to project to a larger audience or say something more protracted or emotionally charged, you do need to take larger breaths. And as an added bonus, you sound better when you breathe more fully.

Your distinguished diaphragm

The diaphragm is a powerful muscle which is fixed to your lower ribs, breast bone and parts of your back.

- ✔ When you breathe in, your diaphragm contracts and flattens downwards, allowing the lungs to expand to receive fresh air.

- ✔ When you breathe out, it relaxes back upwards again against the lungs helping to expel the used air.

You don't actually feel the diaphragm as you breathe. Instead, you're aware of the connecting muscles in your stomach and even lower down, in your groin and buttocks.

When your belly is tight, it restricts the movement of the diaphragm and impedes your breathing. When your diaphragm is free to work well, it is the secret of a powerful voice.

The power of your voice depends on the power of your breath; the quality of your voice depends on the quality of your breath.

When you feel your belly taking part in the action of breathing, your diaphragm is coming into play. Actors and singers are aware of the important role played by the diaphragm. The sidebar 'Your distinguished diaphragm' examines this amazing muscle in greater detail.

Using your diaphragm well is not about blowing yourself up alarmingly with air. In the BBC series of the children's story *Five Children and It*, released in the US as *The Sand Fairy*, the psammead or fairy grants wishes by stretching out its eyes, holding its breath and swelling alarmingly. Some speakers look much like this psammead when they take a breath. Fortunately, breathing for speaking is much simpler and gentler than this!

Don't be misled by the often-repeated phrase 'Breathe *in*.' You aren't aware of your body moving *in* when you take in air. Instead, you feel your body expand *out.*

My friend Anne brought her colleague Sally along to lunch, and the three of us had a lively time together. Sally is a large woman with a mischievous look in her eye. At one point, she told a joke that was so funny we all burst into paroxysms of laughter. Sally's whole body wobbled as she laughed, which made us laugh even more. When we eventually calmed down a little, Anne turned to me with a smile and said, 'You know how you speak about breathing from the diaphragm in your coaching? If people want to get the idea of *every* muscle being involved, get them to laugh their heads off. They'll certainly feel every single one then!' So I am passing her excellent tip on to you!

Keep your diaphragm mobile and flexible! If you aspire to be fit with a flat, hard belly, you may carry a lot of tension in that area which constricts your diaphragm so that it's unable to move. Over time, you lose the habit of keeping your diaphragm flexible. That affects your breathing – both in and out – which in turn affects your voice and eventually even your health and well-being. If you pull your belly in, you can't breathe in deeply, and you have a harder time making good sounds. Allow your belly to expand outwards as you take a breath to speak. Enjoy its ability to move – it has the potential to move comfortably 12 or even 15 centimetres up and down.

Try the following practices to get the correct sensation of breathing when you engage your diaphragm. Practise just two or three breaths at a time to get the feel of the low breath.

- ✔ **Stand facing a wall**. Place the palms of your hands at about shoulder height against the wall. Then lean a little towards the wall with your weight, with your arms slightly bent, and push firmly. As you push, breathe in and out. Release your shoulders as you breathe, without letting your arms collapse. As you release your shoulders more and more while continuing to push, you increasingly feel the lower breath. This practice gives you a solid sense of the connection between your breath and the power in your lower body.

- ✔ **Stand in a balanced position with your legs shoulder-width apart**, **toes pointing forward.** Cross your arms snugly across your chest and hug yourself tightly with your hands clasping your back. Bend forward from the waist until your back is horizontal, still clasping yourself tightly. Keep your knees soft and neck relaxed. In this position, breathe. Feel the movement in various parts of your lower body, including your back and solar plexus. Come back to a standing position gently.

Taking full breaths

Although the diaphragm is the most important muscle for breathing, other parts of your body are involved in the process as well.

The following activity gives you lots of information about your breathing and stimulates your whole breathing apparatus at the same time.

1. **Stand up tall and relaxed and sigh out firmly and quickly through your mouth, making the sound 'Hoo' or 'Whoo', until you've expelled all your air.**

   Doing so gets rid of all the old air in your lungs and allows you to take a fuller in-breath. Don't collapse or slouch in the process.

2. **When your lungs are empty of air, shut your mouth and hold your nose closed with your fingers.**

   Raise your rib cage and stay in suspension for a moment or two without stiffening up in your throat. You'll begin to feel the pressure of a large vacuum growing inside you.

   Don't push yourself until you become dizzy or feel weak, but do wait until your body wants to take in air.

3. **Release the fingers holding your nose and keep your mouth shut.**

   Allow air to rush in through your nose, filling the vacuum.

   Notice how you don't have to breathe in deliberately; the air rushes in naturally to fill the space. Become aware of how the air fills the space in every direction – most obviously in your abdomen at first, but also low down, in your back and your sides.

   Become aware of some or all of the parts that become involved in the in-breath, including your:

   - Belly
   - Ribcage
   - Lower chest
   - Upper chest

After doing the preceding activity a few times and feeling the muscles that take part in breathing, stand tall and open with your feet about a foot apart.

1. **Enjoy a steady in-breath, raising your arms out to the side and up above your head as the air fills you.** Feel as if the breath filling you is actually raising your arms rather than the other way about.

   In your imagination, stay connected with the base of your body grounding you as you raise your arms and fill with air. Notice how the parts of your body you used in the previous breathing practices come into play here too, starting with the lower muscles, then you raise the ribs, and finally top up with air higher in your chest. Enjoy the smooth sensation.

2. **Breathe out steadily while lowering your arms.** Reverse the process. First release the air from your upper chest, then gradually lower your ribs, and finally release your lower muscles. Hear the sound of air being expelled.

   Become aware of the column of air making its way up through your body and out through the mouth without any restriction as you lower your arms.

All the activities in this section help encourage good breathing for speaking. Choose any practices that deepen your breathing easily and organically. There's no ordained way to do it. If you find that you've a favourite, practise that one more than the others.

Breathing to Communicate

After working on your ability to breathe deeply and with your entire body, the next part of the process is to breathe out *steadily* so that you can express yourself in words.

When you read a sentence on the page, it consists of lots of different words

with a gap between each.

But when you listen to a spoken sentence, you hear an unbrokenstreamofsound, which your brain divides into individual words and turns into sense. The following sections link your breathing to actually putting across your message.

Producing a steady stream of air

As you communicate thoughts and feelings, sound ebbs and flows with expression. This process requires a steady stream of air.

Imagine that you're sitting in front of a cake with one candle on it. You take a breath and blow the candle out – whew! So far so good. Now imagine that the cake has 25 candles on it and you're going to blow them all out in one breath. You take a nice deep breath and keep blowing and blowing until every candle has gone out. Whoooooooooooooo. If you blow with great force at the beginning, you run out of breath before you reach the last candle. If, on the other hand, you deliberately hold your breath back, you've insufficient air power to extinguish the candles. Your breath has to last until the very last candle is extinguished so you need to allow it to flow steadily and keep its momentum to the very end.

Your breathing for speaking needs to work in much the same way as blowing out a lot of candles. You take a good breath in and then allow it to come out in a steady stream, which then lasts to the end of your statement.

Have you ever made a sound from a blade of grass? Choose a fat blade of grass and hold it tightly between your thumbs, nails facing you, and find the little gap between the thumbs halfway down. Stretch the grass across that gap and blow through the gap to make a sound. (The blade of grass stands in for the vocal folds and illustrates how they work.) The sound produced when you blow through the grass is loud and piercing and continues for as long as you continue to blow. You can hear clearly whether your breath is nice and steady. And if you're out in the open, people near and far will turn to find out where the piercing sound is coming from!

Avoiding breathing pitfalls

Getting your air flowing easily establishes a firm basis for speaking and prevents quite a catalogue of pitfalls that you can fall into as a speaker if you don't use sufficient air. How many do you recognise? The cure for each of these pitfalls is simply, 'use more air'!

The consequences of insufficient air are significant and well worth avoiding:

✔ If you have little air and it all comes out in a rush – like blowing out a single candle – every phrase you speak tails away at the end and makes you sound tentative.

✔ If you don't have enough air, you're going to be tempted to gabble the words to fit what you have to say into a small breath. In Chapter 7, I share ways to make your speech slower and more authoritative.

✔ If you take more frequent smaller breaths, they are shallower, less efficient and feel more effortful. Your voice tires more quickly.

✔ If you don't have sufficient breath for a whole sentence, you tend to grab lots of smaller breaths and that makes you sound hesitant: 'Hello ... it's great to meet you ... I hope you've ... seen some of what we have to ... offer you today ....'

✔ If you take lots of little breaths, you're going to be tempted to fill in the spaces with 'er' and 'um' and other meaningless sounds. These make you sound, er, even more, well, uncertain about – um – what you're trying to, er, say. I offer some useful tips for avoiding these stumbles and hesitations in Chapter 13.

✔ A quick high breath is often taken with a gasping sound and results in a voice that sounds high and excitable, making your listeners uncomfortable or uneasy.

✔ Taking a high breath often affects the area around your vocal folds and as a result you're more likely to tense your shoulders, neck, jaw and tongue and therefore produce a thinner sound.

✔ If you have little air, you can't project your voice and your listener may strain to hear you – or maybe give up on listening to you altogether.

✔ With too little air, you sound dull and your listener may tune out even through your message is vitally important.

Quite a catalogue of pitfalls! Discover how to breathe well, and you can avoid all these negative effects from poor breathing.

Rather than whistling through a blade of grass, you can try:

✔ Whistling using your lips, producing one note with a single steady sound

✔ Playing a long sound on a recorder or a penny whistle; these small instruments only make a true sound if you aren't too forceful

 As you blow out air, imagine that the sound you're producing is travelling physically away from you in a shallow arc like an arrow in slow motion toward a target in the distance. Focus on the destination of the arrow – the end of your long sound. If you're whistling, try moving your hand from close to your face gradually and steadily out into the distance as an accompaniment to aid you in making a steady sound.

Hissing is another great practice for steadying your sound. Take a breath and then breathe out steadily on the sound 'ssssssss'. You can hear clearly the bumps and interruptions in the sound. As before, think of the sound moving physically. Raise one hand to chest height, and as you start to hiss, move your hand from one side to the other in a smooth horizontal line, and focus on matching the smoothness of your sound to the movement of your hand. After you try hissing on 'sss', you may like to repeat the technique using 'fff' and 'shshsh' for slightly different sensations.

You aren't using your actual vocal folds to make a sound in this practice. The sound is created entirely by the escaping air, not by your voice box.

Speaking on air

In order get the sensation of air moving in your speaking, try forming words with air in a whisper. I've chosen lines from an early 20th-century poem called 'Ghosts' by Fanny Stearns Davis to suit the mood. Whisper the text with a steady stream of air, taking breaths only at the end of each line. I've left the original punctuation, but take just one breath per line, and let the breath flow without any hiatus while keeping to the sense of the words. Allow yourself time to take a fresh breath at the end of each line, but not so long that you lose the flow of the poem. All you hear is wind – no voiced sounds at all – but someone listening to you should be able to make out the words clearly. Listen to Track 5 and enjoy the ghostly atmosphere!

> I am almost afraid; though I know the night
> Lets no ghosts walk in the warm lamplight.
> Yet ghosts there are; and they blow, they blow,
> Out in the wind and the scattering snow.
> When I open the windows and go to bed,
> Will the ghosts come in and stand at my head?

Now try speaking the words again, but this time even more emphatically in a stage whisper, saying everything dramatically as if you were telling the start of a horror tale. Make sure that the end of each line of poetry is just at full and exciting as the beginning.

Of course, you aren't aiming to train your voice to whisper. This exercise is just a way to practise using plenty of air and to feel it moving.

Turning breath into sound

Turning your breath into speaking is what breathing work is all about. After developing your breathing capacity and consistency, you link your breathing to speaking by using all that air to make continuous full sounds. Join in to Track 6.

1. **Take a breath and begin to hum on the sound 'mmm' with your lips gently closed.**

   The experience is similar to the blowing and whistling exercises in the earlier section 'Producing a steady stream of air', with the addition of sound.

2. **Continue to breathe and hum for several breaths while gently moving your head, face, jaw and neck.**

   Turn your neck gently from side to side. Move your jaw as if you're chewing. Allow your tongue to explore the sides and roof of your mouth. These movements should have no effect on the continuous humming sound as you keep your lips gently closed. Notice how little effort it takes to make the sound.

3. **Take another breath and allow the hum to open out into vowel sounds.**

   Start with a hum for a second or two, then open the sound out into 'ow': 'mmm-ow'. Imagine that you're going to intone slowly, 'How now brown cow?' but without the consonants apart from the initial hum – 'mmm-ow-ow-ow-ow'. Or think of it as 'mmm-aaa-oo-aaa-oo-aaa-oo-aaa-oo'. Intone the vowel sounds on one comfortable note (that means singing, but you don't need to be able to sing!). The sound doesn't have to be beautiful. Just create a long sound.

   Keep your breath constant and don't allow any gaps in the sound. Your mouth stays open for 'aaa' and just narrows a little for the 'oo' sound.

4. **After a few practices, eliminate the hum and start with 'a-oo-a-oo-a-oo-a-oo'.**

   Try 'mmm-aaa' a few times, then 'aaa' on its own a few times. The 'aaa' should feel the same with or without the hum before it.

   When you launch straight into the 'a-oo' sound, make the onset really smooth, as similar in quality to the hum as you can. You may be tempted to start the 'aaa' with a *glottal sound* – a little percussive kick from the vocal folds – but don't! After a few breaths, you're ready to turn sound into actual words.

5. **Return to humming again, but this time open up into smooth spoken words: 'How-now-brown-cow'.**

   Try saying the phrase without the initial hum. Keep the sound flowing by maintaining the long 'ow' sounds and lengthening the consonants 'h', 'n' and 'r'. Think of 'Hhaaoo-nnnaaoo-brraaoonn-caaoo.' The short 'b' of 'brown' and the 'c' 'cow' are crisp and clear and don't disrupt the flow of sound.

Become aware of everything that happens as you're making the sound. It's not about getting things right; it's about getting curious. Notice how you feel the hum playing around your lips. Notice how your hum suddenly breaks into more volume as your lips pop apart.

Don't take this practice too seriously! Give it inner life by having fun. Imagine that you're asking a brown cow a solemn question! Then try speaking the same words:

✔ Loudly and joyfully

✔ Quietly and purposefully

✔ Growing louder and building towards a dramatic flourish at the end

✔ Getting quieter towards the end, but making the end sound as important as the beginning

After you've exhausted the drama and excitement of 'How now brown cow', try creating the same feelings in a phrase that you're more likely to use in an everyday setting. Here are a few ideas:

✔ This is the way!

✔ That one for sure!

✔ Down on the ground!

✔ This is for you!

You can also choose your own short sentence – one that makes sense to you in some context. Remember to draw out the phrase with no gaps in the sound, and speak it with meaning.

Play-Acting with Sound and Breathing

The practices in this section all work better when you approach them in a spirit of play. Enjoy them and don't worry if things go wrong; that's all part of the process.

Getting big and theatrical

Continue to explore your dramatic mode by combining the breathing practices I describe in the earlier section 'Taking full breaths' with an energetic sentence. Gradually raise your arms out to the side and up above your head as you fill with air, first in your belly, then your ribs and back and finally your upper chest. Imagine that as you raise your arms, your excitement is building, and when your arms reach the highest point, give them an extra flourish and burst straight into some joyful sentence – one of the following or any sentence of your own that rings out with confidence:

> ✔ I'm on the top of the whole world!
>
> ✔ That's the way it's going to be!
>
> ✔ Listen to this, it's loud and important!
>
> ✔ Here's to you and me and everyone!

Ensure that the breath leads straight into the words with no hiatus between in-breath and vocal sound. I explain more about how this technique helps your vocal tone in Chapter 10. The words should coincide with the flourish of your hands above your head.

Surprising yourself

The in-breath happens easily whenever you're shocked or surprised. You can do the following practice with a friend or colleague. You need to get into a light-hearted frame of mind – no trying too hard!

Stand or sit facing each other, a few feet apart. Person A claps his or her hands. At that very moment, Person B notices something about Person A or the surroundings and acts suddenly surprised or shocked, speaking immediately and spontaneously. After saying a statement, Person B gets to clap and Person A reacts immediately. A conversation (of sorts) ensues.

This practice may run something like the following:

Person A claps.

Person B: *You've cut your hair!*

Person B claps.

Person A: *You're looking amazingly well!*

Person A clap.

Person B: *What's happened to your desk?!*

Person B claps.

Person A: *You're wearing blue today!*

Person A claps.

Person B: *You've got rid of your Ferrari!*

The idea of the clapping is to make the next comment happen suddenly. Don't worry about the comments making sense and feel free to act over the top. You can wait a few seconds before clapping if you like, to keep the other person on his or her toes. As your 'conversation' continues, listen to the freedom of the sound when you burst into speech. This practice reminds you that there are many different ways to take a good breath. I look at more of them in Chapter 10.

Declaiming like an actor

Communication involves more than random short phrases and exclamations. You also need to test your breathing in longer sentences, as Track 7 illustrates. Shakespeare is a great source for this type of material. Many speeches in his plays are written in *iambic pentameter verse* – consisting of lines with five stresses in them. Because the lines are of similar length and the breaths happen at more or less equal intervals, Shakespearean speech makes good practice for breathing.

The basic rhythm in iambic pentameter verse is *di **dum** di **dum** di **dum** di **dum** di **dum***. The rhythm isn't always quite as regular as that, but you always find five stresses in each line.

Although you can recite Shakespeare in many different styles, as a breathing exercise declaim the lines in a full voice with joined up sounds similar to the way you practise saying 'How-now-brown-cow?' in the previous section 'Turning Breath into Sound.'

Imagine that you're a famous actor at the height of your powers. Stand up, give yourself airs and put plenty of drama into the words – both for your enjoyment of the experience and because doing so helps your breath!

Find your own favourite 10- to 15-line passage spoken by a character in a Shakespearean play, or use the following, where King Richard speaks in melancholy mood in *Richard II*.

> For God's sake, let us sit upon the ground
> And tell sad stories of the death of kings;
> How some have been deposed; some slain in war,
> Some haunted by the ghosts they have deposed;
> Some poison'd by their wives: some sleeping kill'd;
> All murder'd: for within the hollow crown
> That rounds the mortal temples of a king
> Keeps Death his court and there the antic sits,
> Scoffing his state and grinning at his pomp,
> Allowing him a breath, a little scene,
> To monarchize, be fear'd and kill with looks,
> Infusing him with self and vain conceit,
> As if this flesh which walls about our life,
> Were brass impregnable, and humour'd thus
> Comes at the last and with a little pin
> Bores through his castle wall, and farewell king!

For the practice, take a breath at the end of each line. Don't read the whole speech at once the first time you practice; just work on three or four lines at a time. Use all your air in each line so that you feel that you need the fresh breath for the next line. When the sense runs over from one line to the next, still take the time to breathe at the end of the line, but keep the thought continuing in your mind through to the next line. If there's punctuation half-way through a line, feel the pause by taking your time, but don't take a new breath.

Pushing the boat out

If you watch news clips or video of a lifeboat being launched down a ramp, there's a moment when the boat, having gathered speed down the runway, goes into the water and forward in a powerful movement. The point of hitting the water provides no sudden jolt; its impact is just the central part of a powerful smooth movement.

Think of this image as you start each line of Shakespeare. Each line moves inexorably towards its end, with a strong word or words near the end of the line. As you speak, aim mentally for the words in bold, and when you reach those words, don't jolt them, but stroke them firmly as if your 'lifeboat' had farther to go. The words in bold remind you to aim for the **end** of each line in your mind.

If it helps, mark the lines as I have, with a tick at the end of each line to remind you to take a breath, and a line under the punctuation in the middle of a line to remind you to sense the little pause but allow the air to keep flowing *without* a breath.

> For God's sak<u>e,</u> let us sit upon the **ground** ✔
> And tell sad stories of the **death** of **kings**; ✔
> How some have been depose<u>d;</u> some **slain** in **war**, ✔
> Some haunted by the ghosts they have **deposed**; ✔

Shakespearean language is heightened and dramatic and may not seem much like the way you speak every day. But take that Shakespearean strength and direction into everyday statements, and they can sound more powerful rather than overblown.

Remembering to breathe!

Of course you're going to remember to breathe before you start speaking! But it is surprisingly easy to forget to breathe *regularly* at the end of each line or sentence.

Getting to the heart of speaking – by breathing

While this chapter looks mostly at the physical act of breathing, it's an important skill for communicating, developing relationships and even growing personally.

When you breathe well, a whole world opens up to you.

✔ You acquire the resources to speak more strongly and emphatically.

✔ You can more easily get people to listen to you – and continue listening to you.

✔ You gain confidence that even in a larger space you can be heard.

✔ You're able to put more variation into what you say and sound more engaged.

✔ Your brain can accommodate larger thoughts because you have the breath capacity to express them. You find that your brain is working better just because you're breathing better. A fresh new breath releases fresh new thinking.

✔ A good breath releases tension when you feel anxious.

✔ You listen better and respond in more focused ways.

In Chapter 10 I explore additional ways in which breath is the life blood of speech.

In the previous practices using Shakespearean verse, you take a breath at the end of each line, whether you need it or not. For this exercise (and in real life), your breath needs to be part of the rhythm of the whole, so you don't have all the time in the world as you do at the outset.

Just like the vacuum you create when you breathe out and hold your nose with your rib cage still open (see the earlier section 'Taking full breaths'), you want air to enter your lungs easily and rapidly when you need a breath in speaking – without any necessity to deliberately breathe in. You need that skill here.

When you say the last word of a line and have used all your air, your rib cage is still open and you haven't tensed up. At the moment you complete that last word, you can open the passageway of your nose and mouth, and air floods in, ready for the next line. This technique takes a bit of practice but it's a skill well worth acquiring.

When you're empty of air with your rib cage still open, it feels like a vacuum inside you. At this point, just allow yourself to fill again with air because your body wants to. Breathing in this way feels more like releasing than deliberately making an effort to breathe in.

Rather than random statements or Shakespearean verse, say something you're likely to come up with normally in the course of your day, maybe at a meeting or while giving instructions to someone. Take the same good breath when you see a tick, join up your sound and aim towards the end, just as you did with Shakespeare in the preceding section. Come up with your own statements or use the following:

> I'd like to warmly welcome you all to today's meeting ✔
> on the new company policy and **direction**.
>
> You'll find the growing number of new aps ✔
> will help you to keep better track of your **records.**

Now take a longer passage from some familiar material, such as a report, or a passage from a newspaper or magazine. Mark in with pencil ticks where you're going to breathe, and apply the technique you used for Shakespeare.

Chapter 5

Rediscovering Relaxation

· ·

In This Chapter

▶ Bringing relaxation to every part of your body

▶ Finding your balance and ideal posture

▶ Linking movement and speaking

· ·

My mantra throughout this book comes down to a single word: relax. Everything about your voice depends upon a relaxed body that is free to make your sound ring out. That's why I've written a whole chapter on the subject! The most important element for speaking well is your breath (see Chapter 4), and breath only works well with a flexible, relaxed body. If you're at all tight, you won't sound good. In the following sections, I explore several ways to release tension, rediscover relaxation, and ready your body to support effective speaking.

Relaxing is not the same as slumping or completely giving way. True relaxation is a potent mix of opposites: stillness and movement, inner calm and energy, peace and power.

At first this chapter's focus on the body may seem odd for a book about the voice. But as the great Polish theatre director Jerzy Grotowski told his students: 'The body must work first. Afterwards comes the voice.'

Finding Freedom For a Fine Sound

Your vocal folds are small and on their own don't produce much sound. But their vibration sets up sound waves that become amplified and re-amplified as they resonate around the bony cavities of your body. This requires freedom. *Freedom* is what gives your voice power and quality.

When I was a student I met a young musician who had just secured his first professional gig to play percussion in a performance for the Bath International Music Festival. His instrument for the first piece was the triangle. Now, the triangle doesn't even look like a serious instrument to me. I played exactly the same instrument in infant school! But I didn't tell my friend that; he was feeling the weight of his responsibility. On the evening of the performance, I was impressed with the large orchestra and the heroic music. But my main focus was my friend, holding his triangle and nervously counting the bars. Finally, in the climax, he raised the triangle on its string and struck it. And then it struck *me* – the power of that simple piece of string that enables a triangle's sound to resonate to the farthest corners of the theatre, loud and clear. The resonant, beautiful sound my friend produced stole the show as far as I was concerned!

A triangle only reverberates because it hangs loosely – because it is free to resonate. Every musical instrument needs freedom to vibrate. A bell has to be suspended; if you grab it by the rim and then strike it, it produces an ugly metallic clack. A giant gong hangs on wires. The strings of a violin, cello, guitar or piano must all be unrestricted so that they can vibrate freely.

Your voice is the same; it needs freedom, and that in terms of your body means *relaxation*. The sound waves set up by your voice resonate in the hollow bony cavities of your body: the chest, pharynx, mouth, nose, face and head. Think of your body as functioning in a similar way to the body of a violin or cello. The vibration only happens if nothing is gripped or held tightly. The resonating cavities then vibrate, producing their own harmonics, which amplify the original sounds.

You need to be relaxed in order for sound to vibrate throughout your body. Only with freedom in the body can your voice ring out in all its magnificence. No amount of pushing or force is going to give you a great voice. If your voice has freedom to vibrate, it sets up sound waves that sound full and vibrant.

Readying Your Body to Speak

You may not think much about your body when you speak. Perhaps you think that you have all you need for conversation in your head: you think of something to say in your brain, you breathe through your nose and the words come out of your mouth. Job done!

Playwright Alan Bennett's *Talking Heads* (1987) was a series of dramatic mono-logues written for the BBC. Each episode featured an unremarkable single character just talking about his or her life. Nothing really happened. But for the listener, the experience was captivating: full-bodied drama, emotion and poignancy were all there beneath the surface and between the lines in *how* the characters said what they said – and in what they left unsaid. Check out (or revisit) Bennett's monologues online; you can find dozens of video and audio clips of Bennett and others performing the pieces.

Your voice is a bit like Bennett's monologues. On the surface, expressing yourself via your voice appears to be a 'head job', the words that come out of your mouth. But everything that gives life to what you say – your determination, passion, emotions and gut instincts – comes from below the neck, in the energy of your body.

Many people use just the top half of their bodies when they speak. They breathe shallowly in their upper chests, focus on thinking rather than feeling and produce sound in their throats. As a result, their voices come out dry and flat, or tight and strained. Narrowing your awareness to just the thinking in your head narrows your voice in the process.

Your vocal cords rely on surrounding freedom to vibrate properly (see Chapter 4). The air passing across the folds depends for its momentum on your breathing muscles, which only operate freely if they're not otherwise engaged in holding up your body. If they take on that job and abandon their role in breathing, then your neck muscles take over and tense up in an effort to push out the air. This tension makes your voice tight and strained.

Speaking is as much a physical activity as an intellectual pursuit. Think of getting your body involved in speaking, much as you would warm up and involve your body in a round of golf or a game of tennis. The following sections guide you through simple warm-ups to get every part of your body ready for speaking.

Freeing up every part of your body

Many people work twice as hard as they need to when they speak by neglecting certain muscles and over-using others to compensate. Every part of your body is involved in speaking well, and the more mobile you are, the better co-ordinated the process and the better you sound.

The first step, to free yourself up for speaking, is to check for tension in each part of your body – and then release any tightness you discover. Use the following sections to guide you through your entire body as you search out and alleviate tension. I start with the spine and work down the body. The important muscles around the vocal cords have their own special section later called 'Relaxing around your vocal cords'.

Do the whole body shimmy-shake

Have you seen a dog emerge from water and shake the water out of its fur? Yes, I know, most canines come right up to you to perform this operation! A soaked dog is your inspiration for this practice.

Imagine that you're a dog who's just emerged from a pool of water. Vigorously shake yourself out all over. At the same time – if you can imitate two animals at once! – make an enthusiastic 'brrrrr' horse-whinnying sound with your lips and cheeks. Stop and take breath; then repeat the process a couple of times more.

Some people just shake their arms and legs, without actually moving the centre of their body between neck and thigh. Make sure that you move and bend *all* parts of your body. Shake your head, shoulders, body, hips, legs and feet. Come alive, remind yourself of all the wobbly bits of your body! A non-serious approach to this exercise definitely works best!

The following exercises are about *freeing* the body, not straining it! Take it easy as you follow the instructions and keep the word 'relax' in the forefront of your mind. Even the smallest movement is fine if you make it with an awareness of what you're doing. Do only what is comfortable.

Spine

Your spine is the structural foundation of your body and supports your frame. Your spine is essential to your breathing, which supports your voice. It even carries the nervous system, so the state of your spine affects how you feel and think as well.

You may have been taught from a young age that a strong spine is ramrod straight and unbending. Not so! A strong spine is actually mobile and flexible.

Gently explore your spine's range of motion. Sitting, standing or even lying on your back, tenderly stretch your spine in all directions, sideways, in rotation, and forwards and backwards in a rolling motion like a crawling caterpillar. Any small fluid movement is good. Feel the spine's stiffness loosen.

Shoulders

Your shoulders are often one of the first places you notice signs of tension, and tight shoulders have an instant negative effect on your voice. Take your time to release them, starting with your hands and arms and then moving your attention to your shoulders.

1. **Shake your hands energetically by your sides for a few moments, gradually making the movements smaller but not slower.**

2. **Raise your shoulders high while breathing in, then let go on the out-breath and allow them to fall down under their own weight to their natural position.** Repeat a few times.

3. **Make two or three big circles with your right arm and then your left, feeling the weight of each arm on the downward movement.**

4. **Swing your arms in circles again, and this time involve your shoulders more.**

5. **Wiggle your shoulders all over the place in every direction.**

6. **Raise your right hand in front of you as though you're holding out a small gift.** Notice that you can do this action at the same time as releasing tension in your right shoulder. Repeat with your left hand.

Shoulder tension inhibits your breathing and tightens your voice, so watch out for the signs – especially when you've sat at your computer for a while or had a stressful day. Give your shoulders a friendly wiggle every now and then!

Rib cage

You may think of your rib cage as a stationary collection of bones, cartilage and other connective tissues, but this entire area has surprising mobility, and needs to be flexible when you breathe. If you hold your rib cage stiffly up to increase your breathing capacity, you only end up tightening your upper chest and stomach, which gives you *less* space to breathe rather than more.

Instead, feel the mobility of your ribs as you breathe.

1. **Raise your ribs as you breathe in and lower them again as you breathe out.**

   Feel your whole rib cage expand outwards with the gentle movement.

2. **Include your back where your ribs connect to your spine in the action of breathing in and raising your rib cage.**

   Your shoulders move a bit during the process, but don't deliberately raise your shoulders or allow them to stiffen.

Diaphragm

The diaphragm is a powerful muscle, but it needs to be flexible when you speak. I discuss this muscle in more detail in relation to breathing in Chapter 4.

Picture a dog panting in hot weather. The fast in-breath and the out-breath are the same length and balance each other. Pant yourself, starting quite slowly and then speeding up. At the same time, move your neck and your shoulders to make sure that you're free there. The more you pay attention to relaxing, the easier panting becomes. Continue for a few seconds, feeling your tummy wobble in and out as your diaphragm moves up and down.

Your diaphragm tends to contract when you feel nervous. Unfortunately, this contraction may happen at the very same time that you want to speak and are attempting to relax it. You end up with the diaphragm pulling in two directions simultaneously and, as a result, it gets stuck and can't move in *any* direction.

If your diaphragm feels locked in place, cramped or just disconnected, take a few moments and think of the flexible movement of panting. That way you can stay connected to your lower body.

Pelvis

Many people hold their pelvis tightly. It's not much in fashion to put a wiggle in your walk, but do that now: walk up and down the room and let your pelvis swing from side to side in a swagger. Practise the pelvic swing as you walk along the pavement outside too! You can also stand on the spot, and picture the pelvis as a bucket containing water, which you slosh around freely. When you come to rest, the water becomes still in the centre of the bucket.

Legs, knees and feet

Clamped legs and locked knees create enormous tension throughout your whole body, running up your spine and to your throat. Death to a good voice!

Before you begin speaking, spare a moment for your knees, particularly if you feel nervous. Softening your knees is one of the most useful reminders you can give yourself when you speak in public.

Your feet are a long way away from your voice box, but they're your foundation and affect your balance. Stand with your feet facing forward a short distance apart. Feel your connection to the ground through your toes and heels, and feel steady and balanced. I come back to your feet in the later section 'Standing Steady and Balanced'.

Relaxing around your vocal cords

Your whole body needs to be relaxed when you speak, and every part is important. However, the parts in the vicinity of your vocal cords are especially significant because here the tiniest difference has a correspondingly large effect on the quality of your voice. And these parts tense up very easily! For these reasons, I devote the following section specifically to the areas around your vocal folds.

Neck and throat

The vocal folds actually live in your throat inside the larynx, otherwise called the voice box. Any tension in your throat makes your voice sound thin and dull.

When your breathing is inadequate – perhaps when you're feeling anxious right before speaking – you may give your throat muscles too much to do and end up tensing them as you attempt to speak. Your words become trapped in your throat. This tension blocks the voice from resonating deeper into your chest and you lose your deeper sounds.

Free your throat by doing all the following:

1. **Turn your head gently to the left, then to the right.**

2. **Let your head drop down until your chin touches your chest and then roll your head gently from side to side.** Feel the gentle mobility of your neck in all directions.

3. **Lift your head.** Feel your neck tall and free with an open passage through the throat.

4. **Do a quick tension check of your shoulders, jaw and tongue.** (Yes, your tongue needs to feel relaxed too. It's amazing what it can get up to!)

If you feel you're getting tense as you speak, gently move your head from side to side to avoid stiffening up.

Head

Human beings have big heads! At least, they have *heavy* heads. Your head weighs as much as a roast goose and can cause trouble if you jut it out forwards or pull it back.

The relationship between the spine and the head is crucial as it determines what happens through the rest of the body. The head wants to feel poised lightly on the top of the spine with an upward feel. The perfect position for your head is floating on the top of your spine, like a ping pong ball caught in an upsurge of air. Of course, it can move easily in all directions as you move your neck. If you're stiff in the neck and head, you're likely to tighten your jaw and squeeze your voice.

To get your head in a relaxed position, let it drop forward, then lift it slowly, paying attention to the muscles of your neck as they pick up the weight of your head and uncurl one by one. After your head returns to an upright position, move it in all directions and bring it to rest upright and balanced.

You may want to keep your head still sometimes when you speak, but don't ever let it become fixed. Let it always feel free and mobile.

After working with your head, focus on your face for a few moments. Relax all your facial muscles and feel any tightness melt away. Imagine that your forehead is as smooth as velvet, your eyes soft and your lips and tongue relaxed. Let all expression melt away.

Mouth and jaw

The jaw is a strong character and can grip sound like a vice. It's the custom in some cultures to move the jaw very little – the traditional 'Oxford English' accent is sometimes a culprit here. Try locking your jaw and stiffening your lips and then put on a posh English accent. You immediately feel rather 'landed gentry' – but your sound is also tight and stripped of much of its expressiveness!

If you lock your jaw, the sound is obstructed and the words can't escape. Locked jaw means locked throat and locked tongue too. The tension is tiring too – for you *and* for anyone having to listen to you.

For a free and clear voice, you want to be able to move your jaw freely. Imagine that you've suddenly spotted something absurd, and let your jaw drop in surprise. Just let your jaw muscles go and your lower teeth drop – allow yourself to look a bit simple!

Voice coaches sometimes suggest that your open mouth should be able to accommodate two fingers held vertically but don't force the jaw open in order to achieve this. Notice instead that the back teeth separate when you open your mouth.

By the way, your lower jaw should be doing all the moving. If you tighten the muscles around the base of your skull, lift your head up and open up the top lip you don't achieve the right result.

After opening your mouth, close it and chew around for a while. Place your fingers behind your ears where the jaw hinges and feel movement. You may find, as you move your jaw around, that you want to yawn. That's a sign that you're releasing the jaw beautifully.

Before you speak, make sure that you're not clenching your jaw or grinding your teeth. While your mouth is still closed, feel your jaw released and 'hanging' freely.

Standing Steady and Balanced

Were you ever told to sit up straight or stand up straight at school? When given this instruction, children often stick out their chests and draw in their stomachs. This action makes them ramrod stiff and they can't even continue breathing normally.

Good posture is certainly about standing tall, but also about standing relaxed. You don't have to 'adopt' a posture, like assuming a pose. Good posture is more of a settling in and a settling down, more about being than doing.

Many people look in the mirror and are not happy with what they see. Perhaps you notice that you're slouching or that your shoulders are rounded. Your bottom may stick out, your legs may be stiff or your knees may point inwards. You may find yourself issuing sharp mental instructions such as 'Stop slouching!' or 'For goodness sake, stand straight!' or 'Stop staring at the ground!' In response to your self-criticism, you may try to sort out particular bits of your posture. You tuck in your behind, you pull your shoulders back and you tighten your slack tummy. But your posture isn't improved by your modifications. You just feel awkward and stiff.

Rearranging your body from the outside, bit by bit, doesn't help. You need to sense good posture from within. Dr Ida Rolfe, pioneer of the relaxation technique known as Rolfing, spoke about 'dis-arming' the body – removing all the tension and stress of posing and pretence and leaving a sense of openness and relaxed optimism. If your body is all screwed up or uneven, or if you're leaning too far forward or too far back, you're tightening certain muscles to stay upright, and the tightness inhibits the sound.

You can demonstrate the effects of awkward posture for yourself. Stand up straight and imposing with your shoulders back and stiff, military fashion, and say a sentence or two. If nothing comes to mind, try 'Good afternoon everyone; I'm delighted to be with you today for our Conference on Cork-Screws of the World.' Now slump and give way; slouch your shoulders, blow out of your lips and bend your knees. Say the sentence again. How is that for you? In nearly all cases, people find that during the second time their voices are freer and more resonant, and the whole task is much easier. You're giving your voice freedom to speak.

Standing in the right way encourages your body to relax, but only if you don't try too hard to 'stand up straight'. Instead, think of standing *balanced,* which allows all your muscles to play their appropriate parts.

Rediscovering your balance

Of course you can speak when you're standing up or sitting down, or even standing on your head. But the quality of your sound depends on balance in your body. Standing balanced boosts your confidence too.

Your body, deep down, already knows how to stand steady and balanced if you just relax and tune into it. Improving your way of standing, and thus your voice, is about removing inhibitions, *undoing* rather than *adding* something new.

As a child you knew how to stand. You probably didn't stand still much, but when you did, your spine was erect and long, your joints free and you effortlessly supported your large head on your little neck. Explore what your younger self has to show you about posture.

1. **Stand up, and imagine for a moment stepping into your body at three years old again.**

   • What do you feel like, as a three-year-old?

   • How do your bones and muscles feel?

   • How do you want to stand and move?

   • How contented and optimistic do you feel? (Choose a happy moment!)

2. **Bring that information to the present and scan your body balance in the here and now.**

   Do this exercise with bare feet or wearing flat shoes. Stand with your arms hanging by your sides and look straight ahead. As you stand, become aware of your contact with the ground and feel the sense of comfort and ease in your body.

3. **Turn your awareness to your balance.**

   a. Point your feet straight forward, about a foot apart, and soften your knees. As they soften, be aware that at the same time other parts of you settle and relax more without slumping.

   b. Stand tall and relaxed. Then sway just a little forwards and backwards until you find your mid-point, neither leaning forward nor back. Ideally, your hips are directly over your feet.

   You may find that you're not sure where your mid-point is. That is quite common. Many people are in the habit of standing unbalanced and have lost their true sense of equilibrium.

   Try placing your feet at different distances apart – about a body's width or so – to help establish a clearer sense of balance. Try standing in front of a mirror so that you have a visible image of balance to help you.

   c. While you're standing in a balanced position, breathe calmly. Feel the gentle rise and fall of your belly. With each breath, feel ever more aware that you're balanced.

Adopting a floating posture

When thinking about your posture, imagine that you're hanging from the sky, rather than having to support the weight of your body. The feeling of lightness this thought gives you naturally adjusts your body and balance to the best posture for speaking. Your imagination often creates a better result than simple physical adjustment. In the following exercise, imagine that you're a string puppet.

Voice coach Kirsten Linklater, who studied at the London Academy of Music and Dramatic Art with influential voice expert Iris Warren, helps people become better speakers by encouraging them to create *internal pictures* that influence their physiology. The following practice is based on methods she presents in her book *Freeing the Natural Voice* (Drama Pub, 2006). Listen, too, to Track 8 on the audio file.

1. **Find your balanced stance.**

   See the preceding section 'Rediscovering your balance'.

2. **Feel your feet in connection with the earth and sense your body rising from the ground.**

   Pay attention to how each bone comfortably separates from the next: your ankles, shins, knee joints and thighs are all rising. Imagine your pelvic girdle and rising from it your hip joints and spine. Feel from the bottom upwards each vertebra of your back rise, continuing to rise up between your shoulder blades and up through your neck. Picture the bones of your neck rising up into the skull, and the skull itself floating at the top like a balloon. As you imagine this, continue to feel your feet in contact with the floor.

   Allow everything to float upwards, while your arms hang by your sides, each bone hanging from the one above, down to your wrist joints and the bones of your hands.

3. **Imagine that you've strings attached to your elbows, wrists and fingers – like a puppet.**

   Let the strings pull your elbows up high in the air, then permit the strings attached to your wrists to pull your wrists up higher still. Then strings attached to the tips of your fingers pull the fingers up higher still.

   Your whole body is held from above and hangs down from the tips of your fingers.

4. **Let the 'strings' go one by one and gently release your body bit by bit.**

   Let your hands drop and hang from the wrists. Then your wrists and forearms relax and hang loosely from the elbow. Your arms drop to hang heavily down from the shoulders.

5. **Gently release the strings holding your head and other body parts.**

   Drop your head forward so that head and neck hang off your body like a headless torso, and then relax your spine bone by bone from the top down until you're bent right over, hanging loosely from your tailbone. Soften your knees as well. Keep breathing throughout and enjoy the feeling of relaxation for a few moments.

6. **Gently uncurl your spine again without tightening your stomach muscles, gradually straightening your knees.**

   Unwind each vertebra right up into the neck and allow your head to float comfortably again. Picture your energy moving upwards.

7. **Stretch, yawn and shake out your body.**

   Notice how alive and awake you feel in your body.

8. **Become aware of how you have the ability to soften all parts of your body.**

   You can, simply by thinking, soften your neck, your shoulders, each vertebra of your spine, your chest and abdomen, your pelvis, your legs and arms.

   As each part softens, it feels lighter too. Everywhere you move your attention, that part of you softens and melts, while your skeleton stands tall.

9. **Turn your awareness to the inside and melt away any tensions you may find.**

   Check for little bits of remaining tension in the mask of your face, your throat, your chest, stomach and down into the groin.

   Be aware of the gentle movement of the breath within those spaces. Enjoy the freedom in your body.

Going Deeper into Relaxation With Body and Mind

This practice – like all the practices in this chapter – is about sensation and feeling. Speaking is as much about feeling as about hearing. (See 'Hearing through feeling' for a compelling example.) After all, when you hear a voice, you feel it in your body too – sometimes uncomfortably so!

Focusing on the internal feeling as you practise relaxation for speaking is more important than getting anxious about how you actually sound, just as swinging a club with ease is more important to becoming a better golfer than focusing on where the ball actually ends up. As a novice golfer, if you concentrate only on getting the ball to the right place, you're likely to acquire a patched-together technique that doesn't serve you in the long run. Sports coaches often talk about 'getting out of your own way', which is about freeing yourself rather than going through the motions of learned (or 'pasted on') techniques. So enjoy heightening your awareness of what your body and mind are actually doing rather than driving yourself towards specific results.

Hearing through feeling

Solo percussionist Evelyn Glennie provides an inspiring example of learning through feeling. She was at first turned down for a place at the Royal Academy of Music in London because she was deaf. The audition panel asked how she hoped to be able to hear well enough to play percussion. She replied that she listened with her whole body – through her hands holding the drumsticks, up through her arms, her cheekbones, scalp, her tummy, chest and legs.

She then demonstrated how when you open your body up and free it from tension, you can allow the vibration to come up through you. The whole body vibrates with sound and every part of your body has a part to play in this. With practice you can feel the most minute differences in pitch with the smallest part of a single finger.

Evelyn challenged the panel's original decision, won her deserved place at the Academy, and by her example managed to change the attitude of many music institutions towards disabled students for the better.

Your posture affects your mood, and your mood affects your posture. A resourceful state of mind can help your posture more than you may think.

Don't think in terms of 'adopting' a posture; that is just 'posturing'. Instead, do as little as possible and just feel the sensation of upward energy and lightness that comes from a relaxed, open mind and body. That sensation itself creates a calm feeling within you, bringing mind and body into harmony.

The famous Israeli movement teacher, Moshé Feldenkrais, suggested that an *open physical stance* allows your mind to open as well, resulting in a sense of objectivity and awareness of alternative possibilities. Your freed body allows more effective thinking, improved concentration and greater confidence – all of which can be helpful for you as a speaker. So a positive state of mind helps you physically, and physical relaxation produces a better state of mind. See the sidebar 'The Feldenkrais Method' for more on this great teacher.

You express emotions through your physical body. When you're tense, you struggle to express certain emotions, such as enthusiasm or pleasure. Equally when emotions seem overwhelming, your body may tense up to protect itself from fear. To some extent, all vocal problems combine physical and emotional causes, and often intellectual or spiritual causes as well. The English language is filled with phrases that express this link between feeling and the physical voice: 'the feeling got stuck in my throat' or 'her heart came into her mouth.' Have a look *Body Language For Dummies* by Elizabeth Kuhnke for more on body/mind connection.

Blending Relaxation with Readiness: Not Too Tight, Not Too Loose

The preceding sections look at relaxing every part of your body. Of course if you totally relaxed your body, you would fall down. Relaxing is not the same as slumping; it needs a sense of life too.

In his excellent book *The Courage to Love* (W.W. Norton & Company, 1997), Stephen Gilligan tells the story of swashbuckling movie star Errol Flynn who was once asked the correct way to hold a sword. Flynn replied that you had to imagine you were holding a live bird instead of a sword. If you held on too tight, the bird was crushed and its life was lost. If you held too loosely, the bird escaped and you were left with nothing. The trick was to hold on 'not too tight, not too loose' with a *felt connection.* This connection is absolutely what you need to speak well.

In order to experience a felt connection, compare two sensations. First clench your fists tightly at your sides and breathe in and out a few times. You experience some sort of connection, but it's tight, tense and restricted. Now gently touch your fingertips together in front of you, using the lightest of feather touches and breathe several times. *That* is breathing with a felt connection.

If you do yoga, the martial arts, T'ai Chi, Rolfing or develop any sport to a high level, you understand the idea of not too tight, not too loose. The feeling is always of movement and elasticity even in a static pose.

Think of anything you do easily and well, and you find that the same 'not too tight, not too loose' description applies. For instance, if you polish a fine glass, you hold it both confidently and delicately. If you paint a picture, you hold the paint brush with poise but without stiffening up. If you hold a tennis racquet, you hold it flexibly yet strongly as an extension of your arm. In all these activities you apply perfect control. The activities in the following sections help your find your best blend of elasticity and relaxation.

Involving your whole body

When I talk about letting go, I often do so with the idea of relaxing muscles that are getting involved in activities that are not their job, and by doing so allowing the appropriate muscles to be used.

Movement teacher Moshé Feldenkrais understood the extraordinary subtlety of movements in any action in which each tiny muscle is allowed to play its appropriate role. (See the sidebar 'The Feldenkrais Method' for more on this great instructor.) The following exercise may seem all too simple, but awareness is all.

1. **Sit upright on an firm chair.**

    Supporting your own back, position your feet flat on the floor and place your hands in your lap.

2. **Slowly – and with full awareness – lower your head and look down to see your belt buckle.**

3. **Return to the original position in Step 1.**

    That's it! That's the exercise!

But now a few questions: Did you move just your head by bending your neck? You might have, but the movement is easier if you bring more of yourself into the action.

1. **Repeat the action slowly and this time pay close attention to your chest.** Place your hand on the sternum bone in the middle of your chest and become aware of your chest tipping down towards your belly, along with your head and eyes. Feel your ribs move. As you reverse the motion, feel your chest help to bring your head back up.

2. **Repeat the action again and become aware of your lower back, just above your waist.** Notice how your lower back moves back and rounds slightly as you look down. Then, notice how it moves forward, arching gently as you come up again. Place your hands there to feel the movement.

3. **Repeat the action again and notice your pelvis.** Feel your pelvis rock gently backwards as you look down and sense how you sit more on the back of your buttocks. Coming back up, feel your pelvis rock forward as you sit more on the front of your buttocks.

Even with this simplest of movements, you become aware that your eyes, neck, head, chest, lower back, pelvis and buttocks are all part of one co-ordinated movement of your whole body.

When you move using all parts of your body, you find that your movement has a grace and ease about it that was not evident the first time you tried it. So too, when you encourage relaxation in your body, your intention to speak stimulates all the tiny movements that contribute to full and meaningful sound. Then, you *really* begin to communicate. When you're tense, you push muscles into play with force, resulting in unpleasant sound and no real communication.

The Feldenkrais Method

Moshé Feldenkrais was a mechanical engineer and physicist, as well as the very first Judo black-belt holder in Europe. He became a great thinker and teacher. After suffering from a knee injury, he taught himself to walk painlessly, which lead to the development of his special method.

The Feldenkrais Method provides a way of discovering and recovering comfort in your body's movements through increasing your self-awareness. Instead of trying deliberately to correct something, you work to become aware of your body, and your body discovers for itself how to self-correct. By moving with awareness, you find ways to vary your movements and make them more effective and spontaneous, much in the way that a baby, with its free body, makes sense of its movements.

People rehabilitating after injury, as well as many athletes, dancers, musicians and speakers, enjoy benefits of exploring movement with the Feldenkrais Method. If you want to explore the method further, you need to work with a qualified practitioner (see www.feldenkrais.com).

Relishing the state of readiness

Readiness in the martial arts combines freedom and flexibility, and the recipe is similar for successful speaking. Readiness allows you to use your body with utmost efficiency – more power for less effort. Readiness is in fact the quality observed in sports people or artists when they're in the zone.

Readiness is a feeling of being 'switched on'. When you begin to speak, you want to feel relaxed yet alert at the same time. Indeed, the highest skill in speaking is the ability to maintain this sense of alive yet relaxed flow in front of an audience, when normal tensions are prone to return.

In the *Pink Panther* films of the 1960s and 1970s, Inspector Clouseau, played by Peter Sellers, is constantly attacked by his Chinese servant Cato, who has been instructed by Clouseau to sharpen his martial arts skills. As a result, Clouseau must be constantly alert – a task at which he fails spectacularly and humorously. Although the films are comedy, you do get the sense of the character's readiness, his senses heightened and ready to respond to the smallest stimulus.

Enjoying perpetual motion

When you speak, you're never static. You move all the time; even when you sit and do nothing, you move. When a plane flies from Los Angeles to Sydney on automatic pilot, its direction is never constant. The plane begins to veer slightly off course and the autopilot corrects it, then it goes a little off course again in the other direction and is corrected again, constantly being micro-adjusted. You do the same with your posture and balance.

Life is expansion, moving and extending. Many musicians develop relaxation through the Alexander Technique. Alexander teachers talk always in terms of movement – *lengthening* the spine, *releasing* and *widening* the shoulders and *broadening* the back. They suggest that you envision a direction for relaxed movement with your thoughts and move in that direction.

Think of expanding in all directions when you stand and speak. Imagine the crown of your head moving towards the ceiling, your back widening and lengthening, and your shoulders moving towards the walls. Feel how this expansion allows space for you to breathe and express yourself more fully.

Alexander Technique

In the 1890s in Melbourne, Australia, a young actor called Frederick Mathias Alexander experienced a problem with recurrent hoarseness and voice loss. It was threatening his ambitions as an actor, so he turned his efforts to restoring his lost voice. Unable to find anyone to help him, he started to observe and experiment on himself and discovered that instead of opening up his throat and body to speak, he was tensing his neck and throat muscles and gripping his entire body – in effect closing down.

Based on this observation, he designed a series of processes to solve his problems. The resulting Alexander Technique is a way to return the body to its balance and natural poise that you've lost through unconscious habits of tension and excessive effort. In following these techniques, you build an awareness of mobility in your body that helps you to develop a freedom and ease in your movements and leads to free expression.

On regaining his voice, Alexander also found that the asthma that plagued him since childhood disappeared – an example of how a poised body and good breathing can affect your whole health and well-being.

Famous early students of the Alexander Technique include George Bernard Shaw and Aldous Huxley, and his work has been endorsed by musicians as diverse as Yehudi Menuhin, Paul McCartney, Sting, Julian Bream and James Galway. The Technique is taught at the Julliard School of Performing Arts in New York, The Royal College of Music in London, The Royal Conservatory of Music in Toronto and at many other educational establishments. If you want to pursue this useful technique, you need to work, preferably one-to-one, with a qualified teacher. You can find more information at www.alexandertechnique.com.

In order to experience the powerful connection between movement and speech, try moving and speaking. Give yourself lots of space. Walk around with purpose and confidence. Raise an arm as you breathe in and sweep it across your body as you breathe out, as if you were introducing an act in the theatre. Make your gesture smooth and theatrical. As you walk around more, make an expansive gesture on the other side. Continue gesturing in this way for a while and eventually begin speaking while you make your large gestures. Say a couple of lines of sweeping verse – perhaps the opening lines of Wordsworth's *Composed Upon Westminster Bridge* (join in to Track 9):

> Earth has not anything to show more fair:
> Dull would he be of soul who could pass by
> A sight so touching in its majesty:
> This City now doth like a garment wear
> The beauty of the morning; silent, bare,
> Ships, towers, domes, theatres, and temples lie
> Open unto the fields, and to the sky.

Speak expansively – nobly even! – with one sweeping gesture per line. Feel how the movement and gestures free the sound and give it rhythm and energy. Freedom and speech together – the winning combination!

Chapter 6

Turning Sound into Speech

. . . .

In This Chapter

▶ Artfully articulating sounds

▶ Helping your listeners easily understand what you're saying

▶ Bringing language to life with your long sounds

▶ Spicing up your speech with your short sounds

. . . .

*W*hen you speak, you want people to understand you easily. How to do that is the principal focus of this chapter.

Speaking isn't just a physical activity. It involves your brain and emotion too. Voice work starts with breathing better (see Chapter 4) and letting go of tension (see Chapter 5), but it also requires developing your physical ability to articulate words in the most economical way and turn your thoughts into effective communication. When you *articulate*, or *enunciate*, your words, people are able to hear every part of each word distinctly.

If you want to be clear, start with a free open sound, which I explore in much greater detail in Chapter 5. Enjoy a feeling of effortlessness. You don't need to listen particularly to the sounds you make; focus on getting to know the free *feeling*.

Making Your Voice Clearly Understood

If someone tells you that you mumble (there's more about mumbling in Chapter 11), you may think that the answer is to speak louder. But being understood doesn't require you to shout, just to be exquisitely clear. Your listeners have to make sense of what you say; if they don't get your meaning, speaking is pointless.

Note that making yourself understood has nothing to do with your accent, education level or class. It starts with *wanting* to be understood. If you're half hoping nobody's listening because you're not sure whether you're talking sense, then you certainly won't be clear.

If you really need to have others understand, you're probably more than capable of making it happen. Picture yourself in a dramatic situation – or in a film thriller. You're the first to notice smoke and flames or someone pulling out a gun. I'm sure that you can clearly yell 'Fire!' or 'He's got a gun!' and make sure that other people understand the situation.

However, in everyday speech you tend not to take such a high level of care to be clear. The following sections give you several articulation techniques.

Forming the words

What does articulating entail? Unlike breathing, which involves your whole body (see Chapter 4), articulating your words *is* just head stuff. In fact, it all happens in a small space in your head. Although saying a simple word such as 'hello' takes the co-ordination of 100 muscles, the actual word-shaping is just your lips closing and opening in different ways and various bits of your tongue hitting parts of the mouth, including your upper gums, the roof your mouth and the back of your hard palate. And that's it.

If your face is active when you speak, you're halfway towards speaking clearly. If your face is usually an impassive mask, you need to get it moving. See the following section 'Warming up your facial muscles'.

Next time you listen to an announcer or commentator on the television, switch the sound down for a few moments so that you're not distracted by what he or she is saying. Just watch the speaker's face and mouth. Are you surprised by how mobile the features are? Now turn up the sound and try saying some of the speaker's phrases yourself with similar facial movements. You probably have to be quite animated to match them.

Various things can get in the way of facial mobility:

- ✔ If your breath isn't properly supporting the sound, your tongue provides compensatory strength and therefore isn't free to take its rightful part in articulation. Check that both the front and back of your tongue can move freely. (See Chapter 4 for tips on breath support.)

- ✔ If you habitually hold your lips tight, you'll struggle to articulate freely. Shake them loose!

> ✔ If you focus too much on manipulating your lips and tongue, their move-
> ments can become too powerful. You end up with clear diction but awk-
> ward exaggerated facial movements and artificial-sounding words. Don't
> try too hard.

In the old days, elocution was about learning to speak 'beautifully,' which
included the right accent. It involved pronouncing UK English like Joanna
Lumley or US English like Frasier in the famous sitcom, with much movement
of mouth and lips. I have vague memories from my early schooldays of reciting 'Jonathan *Joe*, has a mouth like an *O*' with exaggerated facial movements!
This work resulted in people talking with bright, larger-than-life clarity. Listen
to and watch Margaret Thatcher in recordings of her early speeches before she
became Prime Minister for a prime example of this type of classic elocution.

Think of your mouth, lips and tongue being nimble and supple when you
speak, rather than grossly exaggerated. Articulation should consist of natural
easy movements joined with the sound-making breath, and not efforts to push
the sound out *despite* the breath. You want any movement to articulate to be
freeing and liberating, not made artificial by loads of exaggerated motions or
facial contortions.

Warming up your facial muscles

If you're going to do a run or even take a long walk, you probably do a bit of
limbering up first. Public speakers and actors often limber up their voices
and all the supporting muscles around their mouths before giving speeches
or performances.

In everyday life, however, most people are a bit lazy around the mouth
when they speak, and would benefit from warming up their vocal muscles
when they want to be heard. A little vocal preparation can be the difference
between a voice that trudges along with a slouching tread – or one that
swings easily and gracefully in a confident stride.

Don't be concerned that you may look foolish with over-the-top mouth movements when you practise. Be prepared to make funny faces in the interest of
your voice. The following practices are about loosening up your face, lips and
tongue, not developing expressions you can take out into the street – though
you never know where they may come in handy!

Before you start to exercise your speaking muscles, just release any tension
in your body by shaking out your limbs, moving your shoulders, swinging
your arms and loosening your knees for a moment. See Chapter 5 for loads of
ideas to get your body warmed up. Don't do the following facial exercises all

at once – just choose one or two and perform each for a few seconds at a time. When you know how to do them, you can practise your favourites briefly whenever you have a couple of moments alone, when driving or walking for example.

Face

Spend a few moments moving each part of your face:

- Screw up your face tightly, then stretch it out. Using your face muscles, pull it to the left and then to the right.
- Stretch your mouth wide, then pout; wide and pout, wide and pout.
- Raise and lower your eyebrows. Blink fast; then squeeze your eyes tightly shut and wide open, both together and separately.
- Raise and lower your cheeks.
- Wiggle your jaw around and about and up and down. Let your jaw unhinge and hang for a few seconds and then gently lift it.
- Gently massage your face, especially around the eyes. Then, rub your palms together until they're warm. Cup your warm palms and place them over your eyes. Feel any tension in your face melt away in the warmth.

Tension in the face is your enemy. Have you ever noticed people with mask-like faces, so set that they hide every thought and feeling. A tight, impassive face creates a tight, dull voice. Let your face be alive and your voice comes alive too.

Lips

Listen to Track 10. During the following, imagine that you have large soft lips like a horse:

- Move your lips in all directions.
- Make a wide grin, then pout with your lips well forward; repeat a few times.
- With your teeth together, move your bottom lip like a horse showing its teeth, then bare your top lip up as if you're sneering.
- As you take a breath, pull your mouth out wide with your fingers like a child making a funny face; then suddenly let your fingers go, at the same time blowing through your lips like a horse: *brrr*!
- Now, in a whisper just using air, pronounce the following quite fast. Count 1 and 2 for each line – four sounds to the first count, and one long sound for the second. Keep your jaw relaxed and mobile:

1	*2*
Bee bee bee bee	bee-ee
Beh beh beh beh	be-eh
Bah bah bah bah	ba-ah
Boh boh boh boh	bo-oh
Boo boo boo boo	boo-oo

Enjoy moving your facial muscles. These activities can be fun and freeing. Great voices love mobile faces and lips!

Tongue

A major part of forming words takes place way back inside your mouth where you cannot see. This area is often the part of speaking that traditional elocution lessons ignore.

Here's a workout that exercises all parts of your tongue. Before you start, note the position of your tongue when it's lying at rest. The tip should be comfortably forward and the back relaxed and not bunched up in the roof of your mouth.

- ✔ With your mouth closed, move your tongue about inside your mouth to touch one side and then the other.

- ✔ Stick out your tongue and shake it all about, side to side, up and down and round in a circle. Pretend that you're a cat that's just received a saucer of milk and laps up every last drop and then licks its lips all around with pleasure.

- ✔ If you can, roll your tongue into a C-shape.

- ✔ Open your mouth and see whether your tongue can touch your chin and then attempt to touch the tip of your nose.

- ✔ Without employing your vocal folds, whisper on air: *lalalala lalalala lalalala lalalala.* Repeat faster.

- ✔ If you can roll your 'r's, make an r-sound like a motor for a few seconds.

Your tongue is much larger than you may think. The preceding activities exercise just the tip of your tongue. In order to exercise the middle of your tongue, put the tip of your tongue on your bottom teeth and, keeping it there, roll the tongue back and forth out of the mouth and in again. Become aware of the tongue further back as it gets involved in the movement.

Don't forget about the back of your tongue and the soft palate. Open your mouth wide, then relax your lips while your mouth stays open. Whisper the sounds *kaa kaa kaa kaa,* and using the voice, *nga nga nga nga* (the sound here is like the end of the word 'song'). Encourage yourself to do a great round yawn. Then, with the feeling of opening into a yawn, gently whisper *kaa kaa kaa kaa* on an in-breath. The opening to your throat feels wide open at this point. Join in to Track 10!

A well-behaved tongue is going to be tremendously helpful in speaking well. A wayward tongue can be quite a liability:

✔ If your tongue pulls back while speaking, it closes your throat and makes your voice sound nasal.

✔ If the back of your tongue is tense, you lose many of your bright higher tones and much of the middle of your voice too. See Chapter 9 for creating high and low resonance with your voice.

✔ If your breath support is weak, your tongue gets too involved in making sound and muffles it.

✔ If your tongue is bunched up at the back of your mouth, you tend to get too much mucus too.

When everything else is working, your tongue happily does its job without conscious interference on your part. If you think about it too much, it just seems too large for your mouth. A good warm-up helps to ensure that it doesn't block your sound. For the most part, you can just leave it be.

Jaw

You need to be able to release the jaw and move it freely. So just feel it flop open. Imagine that you're a fish and open and close your mouth in the same soft pouty way. Hear your lips give a satisfying popping sound as you release the jaw. Check that your back teeth are separated, which is a good indicator that you've released the jaw.

When you watch someone talking, the jaw looks as if it is involved in the enunciation process, but is only moving up and down with the movement of other facial muscles and tongue. Your jaw doesn't have an active role in forming words, but it does need to be free; and when it's free your voice is able to ring out.

Giving your air attitude

When you've loosened up all your facial muscles, you're ready to give life to your communication. Speaking words is exciting when it's led by your thoughts. You've an energy inside you that wants to communicate; speaking isn't just empty calisthenics.

Articulation gives clarity to your sentences. When you hear a sentence clearly in your own language, your brain divides it into words. But with a language you don't comprehend, you hear a continuous stream of sound and you cannot tell how it divides into individual words. For example, if English is your language, you hear 'What are you going to do?' as five words. In many parts of the US, however, what you actually hear is a single smooth extended sound: 'Whaddayagonnado?' – one word! This joined-up effect is fine and allows language to flow easily, provided that the listener can interpret the sounds. However, unless you and your listener know and understand each other well, you need to make all the individual sounds clear within the flow of the sentence, if you want your listener to follow you.

When you speak a sentence, a steady stream of air carries the sound waves. Articulation just adds interest to the line without making it jerky.

For example, the phrase 'one, two, three' consists of the continuous vowel sounds *uh-oo-ee* with changes of colour for 'w' (which sounds like *oo*), *nn* and *ththrrr*: *oo-uh-nn-t-oo-ththrr-ee*. The only slight nick or break in the sound stream is for the 't' of 'two' and that scarcely disturbs the flow.

Your breathing muscles – your diaphragm and surrounding muscles – produce a continuous flow of air, while the articulation muscles – mouth, lips, tongue and so on – form the shape of the words.

Tune in to Track 11. The differing duties of these two groups of muscles are obvious when you sing, so have a go at singing now. Don't worry, you don't have to be able to carry a tune to get benefit from the following.

1. **Sing a line or two from a simple song.**

   Try a line from a nursery rhyme, such as 'Sing a song of sixpence, a pocket full of rye'.

   As you sing this line, the various sounds are joined up in one constant flow of air. That's exactly how speech works too. You have a thought, which produces a breath, which turns into a sentence with meaning.

2. **Repeat the line of song, but *say* it this time.**

   Maintain a similar flow and rhythm.

3. **Think of something that you may say in your everyday environment.**

   For instance, use a basic introduction (filling in your personal details as appropriate):

   My name is [John Smith] and I live at [Santa Cruz] in [California]. (breath) Each day I am occupied in [selling buns to tourists on the Boardwalk].

4. **Sing this couple of sentences.**

   Don't worry whether a specific tune emerges. Simply enjoy the melody and rhythm and put your heart and soul into it.

5. **Straight after singing the sentences,** *say* **the words with a similar flow, emphasis and rhythm.**

   Notice that the sounds are just as joined up as when you sang the sentences, and the words are beautifully clear.

Reciting high-flown poetry is a great way to increase the feeling of talking on a cushion of air. Take a few lines of Shakespeare and speak them in a declamatory style, like a great actor of the old school. Start off with the following example from *Macbeth*. In these lines, Macbeth is talking about the futility and slowness of time, so stretch out each line in order to emphasise the endless feeling. This stretching involves lengthening consonants and vowels to make your words stretched out and joined up. You do this quite naturally if you think through the sounds and give the words lots of feeling. Speak each line in one uninterrupted breath, and take a good breath at the end of each line.

> To-morrow, and to-morrow, and to-morrow,
> Creeps in this petty pace from day to day,
> To the last syllable of recorded time;
> And all our yesterdays have lighted fools
> The way to dusty death.

Use the mental energy behind the words to direct the sound. Hear the boredom and desperation of 'to-mor-row-and-to-mor-row-and-to-mor-row . . .' Allow nothing to break the direction of the sound as you speak the words.

Bringing Your Words to Life with Long Sounds

I overheard our neighbour's children recently. 'That's not fair!' shouted one, and the high-pitched sound *fai-ai-ai-ai-air* went on and on. I don't know what the children were doing, but I certainly understood that one girl didn't think the matter was fair. Making long sounds is one of the ways that people bring meaning to what they say.

Words are made up of vowels and consonants. On the whole, the vowel sounds carry emotion, while the consonants give your thoughts clarity. The consonants – particularly long consonants (see the later section 'Stretching out the long consonants') can add emotional content too.

In normal conversation you may not be particularly aware of long sounds, but they're certainly the way to sound interesting. For example, if you make an announcement at a meeting about a new project, the entire endeavour sounds more innovative and interesting if you introduce it as the '*ne-e-w* project'.

For the next day, make a deliberate effort to listen out for long sounds when other people speak. Note which words they lengthen. (This is one way to make a boring meeting interesting!) Observe how long sounds add to the sense and significance of others' comments, and note the emotional impact of lengthening these sounds.

Stretching out the long vowels

Vowels in one sense *are* the voice. They're the continuous sounds your air produces. If you make a sound without words, it's likely to be a vowel: when someone stamps on your foot for example – 'Ow!' – or when you don't know what to say next – 'Er?' – or when you're shocked – 'Aargh!'

English has only five written vowels, but many more vowel *sounds* exist. The following are the main ones with pronunciation suggestions to help you; you can adapt these sounds to your own accent. Listen to my vowel sounds on Track 12.

oo	(lose)
u	(put)
oh	(pot)
aw	(corn)
uh	(cup)
ah	(card)
ae	(tap)
eh	(bed)
ee	(bead)
er	(bird)
i	(big)

Try each of the preceding vowels sounds without the surrounding consonants. Check out how your mouth moves to change from one to another. For example: *ah-oo, ah-aw, ah-ee, ah-eh, ee-oh, ee-ah*. Try various combinations, moving smoothly from one vowel to the next. Be particularly aware of how the inside of your mouth changes to form the different vowels. For example, you feel your mouth widen inside as you move from *ee* to *ah*.

Keep listening to Track 12. Two vowel sounds merging together appear often in English. These sounds are *diphthongs.* For example:

> ear = *i-er*
>
> air = *eh-er*
>
> go = *goh-oo*
>
> pay = *peh-ee*

English has *triphthongs* too (three sounds), such as:

> fire = *fah-i-er*
>
> shower = *shah-oo-er*

These words sound clearest when you enunciate each of the vowel sounds. You may be tempted just to let the final one disappear down your throat, muffling the sound – and potentially confusing your meaning.

William Butler Yeats's poem 'The Lake Isle of Innisfree' has plenty of examples of diphthongs (marked in bold), especially in the last verse:

> I will ar**i**se and g**o** n**ow**,
> For alw**ays** n**i**ght and d**ay**
> I h**ear** l**a**ke water lapping
> With l**ow** s**ou**nds by the shore.

As you read the preceding lines aloud, make the most of the long diphthong sounds. Feel them roll around the inside your mouth. Enjoy the atmosphere they create.

In everything you say, the long vowels indicate to the listeners the words that you want them to pay attention to. If you make the vowel really long, the word becomes even more important.

Barack Obama created magic in his 2008 campaign speeches, including through his use of long sounds. These sounds – notably in words such 'schools', 'change' and 'believe' – helped people connect and remember him. The sounds rang in people's ears when he talked about the 'poor' and the 'old'. He was speaking in an honoured tradition harkening back to Martin Luther King and others. Indeed, many people will never forget the precise intonation that King used on the word 'dream' on the steps of the Lincoln Memorial. In his famous speech, he almost sang the words, 'I have a dream'. How long was that dream? Arguably, the longest dream in history!

Pronunciation confusion

Precise vowel sounds are vital for meaning in English, so they need to be clear. Speakers of English as a second language sometimes suspect English listeners of being deliberately obtuse when they don't understand their pronunciations of words.

However, consider how many words sound similar in English. Following are twelve different monosyllabic words starting with 'b' and ending with 'd':

bid, bead, bed, bade, bud, bard, bad, bide, bored, bode, bird, booed.

No wonder confusion results! Of course, listeners who are fluent in English go by the sense of the sentence to figure out meaning, but even so plenty of opportunity for misunderstanding exists. People learning English sometimes get into embarrassing situations by mispronouncing words. If for example you want to say 'I can't go,' people hear 'can' even if you pronounce the 't' unless you make the 'can't' sound long. And not making the vowel long in 'beach' and 'sheet' may have disastrous consequences in certain company!

Enjoying the character of words

Words have character that you bring out in long sounds. Giving words character happens in obvious ways with *onomatopoeia* – words whose pronunciation imitates the sound associated with the word: 'moo', 'growl', 'meow', 'purr', 'roar' and 'murmur'. But apart from these obvious words, lengthening the vowel sound gives additional character and meaning to many words.

Play Track 13. Say the following words with long vowels that bring out the emotion behind the words. Just think of the meaning as you say the following:

I'm *lo-onely.* (Experience the desolate sound of that *o* sound.)

The *va-ast* open plains. (The longer you make the sound, the more extensive the plain. The same effect is possible with words such as 'long', 'tall' and 'wide'.)

The wind was *moa-oaning* in the trees. (Hear the sound of the wind.)

He kept his *coo-ool.* (Linger a moment in the calm of that cool *oo* sound.)

Come and get *wa-arm.* (Sense the heat in the *aw* sound of 'warm'.)

The marble was *smoo-ooth.* (Caress the smoothness of that *oo-oo* sound.)

I'm *deter-ermined* to see it through. (Hear the force of will in that *er* sound.)

Speaking well isn't about making beautiful vowel sounds; it's about putting your energy into the feeling associated with the word.

The Welsh language is characterised by soft consonants and smooth mutations from one sound to the next. The Welsh bring these same features to their pronunciation of English. The Welsh poet, Dylan Thomas, played endlessly with linking series of emotive sounds.

Try reading aloud the following paragraph from the beginning of Thomas' radio play, *Under Milkwood,* which describes the atmosphere of a small Welsh village, Llareggub, (interesting to spell this word backwards!) at night. If you know the Welsh accent, add that! The playwright's instructions tell you to read his words 'very softly'. Keep your jaw loose and be curious about the different shapes that form in the inside of your mouth as you use long vowel sounds, which I mark in bold, to describe the scene. Listen to my attempt on Track 13.

> It is spring, m**oo**nless n**i**ght in the small t**ow**n, starless and bible-black, the cobblestr**ee**ts s**i**lent and the hunched, c**our**ters'-and-rabbits' w**oo**d limping invisible d**ow**n to the sl**oe**black, sl**ow**, black, cr**ow**black, fishing-boatbobbing s**ea**. The h**ou**ses are blind as m**o**les . . . And **a**ll the p**eo**ple of the lulled and dumbf**ou**nd t**ow**n **a**re sleeping now.

To get a sense of the atmosphere, listen if you can to Richard Burton's original recording of *Under Milkwood,* as this charismatic Welsh speaker makes the most of the sounds in his rich tones.

Great speakers from the past knew how to use long vowels. You can hear in old recordings the gravitas these long vowels create. Listen, for example, to President Franklin Roosevelt's 1933 Inauguration speech, especially the famous part about fear. Speak the lines yourself, making the most of the long vowel sounds in bold:

> This is pre-eminently the **ti**me to **spea**k the **truth**, the **whole truth**, frankly and **boldly**. Nor **need** we shrink from honestly facing conditions in our country to**day**. This **great Na**tion will en**dure**, as it has en**dured**, will re**vive** and will prosper. So, **first** of **all**, let me assert my **firm** be**lief** that the **on**ly thing we have to **fear** is **fear** itself

Stretching out the long consonants

Some consonants act like vowels because you can lengthen them in order to give character to certain words.

Try saying the following words with long consonants. I suggest a sentence containing each word – but you can make up your own sentences as well. Put lots of meaning into the word and make the long consonants *really* long. Keep your listener in suspense! Listen to my examples in Track 14.

f	*fffantastic*	That goal was fantastic!
h	*hhhorrible*	The stench was horrible!
l	*llless*	I couldn't care less!
m	*mmmarvellous*	The place was absolutely marvellous.
n	*nnnowhere*	She was nowhere to be seen.
ng	*longng*	The journey was so long.
r	*rrreal*	I just want you to get real.
s	*sssoft*	The velvet was so soft.
sh	*shsharp*	He's young but he's sharp.
v	*vvvalue*	It all depends on the value.
w	*wwwait*	What, we still have to wait?
y	*yyyearn*	He used to yearn for a change.
z	*zzzealous*	She's pretty zealous in her approach.
th	*ththank*	Thank you, I'll never forget it.
th	*that*	*That's* the one!

Several pairs of long consonants are produced in almost identical ways. The only difference is that one uses air on its own (*un-voiced* sound) and the other employs the voice box (*voiced* sound). Try making a hissing sound, *sss,* like a snake. Not do the same thing and add your voice. You're now producing the sound *zzz.*

If your speech gets a bit lazy, the voiced and unvoiced sounds sometimes get muddled up and make you less clear.

Listen to Track 14. Following are examples of voiced and un-voiced consonants. Try them in pairs and notice the difference. You can check the difference by touching your throat. When the sound is voiced, you feel a vibration there, but not if the sound is unvoiced.

Unvoiced		**Voiced**	
s	seal	*z*	zeal
f	fast	*v*	vast
th	thistle	*th*	this
sh	mesh	*sz*	measure

If you want to be clear, you need to be precise with your tongue and lip movements too. You don't need to make a big issue of it, just don't be sloppy or lazy.

Enjoying the expressive qualities of long consonants

The long consonants have various characteristics that you can draw out as you lengthen them. Listen to my examples in Track 15.

- ✔ 'm' and 'n' vibrate in the nose before the sound opens out through the mouth. You can hear the hum of the bees in the phrase: 'murmuring of innumerable bees'. You can express a wonderful finality by lengthening the 'n' in 'no', 'never' and 'nailed it!'.

- ✔ 'l' uses your tongue and can take lots of time about it in 'leisure', 'long' and 'languid'.

- ✔ 'r' is like revving up, ready for off. Hear the suspense and then the sudden release into action in *rrrrrrrrrrrrrrrr-eady*! and *rrrrrrrright!*

- ✔ 'f' (like 'r') has the sense of release when you finally open into the vowel on *fffantastic*, *fffinally* or *phphew!*

- ✔ 'v' is a worthy letter which gives certainty and gravitas to 'value', 'virtue' and 'verify'.

- ✔ 'w' and 'y' are vowels really. w sounds like *oo* and 'y' sounds like *ee*. Hear the wonder in *oooooooooowunderful*! and the inevitability of the opening up in *eeeeeeeeeeeeeyawn!*

- ✔ 'h' is just air, and perfect for breathing down your neck to say scary things like *hhhhhhhorror*, *hhhharmful* and *hhhhuge*, *hhhhairy hhhhag*.

- ✔ 's' is soft, smooth and silky, or, together with 'l', becomes slug-like and slimy.

- ✔ 'z' is much less smooth, as in 'fuzzy', 'blizzard', 'grizzly', 'dizzy' and 'crazy'.

The preceding are word games, of course. Not every word fits. But the idea of finding meaning in the sound of the long consonant is fun to do and helps you sound more interesting as a result.

Listen out for long consonants in the best political speeches, and you will find them everywhere. For example, in Sir Winston Churchill's 'blood, sweat and tears' speech of 1940 that follows, I've marked the main long consonants in bold. Read the passage yourself out loud, lengthening the long vowels as well as the long consonants. Note how the long sounds give your words a truly Churchillian ring:

You ask, **wh**at is our policy? I will say: It is to **w**age **w**ar, by **s**ea, **l**and and air, with all our **m**ight and with all the **s**trength that God can give us: to **w**age **w**ar against a **m**onstrous tyranny, **n**ever **s**urpassed in the dark, **l**amentable catalogue of **h**uman crime. **Th**at is our policy. You ask, **Wh**at is our aim? I can answer in **o**ne **w**ord: Victory.

Adding Sparkle with Short Sounds

If you spoke entirely with long sounds, your speech would be like an endless diet of strawberries and cream without anything spicy or sharp to liven it up. This is where the short sounds come in. They add pace and emphasis. They often surprise you and bring you up short. They add lightness.

Short sounds challenge you too! Think of the old tongue twister, 'Peter Piper', which is abundantly populated with short sounds. Go ahead, give your voice a quick workout:

> Peter Piper picked a peck of pickled peppers.
> A peck of pickled peppers Peter Piper picked.
> If Peter Piper picked a peck of pickled peppers,
> Where's the peck of pickled peppers Peter Piper picked?

You have to be pretty sprightly to get your tongue around clusters of short sounds. Look out for other tongue twisters and try them out. The following sections explore short sounds in all their surprising energy.

Colouring your speech with short consonants

English has eight main short consonants. Like some of the long consonants (see the previous section 'Stretching out the long consonants'), they come in voiced and un-voiced pairs that you produce with similar mouth, lip and tongue movements. The *un-voiced* sound uses just air and the *voiced* sound engages the vocal folds.

Unvoiced		*Voiced*	
p	pat	*b*	bat
c	cut	*g*	gut
t	ten	*d*	den
ch	chug	*j*	jug

Get your tongue around the sounds, reading the lines slowly at first, and then getting faster. Listen to me try in Track 16. Each line has four beats and the last syllable is long. Try all sorts of combinations of short consonants, for example:

1	2	3	4
papa-papa	*papa-papa*	*papa-papa*	*paah*
dada-dada	*dada-dada*	*dada-dada*	*daah*
butter-butter	*butter-butter*	*butter-butter*	*baah*
tippy-tippy	*tippy-tippy*	*tippy-tippy*	*taah*
teddy-teddy	*teddy-teddy*	*teddy-teddy*	*taah*

One challenge with short consonants is making sure that the voiced and unvoiced pairs sound different from each other. For instance, you don't want to sound like someone with a permanent cold in your nose as you order someone not to touch something, 'Don't douch dat!'.

Practise your precision. Say the following easily and fast, first the consonants alone, then with words (Track 16):

k g k g k g k g	catgut, catgut, catgut, catgut
p b p b p b p b	poor boy, poor boy, poor boy, poor boy
t d t d t d t d	to do, to do, to do, to do
ch j ch j ch j	jump chump, jump chump, jump chump

If you want to be *really* clear, you take special care to pronounce the *en's* of your *wor's*. By that, I mean 'the ends of your words'. Some accents tend to cut off the ends of sounds, so that the word ends abruptly before the final conso-nant or just tails off into your throat. I can understand that you don't want to sound pedantic, but these end sounds do help you to be clearly understood by people outside your immediate circle.

The endings that catch many people out are the ones with a cluster of conso-nants. Try saying the following: 'cooked, dragged, stepped, clubbed, fooled, halved, cools, filth, bathed, next, lifts, eighth, masts'. In order to be clear, you need to pronounce both final consonants. Check that you don't put an extra vowel between the consonants, for instance *dra-guh-duh* (dragged). The move-ments required are small, but precise.

Consonants are great for impact, and they save your voice too. If you want to make a strong statement – even an angry one – hit the initial consonants with energy – try the 'v' of 'violent', the 'p' of 'preposterous', the 'd' of 'disgusted'. A powerfully enunciated consonant launches the word strongly and doesn't force your vocal folds.

Expressing emotion with short vowels and consonants

Consonants can carry loads of strong intention and energy. In the British sitcom *Miranda,* the gauche 6-foot accident-prone heroine sometimes catches herself saying a word and then suddenly stops the show as she plays the sound around in her mouth, delighting in its sound. 'Gloomy – guhllllooooommmmy – what a guhllllooooommmmy sound!'

Do the same yourself. Find a few short words and play around with their sounds: 'plop', 'plonk', 'click', 'splosh', 'blog'. Access the child in you and enjoy the mouth shapes and sensation of the words. Each time you pronounce the word more strongly, the more odd it sounds! Lewis Carroll loved such sounds and used to make up words with short vowels and consonants, introducing animals like the *Jabberwock,* the *jubjub bird* and the *bandersnatch.* Find your own phrases or make up words like Lewis Carroll, giving energy to short consonants.

Often, short consonants go with short vowels to give you a wonderfully explosive word like 'bang', 'pop' or 'jab'. They're good for orders, like 'go!' or 'don't!' They can also come upon you suddenly like 'gag' or 'grab'.

A short vowel can also be expressive in the same way as a long vowel, only instead of the sound continuing, you hear the short vowel with a silence after it, before the next consonant. For example, in the word 'massive', you can say it simply with a short vowel, or you can create a silent space after the 'a' which makes the word seem even larger: *ma ssive.*

Make statements with expressive words yourself. Try these sentences for example:

> 'It came as a complete *bo mbshell*'

> 'The service was *drea dful.*'

> 'That's just *ridi culous!*'

Wait a fraction longer than feels natural and hear how that creates an added energy in the silence. Don't use this device too often though, or you will indeed sound ridi culous!

Every time you play with words in this way, invent meanings and put lots of energy into your speech. When you do, you automatically make the most of long and short vowels and consonants – without ever having to be technical about it. You may find it entertaining to find someone to practise with.

What starts out as physical skill-building eventually turns into something more meaningful. Words become clearer as you invest energy and intent into them, and that's how you connect with people too. Then you're talking!

Part III
Playing Your Instrument Well

The 5th Wave   By Rich Tennant

PROJECT YOUR VOICE

In this part . . .

In this part you discover how to make your voice more expressive. Loud and soft, fast and slow – you find out how to ring the changes. You hear how great speakers use rhythm and emphasis to enliven their speeches.

I introduce you to the big secret of influence – a voice that resonates at different pitches. Here you discover the voice of confidence and authority, the heartfelt passionate voice and the light sounds of humour. With these tools you uncover the sounds that are genuinely you – your authentic voice.

Chapter 7

Exploring Volume and Speed

*W*hat are the criticisms you hear frequently after someone's given a speech? Too quiet or too loud, too fast or too slow. One of the easiest ways to ensure others listen to you is to get your volume and your speed right. This means right *for the occasion*, whether that's public speaking, addressing a small group, talking to a colleague or making a phone call. Fortunately, developing your ability to adjust your volume and speed is quite straightforward and makes an enormous difference to your impact as a communicator. When you have full control of the volume and speed buttons of your voice, you can adapt to any occasion, and choose how you want to respond to people.

Turning Up (and Down) the Volume

A business woman meets an associate at a networking event in a large city hotel. 'Hello,' she says smiling. 'I'm Caroline. What's your name?' 'T'ong,' he replies quietly. 'I'm so sorry,' she apologises, 'I didn't quite catch that.' 'T'ong,' he repeats. 'Please forgive me – noisy room isn't it? What was that you said?' 'T'ong,' he repeats quietly looking at the floor. 'Ri-ight . . .' she murmurs in embarrassment. 'How do you spell that?' The associate replies slowly with rising intonation and a quizzical look, 'T - O - M?'

Have you ever been put in a similar embarrassing situation by a speaker who mumbled? Like the woman in the anecdote, three times seems to be the limit to the number of times that people feel they can ask someone to repeat themselves. After that, all most people can do is smile and nod with a glazed look. Few things are more frustrating than not being able to hear what someone says, but people often hesitate to admit that they can't hear and just sit in silent frustration. Don't make people suffer in this way when *you* speak!

Intimate encounters

How do you adjust your volume and speed for intimate encounters, or indeed any one-to-one conversation? Try the following:

✔ Keep your eyes open for visual clues. Notice whether the other person looks comfortable, or whether they're straining forward to hear, or backing away because you're too loud.

✔ Speak at a similar volume to the other person, unless they're excessively loud or quiet. At least move your volume in their direction.

✔ Speak at the other person's speed if it feels natural. If you struggle to match their speed and feel awkward trying, put more liveliness into your speaking instead if they're a rapid speaker, or speak in a calmer manner if they're very slow.

✔ Tune in with interest to what the other person is saying and how they're saying it. With empathy, you adjust naturally to their speed and volume without even thinking about it.

Keep an eye out for people glazing over when you speak. Are they bored, is it time for lunch, or have they given up trying to hear you because you're too quiet or mumbling? If you're speaking in a large space, check whether people can hear you at the back. Encourage them to pipe up at any stage if they can't.

On the other hand, you can have too much of a good thing. Some people produce so many decibels when they speak that you can imagine they served an apprenticeship in public speaking at bustling Pike Place Fish Market or on a hustings at Hyde Park Corner. Telling people that they're too loud feels even more personal than dealing with quiet speakers. If you've an over-loud voice, people don't usually tell you, but they may step back from you or pull their heads back when you speak. Be aware of the clues they give you and adjust your voice accordingly. The sidebar, 'Intimate encounters,' suggests how to find the right volume for one-to-one conversations.

Speaking at the right level for other people isn't an exact science. Finding your best volume depends on your tone, your clarity, the acoustics of the room and your audience's hearing abilities. What's certain is that you need to be able to vary your voice from loud to soft, and tune into your listeners' requirements, as I detail in the following sections.

Projecting your voice

At the music conservatoire, Maestro Magretti was anxious to create a good impression with his singing students' final performance in the grand theatre. He assessed his singers in the small studio where they had their regular lessons, and gave those he thought had the strongest voices prime positions in the programme. A small student with a small high voice was given an inconspicuous slot in the second half. They had one rehearsal in the theatre, during which the maestro stood at the back of the grand circle to make sure that they all came across well. In the enormous venue, some students with large voices didn't sound quite as strong as he'd hoped. After a long wait, the small student came to the centre of the stage to sing her piece. To everyone's surprise, her voice rang out clearly to every part of the huge theatre, amazing everyone with its clarity and beauty. How was the student able to achieve that when bigger voices had struggled? The answer is that she possessed a skill her teacher didn't fully understand. She knew how to create a sound that carries – she had the secret of *projection*.

Projection has nothing to do with strength or force, and everything to do with resonance, or vibration. Three main factors affect your voice's ability to resonate effectively: relaxation, good breathing and strong intention. I cover each in turn.

Relaxation

It can be disconcerting when someone shouts out from the back of a conference room or an auditorium, 'Can't hear you.' If you're like most speakers, your instinct is immediately to make a bigger effort, which may include pushing, tensing and sticking your neck forward to get the tone out. Bad idea!

If you want to project, focus on relaxation (Chapter 5). The difference in your sound when your body is tense or free is like the difference between clinking a wine glass held by its bowl (actually more of a clanking sound) and held by its stem (a beautiful clear ring).

The following practice helps you hear and feel releasing your voice. Find a place where you feel free to make a noise and move around.

1. **Take a breath and shake your body all over: head, shoulders, waist, buttocks, arms, hands, legs and knees.**

   As you shake, release your breath in a long 'haah' sound. Focus mostly on the shaking, releasing more and more of your body as you go.

   Have you released your shoulders? Your neck? Your knees? Listen to how each new awareness of relaxation releases more sound, sometimes startlingly so.

   Every musical instrument, from a triangle to a cello, makes sound by causing air to vibrate, and you too are a vibrating instrument. Stand upright and at ease so that you can create free sound vibrations. The more you relax, the greater the volume you can create. The difference in volume between being tense and being relaxed is extraordinarily marked.

2. **When you feel relaxed and ready, plant your feet firmly, keep your knees soft and hum on a comfortable note.**

   Picture the sound waves echoing from you in all directions, like a light bulb spreading light to every corner of a room.

3. **Continue to breathe and hum, and focus in turn on each of the directions taken by the sound waves.**

   - Sense the sound coming out from your back.

   - With your next out-breath, feel the sound spread out sideways from you.

   - Sense the sound radiating forwards from your chest in a wide arc.

   - Then feel the sound waves move out in all directions at the same time.

4. **Say a phrase, feeling it move forwards, sideways and backwards.**

   For example, say 'This is what I want you to hear', feeling the sound move out in front of you. Repeat the phrase, feeling it travel out behind you. Say it again, focusing on the sound going out sideways; then again, sensing the phrase radiating out from you in all directions.

   Someone standing behind you should be able to hear you as clearly as someone standing in front of you.

   As you speak, check your jaw. If your jaw is tight, it's going to block the sound. You want to get a feeling of letting go all around the area of throat and jaw. See Chapter 6 for more tips on relaxing your jaw.

Breath

When you walk up a hill, think of the moment when you come over the summit and are greeted by a fresh flow of air and a distant view. At that moment, you naturally take a nice full breath to absorb both fresh air and fine view. That's the kind of breath you want for your voice to carry. Imagine yourself at the top of the hill and take that wonderful clear breath now.

This breath is the kind that a Greek actor must have taken in a vast open-air amphitheatre 2,000 years ago, as he breathed in, filling himself with a sense of the large space, before speaking lines that were going to carry to the farthest row far above him. If you like, imagine you're that Greek actor standing confidently with great presence while you do the following. Play Track 17.

1. **Hold up your hand in front of you, palm facing your face; breathe normally and speak in a natural voice to your hand.**

   Say something simple, such as 'Hello, hand.' (Well, that's easy!)

2. **Look at an object about 3 metres away from you, take a medium breath and speak to that object**

Again say something simple like 'Hello, window.' Note the slight increase in energy – the slightly bigger breath and the stronger intention to be heard – that you need to cross the larger space.

3. **Look out of the window to a far point of the external landscape, take a fresh 'top of the hill' breath and say, 'Hey there, horizon!'**

Note how you feel larger and wider as you take in breath and notice the increase in your energy and intention to cross the wide space.

Just before you release the sound, imagine yawning. Don't actually yawn at that moment, but merely thinking about yawning opens your throat naturally to release the sound.

Rather than attempting to produce a louder voice for the larger distance, imagine your sound spinning through space in an arc. For projecting your voice further, picture the sound waves spinning faster and moving out from you in a broader arc to reach the destination.

When you do this, you are, to borrow a phrase from the theatre, *placing your voice*. The further the distance your voice needs to go, the bigger the arc and the larger the breath. For long distances, imagine throwing your voice, letting it go, just like releasing a ball in an arc from your hand. Think of speaking more brightly as your voice travels up the arc.

Feel the in-breath filling not only your body but the whole room surrounding you. Breathe in the room.

Intention

The third element of successful projection is perhaps the most important – *intention*. The words *passion* and *determination* have similar meanings in this context.

If your intention is strong, you automatically breathe deeply and free up your body. If you really intend to be heard, you are heard.

Imagine that you need to yell 'Fire!' Take a big breath, deep down; raise your chest to allow more space for air as your rib muscles expand, and lift up your arms to make room to fill the higher part of your lungs as well. These things all happen naturally in a single movement as soon as you've the urgent need to alert people. Your whole body fills with air, puffing up like a bullfrog! Now give full vent to a word. (Maybe shout 'Fine' instead of 'Fire' so that your neighbours don't come running!)

People speak with strong intention when they swear. I'm not about to write a list of swear words here, but perhaps some Elizabethan strong language can energise you! The follow activity uses words spoken by various Shakespeare characters, talking colloquially to the standing spectators in the pit of the theatre.

1. **Working with a partner (preferably), stand at least 10 metres apart in a space where you can make loud sounds.**

   Call out the following phrases with plenty of exuberant venom. Hurl insults at each other in turn. Put everything you've got into each phrase.

   - Thou clay-brained guts!

   - Thou bolting-hutch of beastliness!

   - Thou poisonous bunch-back'd toad!

   - You juggler, you canker-blossom!

   - Thou boil-brained clotpole!

   - Thou pribbling ill-breeding pigeon!

   What expressive language! Perhaps you can bring some of these brilliant expressions back into regular use!

   How often do you really 'let go' like that? Many people are so 'civilised', they wouldn't dream of raising their voice beyond a certain level. Enjoy the feeling of liberation when you let go of inhibition.

2. **Try hurling more insults at your partner, but this time face away from each other.**

   Many people find to their surprise that the sound is freer and louder when they imagine throwing the sound out of their back. Standing this way prevents you from succumbing to the temptation to push the sound forward.

The energy fuelling your loud voice is your emotion – the strength of your feeling, your passion, determination, fierceness or boldness. You can speak louder much more easily when you put increased mental and emotional energy into what you're saying, rather than thinking physically about speaking louder.

You need a full breath and the ability to free up your body to project your voice. Your voice needs to be free to scream! You can, however, go tense with passion, as many football fans realise when they wake up with no voice the morning after the match before! Turn to Chapter 4 for more on your breath.

ANECDOTE

Intention and awareness in the martial arts

In the martial arts, some sudden moves are accompanied by a loud exhalation sounding like *Hi-yah!* or *Aiyah!* The Aikido shout, known as *kiai*, combines strong intention with relaxation and awareness, a potent combination.

A martial arts master told me the story of walking in a street after dark and meeting a rough group of men who rushed up towards him. The aikido champion let out his loud, powerful *kiai*, and the approaching young men froze mid-step.

When they came to, their aggression seemed to have died.

EJ Harrison, writing about judo in 1912, refers to an incident in which martial artist Yagyu Matajuro fixed his gaze on a few sparrows perched in a pine tree and let out his *kiai* shout. The birds instantly fell to the ground senseless. Just imagine what you can do to a difficult audience with a technique like that!

Gaining attention

I often coach people who have a problem getting listened to. People sometimes have a genuine contribution to make to a debate or conversation, but don't know how to cut into the flow of discussion and get people's attention.

Have you ever been in a meeting when you came up with a great idea but nobody picked it up until *another* team member introduced the same idea later on? If you're like most people, you were probably taken aback or even outraged when suddenly everyone enthusiastically latched onto that idea that *you* had already proposed!

An ear-splitting *kiai* shout certainly attracts interest (see the sidebar 'Intention and awareness in the martial arts'), but you probably should avoid doing that in the boardroom. So how else can you use your voice to gain attention?

Mark Antony has an answer in Shakespeare's play *Julius Caesar*. 'Friends, Romans, countrymen, lend me your ears,' he declares loudly, (an era before microphones remember); the crowd simmers down and becomes hushed. He then launches into a brilliant speech about Caesar that inflames the crowd. He doesn't mention Caesar in the first line, because with all the noise going on not everyone is going to hear. His first line is the *call to listen*.

TIP

Many a skilful teacher knows this strategy, expressed colloquially by a friend as, 'First get 'em to shut up, then tell 'em.' She often gets attention by raising her voice for just a few words, 'Now, class, there's a special trick you can use here…' Immediately afterwards, in the brief lull created by her loud intervention, she drops her voice down much lower, so that her students have to be quiet to hear.

You can do the same in a meeting. Interrupt strongly with a clearly audible statement to get people to listen, such as 'I'd like to make a point about the problem', and then follow up more quietly with your specific argument after people have turned towards you and are paying you attention. By the time you actually make your main point, people are definitely listening.

When you have the attention of your audience, speaking at your normal pitch is probably more influential than using a booming, over-loud voice.

Toning your voice down

Are you a loud talker? Do people flee in droves from your voice? Why do you think that is? Well . . .

- ✔ You may be one of life's effervescent communicators. You don't mean to shout, but everything is just so *exciting* – and you just *have* to express all that *energy*!

- ✔ Perhaps you put on your 'fog horn tone' specifically for presenting, in order to drive your point home to the people right at the back.

- ✔ Your normal way of speaking may push the sound strongly into your nose or clash your vocal cords, creating sounds that are relentlessly forceful and hard to listen to.

In all these cases, the problem for your listeners isn't so much that you're loud, but that the loudness isn't tuneful. I'm talking about speaking here, but a music analogy applies: when a musician plays the big bass drum, the sound is huge, but the reverberation is free and you hear all the harmonics of the sound. When someone shrieks or hollers, the sound is forced and does not produce musical harmonics that the ear can cope with.

Dealing with draughty halls and echoing chambers

Speaking at the right level isn't an exact science. Professional speakers encounter all sorts of acoustics and learn to adjust to what they find. Make use of the following tips:

- ✔ If you have to speak in a huge space or outside, *don't* risk harming your voice; make every effort to get hold of a microphone.

- ✔ If the space is large, make allowances for an echo. Wait for silence, then speak

extremely slowly and distinctly. Even leave a space between each word if the acoustics are particularly bad.

- ✔ Use your skills of projection and 'place your voice'. (See 'Projecting your voice' earlier in this chapter.) *Never ever* be tempted to force your voice to be heard. Ask your audience whether they can hear you if you're not sure.

Blasting people's ears does *not* equal high impact! A pushed sound can have no expression or nuance to it. The effect on the ear is of clashing and crashing – a really unpleasant sensation that gives your eardrums a battering. Pushing your voice with your throat or tongue is bad for your voice and often leads to excessive hoarseness or a persistent sore throat. Pushing hard into your nose or head or throat or banging your vocal cords is also bad for your listeners!

The remedy for an over-loud voice isn't much different from the remedy for a too-quiet voice:

- ✔ Work on powering your voice from the breathing muscles down in your diaphragm and ribs. These muscles can truly support your voice. See Chapter 4.

- ✔ Release any tension in your throat and mouth, so that the sound can vibrate freely with musical harmonics.

- ✔ Remind yourself that being heard is about *projection* – placing your voice with plenty of mental energy, not a war of sounds.

- ✔ Check out how loud you really need to be in a specific location or when speaking to a specific audience. If in doubt, ask whether they can hear you.

As you develop new speaking skills, your voice loses any stridency or excessive nasality. You begin to settle into deeper, warmer tones, which are much kinder to your listeners' ears.

If you think that your voice is too loud, don't speak in a breathy way in an effort to cut the volume. Breathiness is no better for your voice than shouting and severely limits your ability to vary your volume. You're likely just to swap a fleeing audience for a bored one.

Creating magical effects with volume

You would never put up with a diet that consisted of one food alone, even if it were your favourite. Indeed, some of the most delicious foods are appealing because you don't eat them every day. Yet, when you hear people speak about voice, they seem to want the beautiful sound – the caviar – all the time.

The magic of your voice lies in variety; contrast is the name of the game. Soft is as powerful as loud if it surprises and delights the audience. Going from quiet to loud and loud to quiet can build tension or create atmospheres that have audiences sitting on the edge of their seats.

Loudness can have many different qualities. A young woman takes her dog for a walk every morning on the hill behind our house. Her dog is forever getting lost, so we hear her calling 'Daisy! Daisy!' across the fields in a shrill, piercing singsong. On the other hand, I've also heard a loud and stomach-curdling deep howl from an actor playing King Lear as he entered with his daughter Cordelia dead in his arms. His voice seemed to come from the depths of his despair. Different again are the loud tones of a military commander issuing orders and the cheerful calls of a camp leader encouraging children to play a game.

Develop your ability to speak both loudly and quietly in different tones; then you're ready for anything. Chapter 9 on resonance offers various ideas of how to vary your sounds and put emotional intensity into your words.

Appreciating the power of pianissimo

Quiet speaking has an important role, but not the droopy kind of quiet speaking that irritates people because they cannot hear. The difference is one of energy.

- ✔ **When you speak timidly,** your energy is low and your message drops to the floor before it can reach the listener.
- ✔ **When you speak quietly yet with strong purpose,** the quality of your tone creates a strong impact on the listener.

Quiet or loud, if you want to create high impact, employ high energy. This energy consists of:

- ✔ Strong breath and support
- ✔ Clear pronunciation
- ✔ Open sound

When you speak quietly and want to be clearly heard, act the same as you do when speaking loudly, with if anything even more mental and emotional focus. Think of the energy that goes into a stage whisper; the difference isn't in an actor's energy or intensity, but just in the volume.

Listen to Track 18, play with your volume and discover how to bring different energy to your words when you speak loudly and quietly.

1. **Choose a sentence that you can say purposefully.**

   Here are a few suggestions:

- But you didn't do it, did you?
- I'll never forget what you said.
- This is what life is about.

Say the sentence loudly, strongly and meaningfully.

2. **Keep the same strong intention, energy and breath, but speak the sentence a bit quieter, maintaining the emotional charge.**

Enunciating the consonants clearly and emphatically helps this process.

3. **With the same purpose, energy and breath, speak the sentence quietly and clearly.**

When you speak quietly, you may find it easier to communicate the words strongly and emphatically when you speak slower.

4. **Consider how the meaning changes as you change the volume.**

For example, imagine a scenario where you're telling your companion about a terrible disaster. Your home has burned down – and all because the door was left ajar and a sudden wind blew over a candle. You had asked your companion to be careful and to remember to close the door on leaving. Consider the different ways you can say, 'But you didn't do it, did you?':

- You can shout the line in an outburst of desperation and accusation.
- You can suddenly drop your voice and speak the line quietly and clearly – with menace.

What other ways can you think of?

To be listened to when you say something quietly, you usually need to set it up so that people are ready to pay attention to your voice, either talking more loudly beforehand, so that people catch the contrast, or leaving a silence before shifting to a lower volume.

Less is often more. 'When in doubt go louder' isn't always the best advice. Dropping the volume can be amazingly effective.

Building the power and finding the dimmer switch

I talk in the preceding sections about talking loudly and softly. Also important and effective is growing gradually louder or quieter.

The gradual crescendo or diminuendo is something that the best speakers use to great effect. Martin Luther King's 'I have a dream' speech was one long crescendo getting louder and more passionate as it proceeded. When performed on stage, Mark Antony's 'Friends, Romans, countrymen' speech in *Julius Caesar* usually rises from a calm beginning to a riot of angry passion over the course of several minutes of increasingly compelling oratory.

Getting quieter is often used as a device in songs and stories such as the following traditional children's tale, which can start quite loudly, and gradually diminish in volume until it ends very softly and scarily!

> In a dark, dark wood, there was a dark, dark house.
> And in that dark, dark house, there was a dark, dark room.
> And in that dark, dark room, there was a dark, dark chest.
> And in that dark, dark chest, there was a dark, dark shelf.
> And on that dark, dark shelf, there was a dark, dark box.
> And in that dark, dark box, there was . . . a ghost!

You need command of your voice to build up to a grand climax or draw your audience gradually towards a thrilling quiet ending. Start in a small way with the following.

1. **Count aloud slowly and smoothly from 1 to 5, starting quietly and getting a little louder on each number, finishing loudly on the number 5.**

   Make sure that you don't strain with your throat to reach the end loudly. If your breath only allows you to count from 1 to 4, but you arrive at the end without straining, that's perfect. Build the volume gradually.

2. **Count backwards from 5 to 1, starting loudly with 5 and decreasing the volume steadily until you reach 1 on a particularly quiet voice.**

   Decreasing your volume from loud to soft may be more challenging. The '1' needs to be quiet yet significant.

   Keep your breath moving out steadily or you find the tone falls to quiet too soon. Aim to make the change gradual and smooth with no sudden bumps anywhere.

   When you can get steadily louder and quieter to the count of 5, you may like to increase the count to 6, 7 or 8, and build up your volume even more – all without forcing it, remember!

The crescendo and diminuendo effect appears frequently in famous speeches, often in three steps. Take the opening of Mark Antony's speech, 'Friends, Romans, countrymen', which I use in Track 19. You have three words, each longer than the last. You can build the volume, each word a little louder than the one before, in order to make your point. You can equally well start with a strong loud 'Friends', a more moderate proud 'Romans' and a soft intimate 'countrymen'. Either way, the change in volume makes the phrase feel as if it is going somewhere. Try saying Mark Anthony's words yourself both ways and notice the difference in atmosphere between getting louder and getting quieter.

Finding the Best Speed

The other day at a business conference, the speaker glanced at his watch mid-flow and suddenly realised he was running out of time. I noticed the change in his manner as he showed his next PowerPoint slide: 'Ah, well, I'll just skip the next couple of slides because it's really important to tell you about this next one. . .' He began to talk quite fast. 'Here there are five important points to mention; the first is . . . the second . . . ' By now the speaker was galloping along. 'I really want to you to remember all these vital points,' he gabbled, clicking through his slides at a great rate 'which are . . . and . . . Ah, I-really-want-to-share-this-with-you-too. . . .' By now, he reminded me of a film on fast forward. His voice, as well as rushing along, had risen in pitch.

As the presentation neared its end, you felt the audience give up. They seemed to sense that as the speaker attempted to cram in more and more facts, they were unlikely to understand much at all. I began to hear the quiet shuffles of conference manuals closing and pens being put away as they prepared for the lunch break.

If you've been in a similar situation yourself, trying to get through to the end of a presentation that has taken days to prepare, and run out of time, you know how tempting it can be to rush at the end to make sure that your audience gets it all. It's always better to privately cut your losses and concentrate calmly on the few points that are essential to bring your talk to an end with a well-paced delivery.

Most people regularly speak too fast, and speed up even more when they get nervous. You can rarely follow someone who speaks at a great speed, particularly if they lack strong emphasis and sense of direction. By contrast, some people speak too slowly and listeners lose the thread as the speaker plods through the material, particularly if he or she has a growling voice.

Communication is much more than saying all the words you mean to say. You need to check that your listeners are receiving your words in the way you mean them to be received. The test is how well you engage with your audience, and that depends on their capability and level of interest, the subject matter, your voice and your connection with them.

Finding the best speed for each particular occasion is an extremely valuable skill for communicating effectively with your listeners, so I show you how in the following sections.

Slowing down for gravitas and clarity

Speaking slowly in a deep voice is associated with gravitas, so can be useful if you want to be taken seriously. When the Olympic Games are in the news, I enjoy watching TV trailers of conquering athletes crossing the finishing line, arms rising in victory, in glorious slow motion. The slowed-down images give a sense of nobility and triumph. Your voice can have a similar effect. As it slows down, it appears more mature, dignified and statesmanlike.

You need to have a good sense of direction when you speak slowly as a sentence can lose its way. No, really! If you hear someone speak a long sentence at the same speed and intensity all the way through, you lose its meaning.

When you practise counting numbers growing in volume (see the earlier section 'Building the power and finding the dimmer switch'), you need to increase the volume through every number right up to the last. You need a similar directional momentum in every sentence.

Speak some famous phrases really slowly. Every single word – indeed every consonant and vowel – is important, but you also need a strong impulse to carry you towards the important word at the end. Don't grind to a halt! Play Track 20. Repeat the following phrases several times and see just how slowly you can speak them while retaining the power of the statement. Each phrase is designed so that your energy moves towards the all-important last word.

> 'Yes, we can.' Barack Obama
>
> 'The lady is not for turning.' Margaret Thatcher
>
> 'We will never surrender.' Winston Churchill
>
> 'They will always be remembered.' George Washington
>
> 'He that cannot obey, cannot command.' Benjamin Franklin
>
> 'If you can't feed a hundred people, then feed just one.' Mother Teresa

Now apply the same principle to a longer piece. Time for Shakespeare, again! The challenge is to recite the following lines incredibly slowly with no gaps between the words, and with a strong sense of meaning and direction.

Speaking slowly takes a lot of breath, so take a fresh breath at every punctuation mark. These lines are spoken by the old and broken King Lear, so you've permission to sound old and angry – but in the dramatic style of a classical actor. If you read slowly, you need to breathe slowly too, so there will be quite a pause between each line, but keep the sense of momentum. As soon as you've read a phrase, look up to speak it; then look down again for the next.

You see me here, you gods, a poor old man,
As full of grief as age; wretched in both.
If it be you that stirs these daughters' hearts
Against their father, fool me not so much
To bear it tamely; touch me with noble anger,
And let not women's weapons, water drops,
Stain my man's cheeks! No, you unnatural hags!

Get feedback from a friend or colleague on how you read the Lear speech. You may think that you're speaking at a ridiculously slow speed, but I'm sure that they'll like your pace.

Taking time in your head

In a Calvin and Hobbes interchange, Calvin complains that when he's talking, his words can't keep up with his thoughts. He wonders why people think faster than they speak. Hobbes replies, 'Probably so we can think twice.'

If you want to speak at a measured pace, it's a good idea to slow down your brain as well as your tongue. You may think that's easier said than done! Two techniques to help you are making use of the pause and taking a good breath.

Making use of the pause

Two good reasons come to mind for pausing between sentences:

- Pausing gives you time to think.
- Pausing *looks* as if you're taking time to think, which your audience will appreciate.

If you find that any pause seems unbearably long, fill the gap with deliberate action. Take a couple of steps; look down for a moment to gather yourself; or make a calm adjustment to your notes. It all looks beautifully natural. Then breathe in slowly and speak again.

Taking a good breath

When you take a full breath, several good things happen:

- Your brain enjoys the oxygen, and you're able to think better.
- The audience interprets the breath as a new thought and pays you renewed attention.
- You're less likely to rush if you've plenty of air.

Space is good. Your audience needs more time than you may think, for two reasons. If your listeners are bored, they're thinking about what to buy at the supermarket for supper tonight or a hundred other things. On the other hand, if they're fascinated by what you just said, they're beginning to work out how they might implement that idea for their own benefit. In both cases, they've stopped listening, and need time for processing.

So, whether they're interested or not, all listeners stop listening from time to time, and it behoves you to give them time to absorb your message. They take in much more if they're given space to do so.

Enjoying a sprightly tempo

If you naturally speak slowly, you're likely to be easier to understand and may even be considered authoritative. However, a slow voice has its downsides too:

- ✔ If you don't vary your voice in other ways – in terms of volume, pitch and tone – you may sound dull.
- ✔ You find it hard to be quick on your feet with a deep slow voice. Imagine Arnold Schwarzenegger or Henry Kissinger talking fast!
- ✔ Several surveys show that people consider someone with a quicker voice more intelligent.
- ✔ If you're dealing with someone who naturally speaks much faster than you, they may be irritated by your slow pace.

People usually sound unnaturally slow only when their speaking style is monotonous. One remedy is to include plenty of variety in terms of volume, pitch, tone and emphasis. The other remedy is to practise speaking at different speeds. The following practice helps you play with your tempo. This exercise is particularly good if your voice is slow, or low and slow, but everyone can find it useful.

Imagine that you're a traditional storyteller and tell a short children's story, two or three minutes long. Stories always start with words designed to grab the attention, often with the idea that you're letting the listener in on a secret. Start your story with an opening that provokes curiosity, such as:

Guess what happened to me the other day – it was extraordinary. . .

You'll never guess what I've just heard. . .

I had the surprise of my life last week. . .

I've never ever told anyone this before, but. . .

I'll never ever forget the day that I almost died . . .

Good stories have suspense and slow down for impact. They also have momentum, speeding up for enthusiasm or building up tension. Memorable stories have different characters, maybe a giant with the deep gruff voice and a little girl with an excitable high voice. They contain surprise and drama. Play with all these effects to create atmosphere in your story. Of course, if you have real children waiting for their bedtime story to practise on, all the better!

You may think that you can't invent a story just like that. Don't worry about it. You just have to start with the opening, a couple of characters and a prop or two such as a magic wand, hat or a piece of jewellery, and the story takes you where it takes you – *provided* that you switch off your critical internal monitor.

You can find out a lot about serious speaking from telling stories. The secret of volume and speed is to use your whole palette. In the final analysis, after you satisfy the imperative to be clearly understood, there *is* no best speed or best volume – it has to vary according to the *meaning*.

You create a strong effect by having variety in your voice to keep your listeners interested. People may admire you for your voice, but they will admire you much more for what you can *do* with your voice.

Some people find that if they get nervous before a speech, they end up saying more than they mean to, and time passes much more quickly than they think. Other people find just the opposite: that when they're under pressure, they get through all their material in half the time they were expecting to. Try the following in order to be prepared:

- ✔ If you have to give a speech within strict time limits, try it out in different ways beforehand, timing yourself each time.

- ✔ Get to recognise how nerves affect your timing, so that you don't make your speech either too long or too short.

Chapter 8

Filling Your Speech with the Sounds of Music

A memorable piece of music, whether the latest pop hit or an enduring classical composition, contains certain key ingredients: great melodies, contrasts of dynamics and tempo, crescendos and diminuendos, interesting harmonies, repeating rhythms and artfully placed pauses. You need just those same ingredients to speak in a captivating, unforgettable way too.

You aren't particularly aware of the individual elements when you hear a speaker who has a highly developed sense of music in speaking. However, you do find yourself entertained and entranced, and drawn into the speaker's magic circle by the melodic life in the words. Listen to the elderly poet Maya Angelou speak her poem, 'Still I Rise' (you can find it on YouTube). Her rises and falls of pitch and subtle pauses bring a humour and pathos that goes far beyond the actual words. Listen to recordings of Ronald Reagan, especially where he has the opportunity to tell a story or adlib. Listen to the way he uses timing to keep his audience in suspense and then delivers his punch line. It's often said of the best speakers, 'It's all in the timing.'

Listeners tune in easily to musical speaking. This chapter is all about discovering how you can vary your voice to make it more engaging. The basic elements you can vary are:

- **Volume and speed:** Refer to Chapter 7.

- **Pitch and resonance:** See Chapter 9.

- **Pronunciation of vowels and consonants:** Refer to Chapter 6.

- **Emphasis, rhythm, melody and silence:** I look at each of these devices in this chapter.

Making Your Point Strongly

Every influential speaker knows how to make you notice certain words by emphasising them to create an impact. You can emphasise a word or syllable in the following ways:

- Increase its volume.

- Make an initial short consonant stronger.

- Lengthen any long consonants in the word or syllable.

- Raise its pitch.

- Lower the pitch to contrast with the surrounding words.

- Employ a different tone, for example harsher, or more strident.

In practice, when you think of emphasising the word you want to stress – *feel* its importance in the sentence – you automatically employ the relevant skills from the list above and give an appropriate weight to important words.

Find a few speakers you enjoy listening to on television or online. Recorded clips are ideal because you can replay them as many times as you want. Listen to the speakers with an open sense of curiosity and ask yourself *how* they make you want to listen to them. In particular, pay attention to the following:

- How strongly they emphasise certain words.

- Which words they choose to emphasise.

- How frequently they emphasise words in a sentence.

- Whether they vary the emphasis at different times.

Exploring emphasis

Listen to a clip of a speaker you admire and speak out loud along with them, imitating exactly what they do. You don't need to memorise what the person says. Simply hear the words and then, as far as you can, speak them in exactly the same way. You'll lag behind a bit, but you can still catch much of what they say and their way of speaking. After imitating a speaker for a few minutes, reflect on how much you needed to use emphasis. You may be surprised at how much energy you have to put into your speech to match the speaker's voice. What sounds comfortable to listen to when someone else is speaking involves more energy than you may be used to when you try it yourself. Try imitating a few different speakers and compare your experiences.

You may fear that you're going to sound over the top if you put so much energy into your speech. Don't worry, you won't.

Listen to Track 21. Get a partner and practise emphasis with the following activity.

1. **Make up a simple sentence.**

   Here are a couple of examples to start you off:

   > The old man fell in the street.

   > The bus broke down in the rush-hour.

2. **Person A speaks the sentence aloud, and then Person B asks questions about it.**

3. **Person A answers each question, using lots of emphasis.**

   For example:

   > Person B: Who fell?

   > Person A: The old *man*.

   > B: What happened?

   > A: He *fell*.

   > B: Who was it?

   > A: The old **man**.

   > B: Where did it happen?

   > A: In the *street*.

   > B: What did he do?

   > A: He **fell**.

When playing Person A, imagine that you're genuinely trying to be helpful in answering the questions, but are getting increasingly impatient at the apparent refusal of Person B to understand what you're saying, so you stress the words with more and more insistence.

4. **Swap roles and go through Steps 2 and 3 with a new simple sentence.**

When playing Person A, increase your indignation as the game continues, and you'll find that your emphasis gets stronger and seems more and more normal.

Enjoy a bit of braggadocio with a friend. Pretend that you've been fishing and are now comparing the sizes of your catch. Use the following words and any others you can think of to describe your fish:

big	extreme	enormous	colossal	mammoth
vast	giant	massive	immense	immeasurable
huge	limitless	gargantuan	large	gigantic

Take it in turns to show off, and each of you must out-do the other in emphasising the size of your catch. For example:

Person A: The carp I caught was *enormous*!

Person B: Well, my fish was *colossal*!

Person A: Oh yeah? I just can't tell you how *vast* mine was!

Person B: I've never seen the like, mine was *immense*!

Person A: No, but really, this was *gigantic*!

Understanding English emphasis

I can't overstress the importance of emphasis in English. Every sentence is built around its emphasised words, which are a crucial element in conveying its sense. I talk more about emphasis in Track 22. You can create emphasis by lengthening vowels and consonants, raising the pitch and other ways. The synthetic voice that scientist Stephen Hawking uses or that you hear in an automated phone directory sounds strange because these technologies can't fully replicate the emphases of natural speech. Of course, every word plays its part, but if you hear just the emphasised words in most English sentences, you get the gist of what someone is talking about. Consider this random example from a newspaper with the strongest emphases in italics:

The *airline* made further moves to *expand* its *capacity* at *Heathrow* yesterday by acquiring *six* extra *slots*, but the news did *little* for *shares*.

When you listen to everyday, natural speech, the emphasised words come more into focus while the other words in the sentence go by more rapidly or flatly, which increases the spotlight on the important words.

If you want your speech to sparkle, say the emphasised syllables with beautiful clear vowel sounds (see Chapter 6) and let the other words look after themselves. For example, say 'In the middle of the night.' When you say this phrase at normal speed, you probably pronounce it, 'In thə **mid**əl əf thə **night**.' ('ə' is the nondescript final sound in 'better'). As a result, the *mid* of middle and the word *night* are heard especially vividly and clearly.

For this exercise, imagine that you're a newsreader on radio or TV. Prepare a text and read it with lively emphasis. Most people emphasise much less strongly when they read than when they're chatting animatedly with a friend. Emphasising strongly when you read is a valuable communication skill.

1. **Find two or three sentences of printed text to say aloud.**

   The actual words don't have to be anything special. You can use a short paragraph from today's newspaper, a magazine article, or something you find online and print out. The key is to have printed text that you can mark up.

2. **Read through the sentences, decide which words you want to give strong emphasis and use a pencil to underline these words.**

3. **Read your passage out loud, putting emphasis on the words you chose, as emphatically as a newsreader.**

4. **Review your performance, and adjust and repeat until it sounds like an authentic animated news bulletin.**

   If you're like most people, you probably underlined too many words the first time round. Adjust the number of words you emphasise until the sentences sound both natural and full of impact when you read them. If possible, read your passage to friends and get their feedback on how you sound. I'm guessing that they'll enjoy your increased emphasis.

Avoid stressing words randomly. If you sound emphatic without linking your emphasis to meaning, you end up conveying nothing. You *can stress almost every word*, but it sounds like complete overkill. And as for stressing the small stuff, think of the oddness in some *of* the loudspeaker announce*ments* you hear *when* you travel!

Emphasis and meaning are closely linked. With different emphasis, you often get an entirely different meaning. Say the following short statement out loud, placing the main emphasis on a different word each time, and see how the meaning changes. I cover this in Track 22 too.

> *I* want to drive home = I'm the driver. Perhaps you've had too much to drink and should not be driving!
>
> I *want* to drive home = I'm insisting. I actually want to do it.
>
> I want to *drive* home = I want to take the car, not get a taxi.
>
> I want to drive *home* = Home is where I want to go, rather than stay here or go somewhere else.

It's easier to work on your emphasising skills if you combine the practices in this section with body movement. Strike your hand down firmly or grip your fist on the emphasised syllables. You see politicians make these kind of actions frequently: Tony Blair was adept at striking one hand into the other; Bill Clinton raised his fist with the thumb showing. Choose a gesture that helps you sound emphatic when you express yourself and practise speaking. Then speak again just as strongly without the gesture. Gestures are powerful but they can also become the stuff of parody – you don't want to pick up a habit you can't get rid of!

Ending on the low note of authority

If you want to speak with authority, emphasise especially the end of a sentence or thought. Make that final emphasis low in pitch. This low pitch gives your statement completeness and makes you sound as if you know what you're talking about.

People often express the desire for a deeper voice in order to sound more authoritative. Ending on a strong low note achieves the same without forcing your voice.

Try out loud the following sentences or find some of your own in a newspaper. End on a strong low note with a sense of finality (listen to Track 22):

> Police are mounting a review after a woman was arrested on suspicion of *mur*der.
>
> A breakdown of the figures shows that over one million was spent on external con*sul*tants.

The ending must be strong as well as lower in pitch. A low weak ending which tails off suggests that you've lost confidence and people may as well stop listening.

Take a good breath at the start of your thought so that you have enough breath to end with strength. (See Chapter 4 for more on breathing.)

Apply the strong low ending to end of an idea or thought, not every time you meet a full stop. When you say, 'The weather was terrible. They hadn't eaten for days. They needed a safe haven', reserve the strong low ending for 'haven', the end of the complete statement. You can raise your pitch for the endings of the first two sentences to make them significant but not final: 'The weather was *terr*ible (high pitch). They hadn't eaten for *days* (high pitch). They needed a safe *ha*ven, (low pitch)'.

You may find that your accent doesn't naturally end on a low tone – for example, many people from Australia or New Zealand tend to go up in pitch at the end of sentences. If you end a statement on a higher note, you sound as if you're asking a question or seeking agreement. Going up at the end of a statement makes your point less strongly, though it can sound friendly or more consensual. Also, if you end every sentence on exactly the same high tone, people get bored. Variation is key.

Getting into Rhythm

Even if you think that you're all arms and legs on the dance floor, rhythm is deep in your psyche. A baby of just a few months moves in rhythm to the voice of its mother, tuning into the rhythm of language before even tuning into its sounds. You develop language through rhythm in the form of all the ditties and rhymes of childhood. Think of any tune you love, and you find that it has an interesting rhythm and shape to it. Take the most well-known tune around the world, *Happy Birthday to You,* and hear that skipping rhythm on 'happy' and the carrying of the rhythm towards 'you' – 'dum-ti dum dum dum *dum*'.

Music may be the last thing on the mind of politicians giving serious speeches, but great speakers always have a strong instinct for the rhythm of words, and know that certain speech rhythms are memorable. Emphasis plays a part in this rhythm (see the preceding section), as do the rhythms of individual words, phrases, sentences and even groups of sentences. I cover larger chunks of text later in 'Varying the rhythm'.

Thinking of words first, English has a huge vocabulary, and that allows you to choose a word with the appropriate rhythm for what you want to say. You can use short, sharp Anglo-Saxon words, such as 'get', 'go', 'rule' and 'like' or you can express yourself with Latinate words, such as 'acquisition', 'procedure', 'operation' and 'appreciate', which have more length and flow. In the 2008 US Presidential campaign, Barack Obama used the phrase 'Yes we can' almost as a mantra – three strong Anglo-Saxon syllables to pound out to the masses. Think of the impact if he'd chosen instead to say, 'I affirm that it is possible for us.' Almost the same sense, but a very different impact.

Track 23 explores rhythm and impact. The next time you want to create a statement with strong impact, put down your first idea on paper, then open the Thesaurus on your computer (shift + F7 in Microsoft Word) or online. Experiment with alternative ways of making your point. Start with the original phrase: 'Progress is going to be difficult.'

> Adjustment shows signs of being challenging.
>
> New circumstances are guaranteed to be testing.
>
> Transformation is likely to be easier said than done.
>
> Revolution threatens to be brutal.
>
> Change has got to be hard.

Speak these phrases out loud and hear how each rhythm creates a particular effect. Some versions of the phrase clearly aren't as compelling as others. Swap the words around until you create the impact you desire.

Moving to the melody

You can often find your speaking rhythm easier if you move as you speak, because the energy of the words you speak is expressed in your body.

Say this excerpt from *Julius Caesar* in which Cassius displays strong anger. Stride forward, throw your weight about and pause to create an effect. Sweep a hand from across you wide open, gesture, point or clench a fist. Make sure that the movements fit in with the words. 'Experiment' is the name of the game. *Feel* the meaning of the words in your body movements as you speak. Listen to my declamation on Track 23!

> Now, in the names of all the gods at once,
> Upon what meat doth this our Caesar feed,
> That he is grown so great? Age, thou art shamed!
> Rome, thou hast lost the breed of noble bloods!
> When went there by an age, since the great flood,
> But it was famed with more than with one man?

> When could they say till now, that talk'd of Rome,
> That her wide walls encompass'd but one man?
> Now is it Rome indeed and room enough,
> When there is in it but one only man.

Practise the rhythm of words and phrases with poetry! The poet Alexander Pope declared that 'Those move easiest who have learned to dance'; you might also say that those speak easiest who have learned to speak poetry.

Varying the rhythm

Have you noticed how some speakers have a rhythm they repeat endlessly. You can almost hear a tune of '*der* de *der* de *der*' in the following:

> Here we are today. S'great to have you here. S'been a tricky year. Profit down a bit. Markets not so good. But there's lots to do. Gotta keep it up.

The soundbite

Creators of advertising seek endlessly for the perfect rhythm of a phrase – ones that quickly become as familiar and loved as *Happy Birthday to You*.

Try out the compulsive rhythms of these advertising slogans by saying them out loud:

- ✔ 'Because I'm worth it.'
- ✔ 'A diamond is forever.'
- ✔ 'Put a tiger in your tank.'
- ✔ 'Good to the last drop.'
- ✔ 'Let your fingers do the walking.'
- ✔ 'Just do it.'

Masters of the political soundbite look for memorable phrases to energise voters and shift opinion:

- ✔ 'No taxation without representation' (slogan of American revolutionaries)
- ✔ 'Never had it so good' (Harold Macmillan's 1957 UK election campaign)

- ✔ 'A time for greatness' (John F Kennedy's 1960 US presidential campaign)
- ✔ 'In your heart, you know he's right' (Barry Goldwater's 1964 US presidential campaign)
- ✔ 'Let's make America great again' (Ronald Reagan's 1980 US presidential campaign)
- ✔ 'Things can only get better' (Tony Blair's 1997 UK Labour party campaign)
- ✔ 'Are you thinking what we're thinking?' (2005 UK Conservative Party slogan)

Some soundbites capture the public imagination so much that they slip into everyday usage. Phrases such as *power to the people, black is beautiful, the death tax, the buck stops here* and *make love not war* have become part of the English language. Play with language yourself to create memorable phrases. Consider the 'tune' – the rhythm of the words, repetition of consonant and vowels sounds, and other sound echoes as you create your phrases.

This kind of rhythm is a sure recipe for tedium. Rather than lulling your listeners to sleep with regularity, vary your timing and the lengths of your phrases so that you're never predictable.

Consider the following excerpt from Bill Clinton's 2008 Democratic Convention speech. Hear how the sentences grow in length as he catalogues the troubles. Notice too how from line four onwards you have a rising ending and gradual increase in pace on 'hurting' 'declining', 'rising', 'increasing', 'disappearing', and then everything suddenly lands on a strong note for the final three nouns. Clinton is a master of music in speaking. Try speaking the words yourself and feel the rhythm.

> Our nation is in trouble on two fronts.
> The American dream is under siege at home,
> and America's leadership in the world has been weakened.
>
> Middle-class and low-income Americans are hurting,
>
> with incomes declining,
> job losses, poverty, and inequality rising,
> mortgage foreclosures and credit card debt increasing,
> health care coverage disappearing,
>
> and a big spike in the cost of food, utilities and gasoline.

When you read Shakespeare poetry in his plays, the lines are always the same length. The iambic pentameter rhythm he employs can be boring in the hands of others with a rigid *dum* de *dum* de *dum* de *dum* de *dum* rhythm. But the stresses are only like the beat in a piece of jazz. After you grasp the regular pattern, you notice the subtle irregularities that bring the lines alive.

Read out loud the first two lines of a love poem in iambic pentameter by John Donne.

> I *wond*er *by* my *troth* what *thou* and *I*
> *Did* till we *lov'd? Were* we not *weaned* till *then?*

All pretty regular in the first line; then in the second you get *da*-di-di *da* – 'Did till we *lov'd?*' You sense the amazement of the speaker: 'What did we *do? Extraordinary!*' It's as if the words push against the rhythm you expect and make the line more colourful. You're expecting the pattern, but it gives you something different. Listen to my variations in Track 24.

Rap and hip-hop artists do something similar. They get into a pounding rhythm, and then they vary it a bit to suit a particular meaning, giving it freshness and vitality. You can discover ideas about rhythm from many different sources like this.

Playing with pitch

You can also hear music in speech in the ups and downs of pitch. To get the idea, listen to 'Happy Birthday to You' again. If you pay attention to the *notes* of the tune instead of the rhythm, you get a sense of a tune climbing higher and higher and then coming down again at the end.

Tune in to Track 25. Sing 'Happy Birthday to You' yourself, and notice how the highest note in each line climbs higher (I've marked them in bold):

Happy birthday **to** you.
Happy birthday **to** you.
Happy **birth**day dear *someone;*

and then in the last line, the notes fall again in the notes in bold:

Happy **birth**day **to you.**

Now listen to a newsreader or another speaker, and notice how they make a pattern in pitch. Here's an extract from a 1940 speech by Sir Winston Churchill:

You ask, what is our aim? (Churchill ends on a high note)
I can answer in one word, it is victory, (medium note)
victory at all costs, (medium)
victory in spite of all terror, (high)
victory, however long and hard the road may be; (low)
for without victory, there is no survival. (ends extremely low)

The preceding is a typical shape for a strong statement: an initial phrase takes you to a significant word on a high; another phrase takes you to another significant high, and the final phrase takes you to an important final word on a low. It's like a series of mountain peaks, always arriving finally at a low at the end. The high peaks give you a sense of suspense as you travel through a sentence: '*This!* and also *this!* and *this!*' leading you eventually to a low '*this*'. If you speak in this way, you maintain suspense. Your listeners are unlikely to interrupt you mid-statement, but wait until the release of the final low.

You can give a statement shape in several ways. For example, if your statement is a question, it won't end on a low note. Be aware that high sounds mark a word or phrase as significant, and an emphasised low pitched sound gives an air of finality. You can play with these elements to create different shapes for your statements.

Power and persuasion: The art of rhetoric

Imagine a pre-technical world where communicating meant speaking live. This was the world of ancient Greece, where politicians learned the different skills of persuasion and spoke directly to their citizens in grand oratorical performances. Skills included how to create and organise a speech, how to formulate persuasive arguments and how to remember what they wanted to say and deliver it with impact.

The Roman philosopher, lawyer and politician, Cicero (106–43 BC), was considered the best Roman orator of all time. Even though he wasn't of the correct social class, he rose to the rank of consul through his skill with the spoken word. Others of modest birth through the ages have followed his example.

In England, rhetoric began to flourish in the time of St Augustine (AD 354–430) as an instrument of church preaching. Formal education in oratory for students of church and state continued through the middle ages. In the University of Oxford, you can still see the subject 'Rhetoric' from mediaeval times written above one of the doors in the Bodleian Library quadrangle.

After a fallow period, rhetoric blossomed again in the late 18th century in the mouths of political speakers. A work on rhetoric by the Scottish author Hugh Blair became a textbook in many American colleges and schools through the 19th century. Since then, rhetoric has been studied widely to learn the art of speaking and debate, though today's university and college students are more likely to call it Communication Studies and apply it to the fields of marketing and literature, as well as politics. However, the study is still of the fundamental Greek theories such as the modes of persuasion, ethos, pathos and logos. (Pick up *Persuasion & Influence For Dummies* by Elizabeth Kuhnke (Wiley) for the lowdown on this still-powerful tool.) From the Greeks and Romans to the present day, politicians have risen to power through oratory – for better or worse. Without the power of oratory, few presidents and prime ministers are elected. The Greek ideal of the leadership of eloquent men lives on.

Find political extracts on YouTube or tune into news announcers on the television or radio. Listen out for sentence shapes. After you begin spotting them, you start to hear them everywhere, and begin to appreciate what they can add to your own speech.

Pitch variation can certainly be overdone! Listen to house-buying or holiday programmes and you often hear a new style of super-emphasis that swoops from super-high to super-low and super-high again in a series of huge pitch variations without any justification in the sense of the words. This variation isn't shaping; it's swooping! Don't take your listeners on a meaningless roller-coaster ride; aim to match the shape of a sentence to its meaning.

Reviving the Ancient Art of Rhetoric

Rhetoric may be an old-fashioned term, but the ancient art is alive and well today. Rhetoric played a big part in the impact of speakers from the Greek Sophists in 600 BC, and still plays a major role in the speeches of politicians today. See 'Power and persuasion: the art of rhetoric' for more on rhetoric's beginning and on-going influence.

Rhetoric is the art of persuasion in speaking, particularly as it relates to the sounds of language, its repetitions, variations, musicality and rhythms. The point of utilising rhetoric is to influence your listener, often at a level below their consciousness.

The following sections introduce you to a few of the most useful rhetorical devices. Imagine, a classical education – in minutes!

Dancing in three time

One of the most obvious and well-used rhetorical tools is the rule of three. 'I came, I saw, I conquered,' declared Julius Caesar. In the rule of three, the three words or phrases typically grow in intensity with the last phrase being the strongest. The first two are often similar in form with the final one slightly different.

Try saying out loud some of the following well-known rule-of-three phrases. Make them build up to a climax or gradually get softer. You can also try making them gradually slow down at the end. Don't drop the pitch with a sense of finality until the end; keep the momentum going. Listen to my attempts in Track 26.

> This is not the end.
> It is not even the beginning of the end.
> But it is, perhaps, the end of the beginning
>
> Sir Winston Churchill

> Life,
> liberty,
> and the pursuit of *hap*piness
>
> US Declaration of Independence

> Jam tomorrow,
> and jam yesterday,
> but never jam to*day*
>
> Lewis Carroll, *Through the Looking Glass*

The trick when working with the rule of three is to build the tension through the first two words or groups of words and then land with force on the final word or group.

Experiment with the rule of three in words of your own. One way is to repeat the start of a sentence twice, and then alter it slightly for a powerful third statement. Here are some suggestions for starting the first two lines:

> I know that…
>
> It's been hard…
>
> Some people…

Here's my attempt at one of them (listen to Track 26):

> I know that it's been a difficult year for all of us.
> I know that we feel as if we've been struggling uphill.
> I also know that I've witnessed some of the best our people have to offer.

You can use the rule of three in any context, not just in formal speech. By the way, it's a great device for creating comedy too:

> I didn't have time to pack much for the weekend, just
> socks,
> undies . . .
> and my ninja *sword.*

Building up momentum

The rule of three is a great way to build momentum (see the preceding section). The simple device of repetition can build momentum in other ways too, as I illustrate in this section.

Find YouTube clips of great speeches from the past for powerful examples of momentum. Winston Churchill, Bill Clinton and Martin Luther King all built up momentum in their greatest speeches.

Churchill used the image of fighting again and again in this extract from his famous speech in the House of Commons in 1940. Every line begins with the same phrase:

> We shall go on to the end,
> we shall fight in France,
> we shall fight on the seas and oceans,
> we shall fight with growing confidence and growing strength in the air,

we shall defend our Island, whatever the cost may be,
we shall fight on the beaches,
we shall fight on the landing grounds,
we shall fight in the fields and in the streets,
we shall fight in the hills;
we shall never surrender.

When he finally reaches the last line, 'we shall never surrender', in his deepest of deep voices, its impact is extraordinary. Listen to the extract on YouTube and hear how his voice maintains the suspense through ten lines.

John Kennedy built up to a grand climax using these skills in his Berlin speech in 1963. In this speech, repetition takes the form of a refrain. In the last iteration, he creates an impact by slipping in a German translation of his repeated phrase, before saying it again in English with great emphasis for the last time:

There are many people in the world who really don't understand, or say they don't, what is the great issue between the free world and the Communist world.
Let them come to Berlin.

There are some who say that communism is the wave of the future.
Let them come to Berlin.

And there are some who say, in Europe and elsewhere, we can work with the Communists.
Let them come to Berlin.

And there are even a few who say that it is true that communism is an evil system, but it permits us to make economic progress.
Lass' sie nach Berlin kommen.
Let them come to Berlin.

Rhyming and chiming

You can enjoy yourself with the rhetorical devices in this section, which are all about echoing sounds. You can echo through:

- **Alliteration:** Repeating the initial consonants (*p*ickled *p*umpkin)

- **Assonance:** Echoing vowel sounds (Bl*a*ck b*a*ckp*a*ck)

- **Consonance:** Echoing internal consonants (ri*ch* ba*tch*elor)

- **Rhyme:** Similar vowel sounds *and* final consonants. (C*ook* b*ook*)

Flex your alliteration and consonance muscles by reciting three odd lines from a poem of 1918 by Carolyn Wells. Read these lines out loud with flamboyance! Listen to Track 27.

> If you caught a captious curate killing kippers for the cook,
> If you beheld a battleboat bombarding Biscay Bay
> If you saw a drivelling dreamer drowning ducklings in a ditch.

Assonance (echoing vowel sounds) is often subtle with echoes and half-echoes, as in the opening of Aung San Suu Kyi's Keynote Address at the NGO Forum on Women in 1995. She opens with sonorous *or, uh* and *ah* sounds (in bold), and ends with firm *a* sounds (in italics).

> It is a **wo**nderful but d**au**nting t**a**sk that has f**a**llen **o**n me to say a few words by way of opening this F**o**rum, the greatest c**o**nc**ou**rse of women (joined by a few brave men!) that h*a*s ever g*a*thered on our pl*a*net.

Full rhymes (both vowel sounds and final consonants the same), are more often found in poetry, but serve brilliantly for memorable phrases in prose. Think of *brain drain, blame game, fat cat, claptrap* – and Bart Simpson's, 'I am not a l*ean* m*ean* spitting mach*ine*.' What others can you find? Dylan Thomas's radio play, *Under Milkwood*, is brim-full of alliteration, consonance, assonance, rhyming – every kind of language echoing you can imagine. It turns prose into a kind of poetry (I read this on Track 27):

> Come now, drift up the dark, come up the drifting sea-dark street now in the dark night seesawing like the sea, to the bible-black airless attic over Jack Black the cobbler's shop where alone and savagely Jack Black sleeps in a nightshirt tied to his ankles with elastic and dreams of chasing the naughty couples down the grassgreen gooseberried double bed of the wood, flogging the tosspots in the spit-and-sawdust, driving out the bare bold girls from the sixpenny hops of his nightmares.

Use echoes to speed up or slow down your speaking, according to which sounds you choose. In the extract above, the speed of reading naturally changes with the sounds of the words, so that the first dark, drifting part reads slowly, and by the time you reach Jack Black's dream and the 'grass-green gooseberried double bed' you're racing along towards the sentence end.

Enjoying the Silence

After the rhetorical excitement of the preceding section, I want to invite you to pause and enjoy the quiet. If you get at all nervous when you speak, silence is one of the hardest things to endure. Every time you stop, a micro-second feels like an hour, and you become self-conscious and feel everyone looking at you.

Yet the ability to pause in silence for a few moments has much going for it. A well-placed pause:

- **Serves as a great mark of confidence:** When you pause comfortably, people find you self-assured.

- **Gives listeners the chance to process what you're saying:** No one can listen continuously. They need space for reflection. After a pause to think about your words, people are more ready to listen to the next thing you say.

- **Makes people hear the words you spoke just before the silence more strongly:** Those important words hang in the air, and people have time to consider them in the silence.

- **Creates tension or anticipation:** 'And there on the floor he saw . . . *the body.*' or 'This year's winner is . . . *Jane Osborne!*'

- **Gives you thinking space:** Silence may seem unnatural when you're going headlong through a speech, but silence is an important part of the natural rhythm of communication. When you're relaxed in normal conversation, a pause happens naturally as you think of the next thing to say. Without a few thinking pauses, you can quickly sound mechanical or over-rehearsed.

- **Makes the meaning of your words clear:** If you rush through certain sentences with no pause, people can seriously misunderstand you. Take the mystifying statement, 'King Richard talked to his people ten minutes after he was dead', which is actually supposed to mean, 'King Richard talked to his people; (pause) ten minutes after, he was dead!'

- **Clearly indicates that you're going to move on to another section of your speech:** For example, 'So that completed the trial.' Pause; new beginning: 'The next phase of the project was. . .'

- **Can function as a 'back space' key for your mouth after you say something you wish you hadn't:** As soon as you make a gaff, pause, move to another spot (or just shift position in your chair), and then speak in a completely different tone of voice, almost like a new person: 'Ah, that's *not* what I meant to say! What I'd like to say is. . .' Your listeners forget the confusing or incorrect material that came before and you're free to carry on with your message.

A pause can seem difficult because it feels like nothing – a void you feel impelled to fill with something, even if an unhelpful or self-conscious thought. But a pause is never nothing! It's one of the most effective skills in a speaker's toolbox. Always do something with a pause. The silence is a time of doing or becoming. Think of it as *pregnant pause*, a pause full of promise.

Take the simple phrase: 'Friends, Romans, Countrymen' and say each word with a massive pause before the next. Do it with thoughts in between the words and feel their energy moving through the silence. You can move around during this practice, but the exercise is largely a mental and emotional one so concentrate on the thoughts and feelings that build with each breath. For example,

> 'Friends' – Before you say the word, look around the audience for the people who are closest to you. Think of the good relationships you have with them and how they've supported you through thick and thin, how amazing they are. Speak with a voice of intimacy.

> 'Romans' – Before you say the word, turn your attention to those who belong to your city; those people who like you feel a love for this place; people like you who feel so proud that they live in the centre of the known universe, with all its history, its strength and power. Just being near them makes you want to stand taller. Speak with a voice of pride.

> 'Countrymen' – Before you say the word, scan your audience for people who have come in from afar; think of them working the land, providing the grain basket for the city and for this vast empire; think about these people who though from far away are also loyal and true. Say the word with a sense of gratitude.

> Finish the exercise with the final words, 'Lend me your ears', and sense the coming together of this great and glorious people for the message you have to give them.

During a pause, do any of the following:

✔ Think about what you've just uttered.

✔ Move towards your next statement.

✔ Create and share a state of mind – calm, excitement, suspense, determination and so on.

✔ Feel a connection with your audience in that state of mind.

Listen to Martin Luther King's 'I have a dream' speech for a great example of pauses that build. I indicate the pause and suggest some emotional words and phrases that I sense in the air between King's words.

> I have a dream . . . (Oh yes, we dream of a future, could it really happen?) that one day . . . (Yes, how long we have waited and said 'one day', but 'one day' is specific, it *will* happen) this nation will rise up . . . (this *is* our 'nation' and we are part of it, and there's a hint of revolution here too).

What specific words do you hear – what specific feelings do you feel – during each of King's powerful pauses in this speech?

Matching the music of a great speech

One of the best ways to discover the secrets of the masters is to copy. Every day in the great art galleries of the world, you find art students sitting in front of great works with their sketch pads, copying the old masters. They aren't trying to make counterfeit versions of great art, they're simply exploring the masters' genius by attempting to replicate it. Practical skills flourish when you imitate greatness.

You find out certain information about a speaker's skill by taking note of their variables of pitch, volume, pace, tone and so on. But instead, try to *be* them – step into their physical, mental and emotional way of being – and you discover much more. Find video extracts on YouTube or elsewhere of different speakers that you admire. As you listen and watch, 'do' them. Imitate the tone of voice, the ebbs and flows of pitch, volume and pace, and capture what it is that gives them their impact. You may like to record yourself as well to check how close you get to the original. Above all, discover their music. Then gradually you can make it your own, and develop your unique musical style of speech.

Chapter 9

Expressing Yourself Fully with the Power of Resonance

*I*n this chapter I share with you the most important secret of a great voice, the one thing that gives your voice tonal quality, that amplifies your voice and that provides the basis for such a variety of sounds. It's *resonance*.

Resonance is the physical vibration of your vocal folds through your body. When you produce your voice without constriction, resonance produces vibrations in different parts of your body as you express different energies such as determination or empathy. Discovering how to use resonance opens the way to being able to express yourself powerfully and influentially. In this chapter, I introduce you to the different resonators in turn.

Beginning to Explore Resonance

If your voice didn't resonate, it would be feeble. Your vocal chords are like tiny rubber bands and don't produce much sound on their own. They need the resonating cavities of your head, chest and the rest of your body to amplify your sound and create a powerful, dynamic voice.

Experience how vibration and resonance works with this little experiment. Hold a rubber band loosely between your thumb and forefinger and pluck it. In its flabby state, it makes practically no sound. Then loop the band over your thumb and little finger and stretch out your hand to extend the rubber band. Now pluck it. It makes a pinging sound, more resonant but still fairly quiet. Finally stretch the rubber band across the top and around the bottom of a fairly steep-sided bowl. Rest the bowl on a hard surface and pluck the band within the concave shape. You hear a sound that is considerably louder and more musical. That's resonance!

The strings of a violin stretched across the instrument's hollow body work in a similar way to a taut rubber band stretched around a bowl. The strings are fixed at each end, leaving the body of the violin free to vibrate. These vibrations produce the warm, powerful sound of the instrument.

When you speak, your equivalent of the violin's wood structure is your head and your body. The vibrations produced by your vocal folds (refer to Chapter 4) multiply as they encounter the bony surfaces and cavities within you, setting off harmonics that make the tone satisfyingly rich and complex.

Your unique body shape creates your sounds. The legendary tenor Pavarotti's beautiful sounds were enhanced by his vast bulk. Another great singer, Maria Callas, sacrificed some of her rich vocal tone when she lost a considerable number of pounds to look more the part of the consumptive heroine. Don't worry though – a violin sounds just as good as a double bass – and vice versa!

Expressing resonance

Resonance loves bones! They're excellent conductors of vibrations. The hard surfaces of your body provide the strongest resonance. The bones of the skull and the chest are particularly good, but all bones contribute – even the vertebrae of your spine. Cartilage and muscles (if toned up!) also amplify the sound well. Resonance especially loves hollows and other concave surfaces, which you find in the lower throat, the mouth, the nose, the sinus hollows and the skull.

Don't hold yourself too tightly. Sound needs freedom to echo around your body without meeting rigidity. However, you also need to avoid slumping or sagging. Resonance does *not* love the flabby, squishy parts of the body because they absorb and deaden sound like heavy curtains and a thick carpet in a sitting room. If you want your voice to resonate well, you need to feel the elastic strength of your body – neither tight nor flabby – as you hold yourself open and free. See Chapter 5 for further descriptions of elastic relaxation.

As I explore in detail in the following sections, resonance in different parts of your body happens naturally as you access different mental and emotional energies. In order for resonance to happen, however, your body needs to be free and flexible, and your mind and emotions must permit you to express what's going on. If either of these provisos isn't in place, the natural process is disrupted and you experience vocal problems (which I explore in Chapter 11). For now, I assume that you're free and flexible and willing to express yourself fully.

When you produce your voice with freedom, every different thought, feeling or impulse affects the resonance, and your voice expresses ever-varying combinations of these different energies with extraordinary subtlety. When you do the exercises in this chapter, you focus on just one resonator at time. You don't do this in real life, but isolating them one at a time enables you to understand the function of each resonator separately, and to work on particular resonators that you may have neglected until now.

Varying your pitch

As your voice resounds around your body, it also has the ability to vary in pitch. Most people have a vocal range of three or four notes when they speak, but they *could* have a range of three or four *octaves* if they trained their voices with the dedication of singers.

Your range is defined not only by the physical limitations of your individual physiology but also by your conditioning. You may still be *able* to scream on a really high note, but you probably last performed that feat in your cradle.

A wider pitch range involves greater emotional freedom and intensity than you probably demonstrate in daily life. Many people keep the resonance of their voices down in their throats and chests, confirming the common view that expressions of passion or joy don't have a place in everyday speaking. Most people are quite inhibited!

Actors, because they train their voices, have a bigger pitch range than most people. Every new part demands something different from the voice. The great British actor Laurence Olivier frequently rose to the challenge. But when he accepted the part of Othello, he decided that something exceptional was needed from his voice. He undertook a period of intensive preparation, including body work, to give himself greater muscle tone and strength and voice work to lower his voice. People who heard him in the part remarked upon how deep his voice was; he succeeded in adding several notes to his lower range. Incidentally, reports said that Olivier warmed up his voice for the role by bellowing at a herd of cows for an hour!

Different parts of your body come into play when producing different pitches:

- ✔ The chest for low sounds
- ✔ The throat, palate, teeth and jaw for middle sounds
- ✔ The sinuses, cheekbones, nose, and the upper sinuses and skull for the highest sounds

In the following sections, I offer activities to develop each resonator in turn. That said, the whole body is constantly involved in creating sound because a resonance in one part of the body sets up other resonances, harmonics and overtones elsewhere.

Try out different pitches to explore your range with this playful practice which I demonstrate in Track 28. Tell yourself – or a captive child – the story of 'The Three Bears', getting fully into the various characters. Enjoy the parts where the three bears speak and see just how different in pitch you can make the voices. Try this part for example:

'Somebody's been eating *my* porridge,' said the Daddy Bear in a deep gruff voice.

'And somebody's been eating *my* porridge,' said the Mummy Bear in a gentle medium voice.

'And somebody's been eating my porridge, and they've eaten it *all up,*' said the Baby Bear in a high squeal of a voice.

You can practise these skills in slightly more serious mode using the following extract from the love poem 'The Good Morrow' by John Donne. In order to get into dramatic mode, stride around the room using broad gestures as you recite the lines:

I wonder, by my troth, what thou and I
Did till we loved? Were we not weaned till then?
(high voice of surprise for these lines)

But sucked on country pleasures childishly?
(middle voice for this line)

Or snorted we in the Seven Sleepers' den?
(deep voice for this line)

'Twas so
(deepest of slow deep voices for this phrase)

In the previous two practices, concentrate on the *meaning* of the words and the *feeling* of the different pitches rather than on what you hear. Your ears may deceive you!

Avoid pushing down physically to make your voice deep. Don't force anything. Just imagine and feel a low voice coming from deep in your body. Whatever sounds come out are fine.

Championing Your Chest Voice

When you state something you believe to be true and want to share your belief, your voice naturally vibrates in your chest. You hear the connection between this part of the body and truth in language too: you 'get things off your chest' and 'make a clean breast of it'. If you want to develop a voice with more authority and gravitas, this is the resonance you need to develop.

The voice that resounds in your chest is easy to listen to, not too high and not too low, and it carries well. It has the ring of authority and tends to be trusted. It sounds confident and assured. See the later section 'Using your chest voice' for more on situations in which your chest voice is particularly effective.

Producing your chest voice

Stand tall and open for all these resonance practices. Stay relaxed, particularly in the upper part of your body, with your shoulders loose and throat free. For the lower resonances, think low and settle down into your body with no upward tension. See Chapter 5 for more relaxation techniques.

In order to produce your confident chest voice, you need to locate the area of your body that resonates most strongly when you produce these tones – your sternum (breast) bone. You can feel its hard flat surface when you touch your chest. Listen to Track 29.

1. **Put your hand on your chest and breathe in.**

2. **As you breathe out, settle into the easy humming sound *hermmm*.**

   Have a feeling of relaxing downwards – without any pushing or strain.

   You may choose instead to start on a hum at a comfortable pitch and slide the sound down in pitch until it feels as if it reaches your chest. Then open the hum out into the lengthened word *mmmore*.

3. **Feel your sternum bone vibrate under your hand.**

4. **Continue to breathe and make an *aah* sound while patting your chest repeatedly with your hand.**

   Notice how the movement of your hand interrupts the sounds – *if* your voice is vibrating there. The sound ululates like Tarzan when he does his famous cry.

5. **When you find the place where your chest vibrates, let yourself go with the full-bodied Tarzan cry, beating your chest vigorously.**

   Enjoy the robust sounds that vibrate in your chest!

Tarzan cries are a great way to get an accurate feeling of sound resonating in your chest. Another way is to locate the correct place and speak from that resonance (Track 29):

1. **Lay your hands lightly on your belly and take a good fresh breath.**

   Feel your hands gently rise as you take in air low down.

2. **Make the sound *ffff* on the out-breath, keeping your hands in gentle contact with your belly to monitor the smooth flow of air.**

   Continue making the sound for a few seconds, keeping the air flowing in a beautiful steady stream.

3. **Repeat Steps 1 and 2, but this time make the sound *vvvv* (which engages your vocal cords) on the out-breath.**

   Think fairly low, but let the pitch decide itself. Keep the air flow free and steady. Be aware of vibrations in your body. If your chest vibrates, that's perfect.

4. **Speak from same place as the *vvvv* sound you made.**

   If you like, go straight from *vvvv* into a sentence within the same breath: 'Vvvveronica loves to play chess.' Hear how the tone is low and resonates in your chest.

During resonance practice, imagine that you're breathing *into* the resonating place and connecting with its energy before you speak. Think of confidence and strength as you breathe into the resonance in your chest.

Having found the resonance through physical practice, you can also discover it – often more strongly – through mental intention. Most people resonate their voice naturally in the chest when they have a strong opinion about something, especially if the opinion is negative. So now, with someone to listen to you if possible, speak strongly about something you think should happen or shouldn't happen, something that is wrong, ridiculous or shocking. Find a subject that you have a strong opinion about so that you can put genuine energy into it. When you make your statement real, the sound resounds in your chest.

Using your chest voice

The chest voice is ideal for public speaking and for all situations where you want to be taken seriously. The big sternum bone provides excellent resonance without straining your voice, so this way of speaking is kind to your vocal apparatus too.

Deep resonant voice won the US presidency

In 2002, Stanford W. Gregory Jr. and Timothy J. Gallagher of Kent State University in Ohio produced a paper in *Social Psychology Quarterly* predicting the result of US presidential elections purely on voice quality. They undertook audio-spectral research into the fundamental frequency or pitch of the candidates in various US elections and discovered that the candidate who had the voice frequency they labelled 'more dominant' always won the popular vote. So Kennedy won against Nixon, Carter against Ford, Reagan against Carter, Reagan against Mondale, Bush against Dukakis, Clinton against Bush, Clinton against Dole and Gore (as winner of the popular vote) against Bush in 2002.

The researchers were looking in particular at a critical low-pitched frequency in vocalisation, which they filtered out electronically and called F^0. This frequency is the frequency of sounds produced when an individual speaks from a place of conviction (and I contend, a voice relaxed enough to resonate freely in the chest and below). To voters, this voice resonance conveys power and leadership. These methods would have predicted a win for Obama in 2008.

You hear chest resonance often in the speeches of western political leaders. Listen to former US President Bill Clinton or the first female president of Ireland, Mary Robinson. Margaret Thatcher spoke powerfully in Parliament in her time as leader of the opposition but lacked this authoritative deeper chest voice. As prime minister, she put in a lot of work with a voice coach to acquire the deeper authoritative chest sounds that became her hallmark.

Centring in on your chest resonance is difficult if you fear expressing opinions that people may disagree with. Listen to others in the public arena, and you can hear how their voices slip away from strong resonance in their chest to a slightly higher place in the body when they lose confidence. Being able to produce the chest voice is about trusting yourself to state your case firmly without being swayed by what others think.

When trust is absent, your voice sometimes tells the truth more surely than your words! Tony Blair, as prime minister, was an excellent speaker who carried audiences with him, and his voice had many qualities that made people warm towards him. However, the voice of the chest – the voice of truth that isn't swayed by outside influence – sometimes eluded him. When asked in media interviews to justify his decisions over the war in Iraq, you can hear how his voice tightens and thins instead of resounding clearly in the chest. Blair reveals his discomfort even as he states his case with emphasis, ultimately creating a feeling of uncertainty as you listen to him.

Getting Excited about Your Head Resonance

Your voice does something special when you get excited about something, and this brings me to head resonance.

I demonstrate the head voice in Track 30. Speak the following phrases with excitement – the exclamation marks are your reminders to get genuinely excited!

> You'll never guess what's happened!
>
> I won! I know, it's amazing!
>
> It was the most extraordinary thing I've ever seen!
>
> Did you really? You couldn't have!

For most people, when you read the preceding phrases with excitement, your voice goes higher, throughout the phrase or at the strongest point within it. The more energetic, enthusiastic and excited you feel, the more your voice rises.

Consider different scenarios. Play the part of greeting each of the following people in turn:

- ✔ Someone who turns up and he or she is the last person you want to see.
- ✔ A business associate you don't know well.
- ✔ Someone you really care about, who turns up on a surprise visit.

How was your voice different with each person? I'm guessing it was low and flat for the first, mid-range and business-like for the second, and high and excited for the third.

Your tone is usually a fairly accurate indicator of your enthusiasm. Have a listen to other people. If nothing excites them much, you find their voices don't go up often. If you know someone whose life is a roller coaster, swinging between enormous enthusiasm and utter despair, you're likely to hear a voice that swoops up and down with the changes of mood, perhaps even within a single sentence or phrase. Teachers recognise children's characteristics through their tone in their classrooms: the quiet low voices of the timid and the high 'have to speak' tones of, 'Me! Me! Me Miss! I know the answer!'

Producing head tones

Your high tones ring in your head, which is a powerful resonator full of bony tunnels and cavities. Find your head tones with the following activity (Track 30):

1. **Make a long *whoo-oop*! sound that starts at a comfortable mid-level and rises quickly to your highest pitch.**

2. **Do the rising 'whoop!' again and then repeat just the high sound on its own: *oop*.**

3. **Explore the different resonators of your head.**

   Speak in a funny, high voice in your nose like Gollum in *Lord of the Rings*, using lots of 'n' sounds, for instance: 'Nn, nn, nno, never! Never!'

   Become aware of your cheek bones and speak with lots of squeaky 'w' sounds: 'Why? Wow, that's wonderful!'

   Speak imagining sound coming out of your ears: 'Eeeears! Out of my eeeears!'

   Make sounds that issue from the very top of your skull, the highest sounds you can ever imagine: 'Eeee! Wiiiii! Wee Willy Winkiiii!'

   Yes, I know! These sounds don't seem like the kind you're going to use often in sensible adult conversation. But play along; these tones are vitally important components of your voice and probably under-exercised and under-used.

The following practice (also covered in Track 30) is to develop your head voice on its own to enjoy all the head cavities. This one is easier to practise with someone else.

1. **Imagine that you and your partner are both children in the playground.**

   No need to take to take this step seriously!

   Children have high voices, get excited, sometimes squabble and are often exceedingly insistent. Include these elements as you speak, shout and yell to each other in high voices. 'That's my ball!' 'No it's mine! Here it comes! Whee!' 'Oh you've lost it!' 'Hee hee, that's so funny!' . . . you get the idea.

2. **Choose a more everyday subject and have a more realistic conversation, using your adult voice while still including high tones.**

   Talk about your experience and, with each comment, try to outdo the other person in insistence that your experience was more exciting than theirs. Escalate the excitement as you go.

   In the example below (in which two people talk about holidays), the high sounds are in italics – they come out naturally high if you're insistent and enthusiastic:

   Person A: We've just been in Cumbria. The landscape is *magnificent!*
   Person B: Ah but the Alps – those mountains are *amazing!*

Person A: True, but the craggy Dolomites – just *stunning!*
Person B: I'll tell you what – if you want splendour, try New Zealand – *astonishing!*
Person A: Good I'm sure, but for a complete one-off try the Galapagos Islands – they're *unbelievable!*
Person B: Okay, but check this out! The Great Barrier Reef – it's *extraordinary!*

Just use your own words for expressing wonder – *terrific, fantastic, brilliant, wonderful, super, superb, stupendous* and *marvellous* are other examples – and let your voice hit the roof.

You may find that your voice doesn't rise naturally on the italicised words; for this exercise, encourage it to do so even if it feels awkward. Usually, you find that just the accented syllable in the word sounds high, as in 'a**ma**zing' or 'te**rri**fic'. That's fine, and sounds more natural than saying the whole word on a high pitch.

Don't confuse these enthusiastic high tones with the lacklustre thin high tones of someone who feels submissive or fearful. This high resonance always has lively energy behind it. See Chapter 11 for more about how to deal with fearful or squeaky voices.

Using your head voice

Your high resonance is like the sparkle on a Christmas tree decoration. It adds interest to your conversation. You don't use it all the time, but when you do, people catch instantly your excitement, enthusiasm or the special significance you're giving to a certain point.

You hear these high tones of enthusiasm all the time on chat shows in the media. Listen, for example, to the actor Jane Horrocks or show host Jonathan Ross to hear frequent head tones giving high energy to their delivery.

Another vital use of high resonance is to give your voice stronger carrying power. The more you want your voice to project, the more you need to include the resonance of your nose, cheeks and the bones of the front of your face – your *mask*. I don't mean that you use *just* those high tones, but they join with your chest resonance to give your voice a brightness that projects well. You can discover more about projecting your voice in Chapter 7.

As a general rule, don't use your head voice on its own for any length of time. For example, if you're speaking in a serious forum, intersperse your speech with high sounds to show enthusiasm or significance, but don't use high sounds continuously. This advice is especially good for women, as a constant high pitch can sound shrill and unpleasant – and attract accusations in public life that you're a witch, a harpy or worse!

Warming to Your Heart Voice

Consider the following media descriptions of the finest speakers:

- ✔ 'One of the greatest communicators of our time . . . speaks from the heart.'
- ✔ 'One of the most gifted communicators on the planet – speaks from the heart in a human voice.'
- ✔ 'She is fervent and articulate . . . speaking with passion, eloquence and dry humour.'
- ✔ 'Speaks with passion and conviction.'

Who does each description refer to? In order: Colin Powell, Bill Clinton, author Arundhati Roy and Mother Teresa. A diverse group, yet one important quality they all share is passion. And passion persuades. Eloquence may impress, but strong feeling changes hearts.

Whenever a speaker is genuinely speaking from the heart with feeling, you hear the soft-edged low-pitched tones of this resonance. You hear it in the voice of Nelson Mandela, who once said that a good head and a good heart are a formidable combination. The conductor Benjamin Zander and the politician Shirley Williams provide other examples of heartfelt voices.

In this section, I introduce what I call *the voice of the heart.* You display a different kind of energy when you care about something, and that energy naturally colours your voice, giving it a deeper sound and a softer persuasive edge. Emotion has a way of travelling straight from your heart into the hearts of your listeners.

Voice is coloured by emotional energy in every kind of communication. Even in classical singing, an art characterised by extremely difficult technique, the most adored singers are those who put heart into their voices. The famous tenor José Carreras suggested that singing from the soul is what distinguishes the good from the great. Or, as the poet Maya Angelou said, 'People will forget what you said, people will forget what you did, but people will never forget how you made them feel.'

Finding your passion

How easily you produce your heart voice depends on how willing you are to show others how you feel. Speaking from your heart is simply about *feeling while speaking.* At the precise moments when you feel moved in some way while speaking, your voice takes on a softer-edged quality.

This ability isn't the same as being able to talk *about* feelings. Many people are able to talk only too easily about feelings they have or have had: 'I felt he didn't understand me' or 'I feel it's just so awful that it's happened.' You can often spot a sentence that is *about* feelings rather than feeling itself because you can slot in the word 'that' after the word 'feel' or 'felt' without changing the sense. You also hear the unemotional reporting tone in the voice.

Revealing your emotional state to your listeners feels intimate and can make you feel vulnerable. When you do share your present feelings, however, you have great potential for connection and influence. Emotion moves people and makes them connect more with you and register more strongly what you've said. If you want to be influential as a speaker, you need to discover this resonance.

I demonstrate the heart voice in Track 31. Practice sharing something you care about with a friend or colleague, or preferably with a small group:

1. **Choose someone or something you love or care about.**

   Think about a person you know or an animal or a place that is special to you. Think about an activity you enjoy that allows you to feel most yourself. Or a cause that you passionately care about.

   Choose one of these subjects as the topic you're going to talk about.

2. **Absorb yourself in enjoyable memories of the subject for a moment, then take a couple of minutes to talk about your passion.**

   You may not instantly 'switch on' to your passion, but don't worry; you get into it as you talk about it. Think especially of what you enjoy and care about and what 'turns you on' or moves you about it.

3. **After you finish, ask your audience what it was like for them to listen to you.**

Most listeners discover that they're moved by a speaker who employs this kind of feeling, even if the subject isn't one they usually relate to. Feelings are extremely contagious.

Even feelings can do with practice! The next time you experience or remember a happy time, take a few moments to relive the emotions. Enjoy them and even amplify them. File away the experience of happiness in your mind, so you can recall it and use it later. Do the same with other positive emotions, such as determination, confidence, joy and empathy.

The emotion of fear gets in the way of other emotions. Fear makes you self-conscious. That leads to you to try to make an impression rather than honestly feel a feeling, and true connection goes out of the window. Maybe the biggest fear is that if you feel an emotion deeply you won't be able to cope with it in front of other people, so you end up suppressing all emotion. It's a shame if you do, as heart-felt communication is beautiful and powerful, whether you're speaking to a group or to one person. Moreover, after you do dare to share your emotion, you release yourself from performance expectations, all those 'shoulds' and 'shouldn'ts'. You realise that a real connection has been established, and can let go and enjoy the experience. The same is true for everyone who listens to you.

Using your heart voice

Many professional speakers and business leaders avoid the voice of the heart, considering it 'unprofessional' or not appropriate in the office or conference room. When you eliminate this voice entirely from your repertoire, you're missing a powerful element of public speaking.

You don't need to use the voice of your heart all the time. In fact, wearing your heart constantly on your sleeve is probably not the best idea. But when you use your heart voice, it's powerful and it moves people. In expressing your emotions, you get in touch with a powerful element of your life force.

The heart voice is always personal; it's always 'I'. It can't be the company voice or considered opinion. This is its strength; it is one person's feeling, and therefore never to be contested or denied. What you feel is what you feel, and it shows in your voice.

The power of going off-script

Tom, the leader of a small company, knew he had to motivate his employees to keep ahead of the curve during the downturn in the economy. As he prepared his annual conference speech, he concentrated on finding powerful ways to get his points across.

On the day of the conference, he summoned his resolve, stepped up to the podium and spoke the piece he had carefully prepared. It was a strong speech. He told his employees tough truths, not mincing his words. He spoke of his determination to forge ahead despite the challenges and to stand together with the whole company in putting their every effort into the way ahead.

As he spoke, he caught the eye of one of the recently graduated, young employees in the audience. Tom remembered his own early years as a fresh ambitious recruit. Suddenly, he felt almost choked up – so much of his life had gone into this business. Unable to continue as he'd planned, he spoke improvised words in an emotional voice. 'I've been with this company for 15 years,' he said. 'It means the world to me. I don't want to see us fail.'

Tom's speech received enthusiastic applause, and afterwards people kept coming up to him. The theme was always the same. He had really motivated them *because* he had got emotional. 'I never realised before,' said one of his team, 'But I understand now – you really care about this company, don't you? We won't let you down.' Tom hadn't meant to show his emotion, but through doing so he influenced his audience more than at any other time in his speech.

The voice of the heart also uses personal language. You can't be heartfelt in the non-sensory language of business. 'It has been determined that the strategic approach will afford the company considerable benefits' can never have the emotional impact of 'I'm fiercely determined to think long-term and win through.'

You may find yourself wary of sharing what you genuinely feel because in the past your voice has cracked or you found yourself fighting back tears. Some people stick to a flat unemotional delivery in order to keep tight control of their feelings. But feelings include determination, passion, motivation, empathy, joy and almost everything that connects powerfully with your listeners. You feel in your body, not your head. Blocking feelings entirely is like throwing out a valuable baby with the bath water! Practise revealing your feelings occasionally in safe situations at first, and discover how well people respond when you do.

Going with Your Gut: Speaking with Gravitas and Authenticity

I was in one of those meetings where everyone was getting excited. A confident voice declared, 'Well, I think . . . ' only to be have another heartfelt voice interject, 'But I really feel . . . ' while an excited voice cried out, 'Why don't we . . . ' The voices batted to and fro without a pause, and then somehow, with no gap in the talking, a low voice made itself heard and everyone stopped in their tracks and turned to listen. 'This is what we have to do,' said the deep voice. Why did everyone stop to listen even though the voice wasn't loud? And somehow we all heard it!

The conversation stopped because the speaker's voice came from a place deep in the gut, producing a sound that impels people to listen. This is the voice of the whole body, one that resonates deep down and finds harmonic resonance throughout the body. It conveys a sense of commitment that is hard to resist. I call it the voice of the gut.

Producing the voice of your gut

The easiest way I can describe how to produce the gut resonance is to do the following activity, based on creating the low sound *ohm* used in meditation. Listen too to Track 32.

1. Stand open and relaxed.

See Chapter 5 for more on relaxation.

2. **Take a fresh breath and launch smoothly into the long sound *ohm* on a low note that is comfortable for you.**

3. **Become aware of vibration.**

   Be aware of vibration in your body wherever you can sense it – your chest, lower in your belly and your back, in your arms and hands, the tips of your fingers, your legs and throughout your frame.

4. **Take a breath whenever you need to without strain, and pay attention to each part of your body in turn.**

   Focus on any parts of your body where you can sense vibration, from the top of your head to the soles of your feet.

5. **After feeling the vibration in your body, take another breath and say some words quietly using the same vibration.**

   This is the wise voice of your instinct. Choose a few words that come from deep within you. Maybe start your sentence, 'I hold the deep belief that . . . ' or 'My gut instinct is . . . '.

Another way to discover the resonance of your gut voice is to sing and speak.

1. **Hum or sing a low note on any vowel you choose.**

   You're not trying out for a televised singing contest here! Just think low and intone. Do nothing to push the sound down: don't tuck your head in or pull it back. Just think low and intone in a free and natural way.

   Use may like to use a piano or keyboard if you have one to check where you are.

2. **Speak calmly and easily without strain from exactly the same place.**

   Say something short that comes from that sensation of using your whole body. What can you say that comes from the whole of you? The phrase I think of is: 'That's what it's all about.' The meaning is just for me! What will you choose?

3. **Be aware of the vibrations that your voice creates.**

Using the voice of your gut

You hear the deep gut voice when someone is stating a truth that is fundamental to him or her, beyond enthusiasm, beyond conviction, beyond emotion – just from the person's whole inner being. The gut voice is most typically the voice of an older person who has deeper understanding. This voice is entirely free of self-consciousness, role playing and any other posturing or ego-positioning. It says simply, 'This is how it is.'

You use your gut voice only when you're accessing your gut instinct or speaking a truth that is fundamental to you, so people won't hear it in your voice all the time. In fact, this voice is likely to appear fairly rarely.

Listen out for gut voice tones from time to time in the voice of the ex-Secretary General of the UN, Kofi Annan. Being a voice associated with ancient wisdom, you will hear actors taking on these tones in the voice of Ian McKellen as Gandalf in *Lord of the Rings* and Michael Gambon as Dumbledore in *Harry Potter*.

The gut voice is available to everyone, regardless of age (or wizardly powers) when they dig down into their sense of fundamental purpose. This voice is the resonance you may use if someone asks you a serious question, such as, 'What does life mean to you?' and you're able to answer the question openly and fearlessly from your deepest being. The expression doesn't leave you untouched; you have the sense of your boundaries being expanded.

Understanding the Gatehouse of Your Voice: Your Throat

In between the bright sounds of your head and the confident and heartfelt sounds of your body, you find your neck.

If you think of the human body as an hourglass, the throat is the narrow passageway where the sand trickles through. If you're relaxed and free, the passage allows the vibrations of the vocal cords access to all the resonators of head and body, but if you're tense or fearful, the passageway blocks, preventing certain parts of you from resonating.

The narrowing of your throat makes it a powerful gatekeeper.

- ✔ For some people, the throat permits none of the lower resonance, and they have voices that just resound in the throat and head – childish, geeky, clever intellectual or over-pleasant voices.

- ✔ For others, the throat blocks off all the joyful excited noises of the head and they have voices that resound just below the throat or unvaryingly in the chest – inhibited, boring or relentlessly certain voices.

The tensions put up by the gatekeeper throat can be formidable. The jaw can clamp like a vice. The neck can be held ramrod stiff. The tongue can solidly block the entrance to the throat. When these tensions lock the area, resonance is deadened and the voice has no life in it. See Chapter 11 to find remedies for these blocks.

The throat's proper purpose in speaking is as a channel for sound. Someone called it 'a chimney for the heart', the conduit for sharing your real feelings and energies with the world. For this it needs to be open and free. See the sidebar 'The fifth chakra: Self-expression' for another take on the throat's importance.

Giving yourself permission to speak

If you talk to someone in a quiet voice, you produce sound naturally from your throat. That's fine, though if you speak always from the throat, your voice doesn't have much variety in it. A problem arises when instead of using the resonance of head and body to vary the sound, you try to produce different tones by forcing your voice at your throat.

The throat is vulnerable to what is going on in head and heart. Fear, excitement, inhibition, nervousness, apprehension – all affect the throat physically in different ways. If you track your well-being, you may be aware that sore throats sometimes coincide with periods of tension, and colds and congestion with challenging upcoming engagements.

Writing my first book, *Voice of Influence,* was an extended personal journey for me. After having looked forward to its publication with excitement for months, I suddenly began to worry about what may happen when my personal thoughts and ideas were officially (and permanently!) out there for anyone in the world to question or ridicule. A week or so after publication I was due to give a speech about the book, and just before the speech I caught laryngitis and was unable to speak. The gatekeeper had put up a block. Yes, I do appreciate the irony of the voice expert losing her voice!

The fifth chakra: Self-expression

The throat has a noble and appropriate place in the ancient eastern system of the *chakras*. The seven chakras are subtle energy centres that align along the spinal column and connect to specific major organs or glands. Chakras are focal points for receiving and transmitting energies. Each chakra isn't only associated with physical health but also affects your emotional, mental and belief system. The chakras take in the energy of the environment, including people's moods, and also radiate an energy of vibration out into the world.

The fifth chakra is located in the throat and is associated with communication, in particular with your willingness and ability to express your true self. The lesson of the fifth chakra is said to be about discovering how to express yourself and your beliefs, and the ability to trust yourself.

In this thought system, it seems appropriate that the throat is where you give yourself permission to communicate openly – and also the place where you veto true expression.

I notice when people come to me for coaching that success in speaking with different resonances depends upon their giving themselves inner permission. If you're unable to speak firmly with chest resonance, for example, the reason is seldom because of physical incapacity but rather that you cannot see yourself as 'that kind of person'. In other words, you don't give yourself internal permission to *be* that way. This lack of permission is particularly noticeable with the joyful enthusiastic head voice. If you don't give yourself permission to be child-like or playful – to do 'whoopy' – you find yourself separated from your head voice.

The journey of your voice is psychological as well as physical. Granting yourself permission to express your different energies is the biggest step towards a freer voice. Though joyful and freeing, the experience can be cathartic too.

As you get to know your voice better, you become aware of all the signs of your 'gatekeeper' throat pulling up the moat when you get anxious. Perhaps your throat tightens and your shoulders stiffen. When that happens, just remind yourself that you're most powerful when you don't close down. The psychologist Karl Rogers, who found public speaking daunting, used to remind himself on such occasions, 'I am enough', and those simple words gave him encouragement. See Chapter 11 for other ideas for combating fear when you speak.

Using Your Whole Vocal Range

I discuss each main resonator separately in the preceding sections, but the voice isn't designed for resonances to work in isolation. When you speak, your various resonators interplay with each other.

If you have a voice that is completely free and open, you can create wonderful subtlety in the sounds you make; resonators come in and out of play to different degrees by the moment. For instance, you may start with a relaxed comfortable sound, resounding in your throat and chest, and then a slight element of surprise increases your energy and adds higher vibrations to your voice. As you become more excited, sounds are released into the resonators in the skull, while meanwhile you feel an empathy that gives your sound an element of softness as resonance finds the lower body. So, as you continue, the sounds are constantly varying combinations of resonances, interacting with each other, producing harmonics, and creating wondrous nuances that make meaning for the aware listener. That's the ideal free voice!

If you want to be able to express yourself fully, you need to be able to use all your resonators. Doing so has physical advantages too:

✔ Speaking just in one or two resonators, such as your throat and chest is much harder on your voice. If you resonate throughout your body, your voice is working more efficiently.

✔ Resonances work together so, when all are available, your voice sounds richer and fuller.

✔ If you include your head resonators in your kit, you have the ultimate tool for being heard anywhere.

✔ Breathing and using all parts of you in expression is good for your physical well-being.

Celebrating your own box of sounds

You can discover your own potential most surely if you take a playful approach to practising resonance. Following are a few of my favourite ideas.

Pretend that you're a Shakespearean actor working for three different directors, each of whom requires a different style of performance. You need to exaggerate in order to make your point.

1. **The first director demands Harold Pinter style – banal, 'kitchen sink' and understated.** Make your statement dull and indifferent.

2. **The second wants extreme over-the-top declamation, almost to the extent of insanity.** Speak smoothly and grandly, extending all the sounds, and cover an enormous range from high to low with your voice.

3. **The third wants psychological intensity, where every thought comes from deep within your brain, heart and very soul.** Read the speech as poetry, connect to the meaning as if you're speaking to yourself.

The text for your practice is the famous Hamlet soliloquy where he contemplates ending his life:

> To be, or not to be: that is the question:
> Whether 'tis nobler in the mind to suffer
> The slings and arrows of outrageous fortune,
> Or to take arms against a sea of troubles,
> And by opposing end them? To die: to sleep;
> No more; and by a sleep to say we end
> The heart-ache and the thousand natural shocks
> That flesh is heir to, 'tis a consummation
> Devoutly to be wish'd. To die, to sleep;
> To sleep: perchance to dream: ay, there's the rub;

This exercise gives you the opportunity to practise the four main areas of resonance that I cover in this chapter. Listen in to Track 33.

1. **Find a subject to make a short speech about.**

   Although you're only going to speak for approximately four sentences, choose an interesting topic – perhaps a project you're working on or a personal activity.

2. **Taking each of the main resonances in turn, make a statement which fits each resonance.**

   Start each sentence as follows:

   - Head resonance: enthusiasm and excitement.
     'I'm very excited about . . . '

   - Chest resonance: confident facts and logic.
     'The most important facts are . . . '

   - Heart resonance: feeling and emotion.
     'This makes me feel . . . '

   - Gut resonance: deep instinct and inner truth.
     'Fundamentally, deep down . . . '

3. **Join up the four statements to create one flowing and convincing speech on your topic.**

   Exaggerate the resonances to distinguish clearly between the four different voices. Enjoy exploring your range!

Exploring your limits

Resonance is revealing because your missing voices let you know which ways of being you allow or don't allow yourself.

- ✔ **If you care too much what people think,** you have problems finding your centred chest resonance.

- ✔ **If you're not able to show your feelings,** the softer heart resonance isn't heard in your voice.

- ✔ **If you take life too seriously and have forgotten your sense of excitement and fun,** your voice won't find your exuberant head tones.

- ✔ **If you play a role of any kind,** you're not able to speak from the deep authentic place in the gut.

- ✔ **If you resonate just in the head,** life's emotions and gut instincts are beyond limits.

You need your whole voice to be fully expressive. Any resonance that's 'locked out' reveals a part of your life that you aren't expressing – or living.

The following meditative practice enables you to connect your thoughts and various parts of your body. Use some simple thoughts and feelings, for example:

> I feel curious.
>
> I am determined about this.
>
> That's beautiful.

Relax and be quiet for a few moments. Take a few deep breaths. Now, say one of the statements in your mind and tune into the sensations of your body. Place a hand on the part of the body that most responds to the words. For example, many people point to their heads when they tune into curiosity, while others feel strength in their chests when they think about determination. What you feel is individual to you.

If you find yourself intimidated by the process of discovering aspects of yourself that you haven't given expression to, consider the power of 'as if'. The great theatre director Constantin Stanislavski called it the key to unlocking the imagination. You don't have to commit to being a particular way – you just 'try it on' for a while. If you were happy right now, how would that be? How would you stand, sit, move and gesture? What would you think? How would you feel? How would you speak? When you follow the 'as if' path, *nothing* is off limits and *all* is possible.

Chapter 10

Uncovering Your Unique Voice

*T*hink of this chapter as great adventure, with me as your guide on the quest to discover the voice that expresses the best of you – your own authentic voice.

As a first step, take a moment to make a list of some of your favourite communicators from various sources: show hosts, commentators, actors, comedians and others you've heard on radio, television or in film. Your list may also include people you know, such as a professional colleague who's a great presenter, a team member who's convincing at meetings, a friend who draws an eager crowd in the pub or a member of your family who's fascinating to listen to. For each person on your list, write down a few words about their voice to describe what in your view makes them a good communicator.

Most people discover that they like a range of different qualities and that the appeal of each speaker is different. Whenever you warm to a speaker, you're responding to something in the voice that is unique to that person. There are as many different ways to communicate successfully as there are people. Now is your opportunity to explore what is unique and special in *your* voice.

Moving Beyond Technique

The other day I listened to a recording of a speech that had won an international speaking competition. The skill of the speaker was evident in every phrase. If I'd been judging on individual skills, I would have ticked almost every box: organisation of speech, resonant voice, variety of tone, pace, contrast, use of rhetorical devices, facial expression, use of silence. But there was one box I wouldn't have ticked – inspiration. The speech was wonderfully competent but the skills failed to add up to something greater than the individual parts. It left me cold. The speaker's technique *led* the delivery; it was a display of brilliance more than a communication.

On the other hand, certain speakers don't have the finest voices and rush sometimes in their eagerness to get the words out or occasionally pause, unable to find the right word. Yet you find yourself inspired when they speak, because of what they have to say and how they're able to connect with you.

When people listen to you, they're not actually interested in *how* you speak, they want to hear *what* you have to say. They don't want to be impressed by your technique, but rather to connect with what you're offering.

While lack of technique may get in the way of communication at times, over-displayed technique is just as problematic, often more so. Technique that is patently visible actually impedes understanding. You find yourself admiring the skill rather than connecting with the message. On some level, the audience knows when a speaker is feeling self-important and indulging too much in their prowess as they show off the brilliance of their range and power. In times of political conferences and elections, you don't have to look for long before you hear such a speaker.

Inspiration doesn't stem from technique. It comes from an energy within – a glorious combination of thinking, emotion and purpose – that creates nuanced sounds. Being born of inner impulse and outer expression, your voice is produced by both a physiological and a psychological process. Change to your voice can happen through either route.

Working with your inner energy

Your voice responds best when your internal energy works harmoniously with the physical breath and sound. When you're feeling passionate, your voice wants to respond vigorously; when you're moved to sympathy, your voice wants to express that different energy. When you allow this to happen, your inner feelings are reflected in your outer expression.

When your body responds to the inner energy, your communication has an authenticity and ease that transmits to your listener, energising your audience. You yourself feel energised by the process.

The opposite is true if your energy and voice are mismatched. This creates tension and wastes energy. If, for example, you force the energy, using too much breath and pushing the sound, the result is tiring – to you and your listener. You'll also both get tired if you have a message of excitement and passion but hold back and speak in a boring voice. Moreover, the audience feels the disjunction and steps back emotionally.

The following are three ways for you to access this energy. Practise any and all of the activities before important speaking occasions to get your energy moving, ready to hit the ground running.

Finding the state of readiness

The state of readiness is familiar to practitioners of martial arts. You can call it being 'switched on'. The following practice gives you the idea.

March around with energy, as if you have an important appointment to keep and know exactly where you're going. Look out into the distance as you march, swinging your arms with a sense of freedom. If possible, practise in the open air in a park or in the countryside. Breathe in the fresh air, and stride out.

After moving for two or three minutes, pause for a moment. In the stillness, feel the energy coursing through your veins. Your body has come to a stand-still, but every cell of your body is alive. You feel alert. *That's* the state of readiness.

Using your whole body

Speaking is never just a cerebral activity; it engages the whole of you.

Remind yourself of the physical energy behind what you say. Try the following, and think up some examples of your own:

- Remember a time when you were determined when you said 'no' to something. Lift your arms and your whole upper body, make fists of your hands and bring them sharply down, at the same time declaring in a determined voice, '*No!*' or 'I will *not!*'

- Remember a time when you felt warm and comfortable and you sighed with utter bliss. Take in the full happy breath of contentment, and as you sigh, let your shoulders sink down with the feeling of pleasure and say, 'What a *beautiful* day it is.'

- Stomp up and down for a few moments feeling impatient while picturing a ticking clock. You're about to miss that deadline! Then stop and speak with all the energy of the movement, 'It's got to be done *now!*'

Filling the space

Energy is necessary to fill any space – and the larger the space, the more energy you need. Practise filling the space in different-sized rooms with the following steps:

1. **Walk into the centre of the room with confidence as if you're about to give a speech.**

2. **Stand there open and relaxed, and raise your arms straight out in front of you.**

   Imagine that your fingertips are touching the wall in front of you.

3. **Open your arms out expansively and imagine that you're touching the walls at each side of you.**

   This space is yours, and you own it!

4. **Lower your arms, and become aware of your body as you stand there.**

   Expand your awareness and discover that you're larger than your body. Feel your body expand outwards beyond its edges into the space. Fill the space mentally. This expanded energy commands attention.

5. **Open your eyes and make a large slow upward gesture with your arm to express this feeling.**

   Sense that your fingers can reach to touch the walls.

Note that this feeling is the opposite of that cramped sensation you get when you feel frightened. Carl Jung suggested that people are too limited; he said, 'We walk in shoes that are too small.' Be your expansive self. Imagine that your chest has wings that open, and feel them begin to fly.

Finding your inner voice

The energy that produces powerful sound and broad gesture starts within you in the core of your being with a spark of desire to communicate. Finding your voice is about connecting with that inner spark.

The ability to connect your inner impulse or desire with action is shared by the best performers in different fields. The great tennis shot begins with the desire to put the ball somewhere, and that desire connects to the movement of the body. The spark of creativity in the artist turns into the subtle movement of the hand holding the paintbrush. In terms of voice, the spark of desire turns into the muscle movements that produce sound. Your voice reflects your inner world and connects with what is real for you. This connection doesn't require your body to be physically active in any noticeable sense, but inside you're aware of something intensely alive. Your life force is not the same as anyone else's. It is yours and yours alone.

When you tune into this life force, your listeners get your message. You aren't tuning into your own life force if:

✔ You're worried about what others are thinking.

✔ You're hoping to impress.

✔ You think that you should sound a particular way.

✔ You want to think the same as everyone else.

✔ You want to be one-up on someone else.

Tuning in requires you to be internally referenced, at ease with yourself. You can find some helpful tips for combating such concerns in Chapter 11. How to get in touch with your life force is similar to having a strong intention, as explained in the next section 'Grasping the power of intention'.

Grasping the power of intention

Intention is the desire or energy that fuels your voice. It's quite different from wishing. If you say, 'I wish I could finish', you can hear doubt. If instead you say, 'I intend to finish', you can hear the strong energy, involving mind, body and emotions, behind the words.

The inner spark of intention enlivens the breath, and the quality of the in-breath determines the sound you make (see Chapter 4). In order to shout, you take in a quick energetic breath; to describe a beautiful place, you take in a gentle slow breath. The breath is as much a part of producing your voice as the sound you make. Particular breaths create particular sounds.

The word *inspiration* is made up of 'in' and *spirare*, 'to breathe'. Your in-breath is indeed your inspiration. You never need to put on a voice to be angry; the angry breath produces a hard voice. By contrast, you never need to put on a sympathetic voice. As soon as you feel empathy, your breath softens the sound you make. And if you feel joy, the lively feeling spreading across your chest gives warmth to your voice.

The connection between your inner impulse and your sound only happens if you go straight from breath into sound without a little gap in between. This is the secret of the expressive voice. (If you do leave a little gap, find remedies in the later section 'Speaking mechanically: The personality-free role'.)

Find a space where you have room to move and then do the following:

1. **Think of something in your life that you passionately say 'yes' to or are determined to say 'yes' to.** This can be anything – a person you want to say 'yes' to, a cause that you completely believe in, something you're determined to achieve, a big yes to life – anything that makes you want to say a full-hearted 'yes'!

2. **Take a big step forward, breathing in as you take the step and breathing out as you land on your front foot.**

   Don't over-extend as you step forward, but make the step big enough so that you feel a clear change in body weight as you come off the back foot and land on the front one.

3. **Bend your knee as you land, and at the same time come out with a passionate, 'Yes!'.**

   Feel strongly the passion of that 'yes' as you breathe in and take the giant step forward.

   You can also try this practice with the word 'no', thinking beforehand of something you strongly say 'no' to or intend to say 'no' to. Think of activities in the world that you feel shouldn't happen, someone you want to say a loud 'no' to, something you're determined to do no longer, or anything you can say a loud strong 'no' to.

Focus on the feeling of that 'yes' or 'no'. You don't need to have any preconceived idea of how you should sound. Nor do you need to try to 'produce' a particular kind of voice. Your voice is liberated by your intention and sounds authentic and free.

When I reprimanded our young children, I often talked urgently and stridently to them, commanding, 'Don't do that!' 'Come away from there!' and so on to ever-diminishing effect. But sometimes a resolve took hold inside me, and I thought to myself with a kind of internal knowing, 'This is enough. I truly am not going to allow this any more. This is really enough.' At these times, I breathed much firmer and slower. What came out of my mouth was something much quieter, from deep in my body. When that happened, the response was immediate – the children took it very seriously indeed. I was surprised by the response every time because I hadn't been thinking about putting on a particular voice! The change was in the strength of my intention.

Your intention profoundly affects your voice and body language. Change your intention and you get a very different result.

Playing Roles

If you aren't getting the reaction you expect when you speak, a mismatch may exist between your conscious intention and what you're truly feeling about a situation.

Perhaps you sometimes spend a lot of energy thinking about the impression you want to make and in consciously creating ways of speaking that you believe will get you approval or respect. You straighten and stiffen your shoulders as if you're wearing the epaulettes of high rank, and you put an artificial energy into your voice. If you do that, you may create the impression you want, but your voice has a curious way of revealing how hard you're trying. The energetic pace and emphasis are there – but the tension created by your effort restricts your breathing, which is reflected in a tightening of your voice. If you counteract this effect by forcing your voice to do your bidding, your sound becomes tight and pushed. You end up sacrificing freedom and subtlety for something strained and predictable.

The answer is to stop trying so hard, and to regain a sense of ease, so that breath and sound can work smoothly. When you do this, you access your authentic energy, which is much more powerful than false confidence and posturing. Whether your role is CEO, manager, team leader or parent, trying to look assured and professional while you're feeling the opposite isn't likely to work. The following sections describe various ways in which people try too hard, and shows you how to avoid them!

Speaking mechanically: The personality-free role

A safe but defeating way of playing a role is to cut all the personal characteristics out of your voice. Doing so is a surprisingly common – albeit unconscious – strategy, and an understandable one when you feel unwanted emotions like vulnerability and fear.

Listen to the example on Track 34. The following activity shows what happens when you strip most of the personality from your voice. I want you to able to recognise it, so that you can take measures to avoid it!

1. **Think of something important you want to say.**

2. **Breathe in and feel ready to speak – but stop for an instant and hold your breath.**

3. **Speak without taking another breath and notice the sound you make.**

Most people, after the hiatus, start their voice with a little kick, sometimes with an audible click as the vocal folds come abruptly together. If you say a word starting with a vowel, such as 'egg' or 'apple', quite sharply, you will hear what I mean. It's called a *glottal attack*. In any case, you lose the connection with the energy that prompted your remarks; all energy drains out of the voice leaving it stripped of its expressive energy. The voice feels tense and you have nothing with which to power the sound.

You often hear voices produced in the preceding manner, especially in business or formal social settings. This kind of voice is sometimes called a 'social voice' because people use it when they're going through the motions of being polite, interested and so on. Unfortunately, it doesn't express the message that existed in the energy of the breath. The voice seems cut off from genuine communication.

You may be so used to producing your voice in this way that you've no idea that you're doing it. It happens every time you take a half-second to consider or veto your emotional response instead of responding with the natural feelings of the moment. (Go to Chapter 11 for a more in-depth explanation of what happens when you block your voice and how to respond effectively.)

If you ever get feedback that you sound boring, monotonous or mechanical, you're very likely adopting this way of speaking, dissociating feeling from response. You can find relevant and useful material on dissociating in *Neuro-linguistic Programming For Dummies* by Kate Burton and Romilla Ready (Wiley).

Try the exercise on speaking with intention (see the earlier section 'Grasping the power of intention'), to practise going from thought and feeling straight into sound, and hear the difference in your voice.

Playing the prima donna: Putting on roles

Another way of speaking in which the breath is similarly cut off from sound is the 'created' or 'manufactured' voice, where the speaker has found a way to make sounds that create a particular effect. This act can be performed deliberately in the moment, but more commonly it's a way of speaking that was picked up early in life and is now involuntary and automatic.

Various versions exist, and I explore them in Track 35:

- ✔ **The Mussolini voice,** named after the Italian dictator, involves pushing down into the throat and chest to make yourself sound imposing, authoritative and in control. You push out air too forcibly, giving the sound a hard tuneless edge that bulldozes the listeners' ears. In London,

Speakers' Corner offers many examples of ranting in public, and you often hear this voice at union or political meetings in the open air, where the speaker lacks a proper microphone. Unfortunately, many speakers also bring the voice inside! US Congressman Anthony Weiner, among others, uses this voice to push his point home.

✔ **The Establishment voice,** like the Mussolini voice, is also created low down in controlled fashion, producing a voice whose tone is rich and deep but unvarying. The person breathes, pauses for an instant to put on deep cavernous tones, and then speaks. The Mayor of London, Boris Johnson, has a voice that comes into this category. It has a rich Eton 'plumminess', which changes very little whatever mood he is intending to convey. The politician William Hague does something similar with his voice. The tone is distinguished by its unvarying quality; pleasure and horror are expressed in the same rich tones.

✔ **The 'Barbie Doll' voice** remains sweet and high pitched whatever barbs are thrown its way. It proclaims in its gentle tones that the speaker is a sweet person, but more often reveals that the speaker is trying too hard to sound pleasant and can sound patronising. It was the fashion for women to speak in this way in the 40s and 50s, so you can find many examples in recordings of that period. A great example is the character Dolores Umbridge, played by Imelda Staunton in the Harry Potter films.

People who use any of the preceding voices have to take a second after breathing to engage their special voices. These voices don't tune into others or respond to the energy of an audience (see Chapter 10); they're simply sound created in a vacuum for a particular effect. Your first impression on hearing such a voice may be good, but listen for a while and the artificiality becomes boring or irritating.

Being Authentic

Being authentic is one of the most powerful ways to be believed and respected, which makes it extraordinary how far people go to hide who they really are.

When you're authentic, you create aliveness and excitement. People instantly tune into you and find you interesting. Sanitised and predictable speaking on the other hand, whether unconscious or deliberate, cuts off connection and creates boredom, disappointment and even mistrust.

If you watch any audience – or read the tabloids or pay attention to non-scripted television – you quickly see that people are curious about other real people and aren't very interested in people who always perform a role. Much of what people hear in speeches and presentations is predictable and its delivery stiff and formal; the official behaviour of business leaders in their work roles is usually predictable too. Audiences love the genuine aside, the odd mistake, the burst into normality. The more real you are, the more convincing you are – and the more you feel yourself. The opposite is also true: the more rigid you are, the less you feel like yourself, and the more artificial you seem to others.

Finding out how to speak authentically is about reconnecting the energy of your thoughts and feelings with your voice. In other words, you express on the outside what is within you. This approach, pioneered by voice teacher Iris Warren more than 60 years ago (see the sidebar 'Iris Warren, vocal revolutionary'), is still among the most effective today.

Authenticity in your voice is certainly about being emotionally truthful. When you are, the sound of your voice, the look in your eye, your facial expression and the balance of your body work in harmony, so that all parts of you are telling one story. Authenticity puts your listeners at ease and makes them trust you. Mismatching your signals, on the other hand, creates annoyance, confusion and disbelief. 'Wipe that smile off your face,' snaps the teacher, for nothing's more annoying than a pupil apologising with a mismatching grin.

Iris Warren, vocal revolutionary

Prior to the Second World War, voice training was about producing a particular tone of voice rather than using your voice flexibly to express different thoughts and emotions. The person most responsible for changing this approach to voice production was Iris Warren, a voice teacher who taught at the Royal Academy of Dramatic Art in London in the 1940s and then joined the London Academy of Music and Dramatic Art. She never published, but her pupil Kristen Linklater followed her method and later moved to the US where she became one of the major influences on voice teaching in both the US and UK.

Warren was a tremendous character, according to those who worked with her. She developed an approach to training actors' voices that worked from the inside out. She believed that each person has a unique voice and aimed to 'free the actor into the voice' rather than 'train the voice in the actor'. She famously said, 'I want to hear the person, not the voice.'

She moved away from the popular notion of 'the beautiful voice' to the ideal of a voice that is capable of expressing powerful emotions. She stressed the importance of imagination and play in creating a free voice, and worked on the actor's psychology with the purpose of reconnecting thought and feeling with its expression.

A whole generation of actors and speakers was influenced by her, and the waves of this are still felt today in the influence of teachers on actor-training programmes worldwide who learned their craft from Warren or her protégé, Linklater. Find out more about Warren's method as developed by Linklater at www.kristin linklater.com.

Expressing different 'parts' of yourself

I'm encouraging you to be real and to be yourself to make your voice more authentic, but a snag may have occurred to you. If you're feeling unconfident, or even pathetic and hopeless, you may wonder how 'being yourself' is going to help you. This situation is where it's useful to be able to access different 'parts' of yourself when needed. For example, while you may lack confidence when you present in public, you don't feel unconfident *all* the time – it doesn't represent the whole of you. At times you feel positive and sure of yourself, when you're with friends, or playing golf, or baking, or fishing, or tying your shoelaces! If you can recover the state of mind you have at *those* times and access it when you have to give a speech, then you're laughing.

If you need to be confident, but don't feel it inside, try the following:

1. **Remember a time you *have* been confident, and imagine yourself in that situation.**

   Remember vividly the feeling of confidence of that time. Get to know it well. How do you stand and hold yourself when you have that feeling? How do you breathe and speak? What physical sensations accompany that feeling? That feeling is gold dust.

2. **Take that confident feeling into a situation where you need confidence.**

   When you find yourself in a daunting situation, recall the feeling of confidence that is now familiar to you. Note how accessing the confident feeling changes your experience for the better.

This skill is one that many actors use in order to portray characters authentically. You can use this technique to access other feelings useful for speaking, such as calm, ease, enthusiasm or determination. When you adopt this technique, you aren't stepping into a pretend role; you're accessing a part of yourself that is true – but just hasn't shown up at a crucial time!

Truth is always powerful. It won't stop you feeling vulnerable at times, but the instinct to hide your vulnerability can be misjudged. You look stronger to others when you dare to show your vulnerability than when you attempt (often without success) to mask it and in the effort deaden your voice. When you don't hide your vulnerability, it turns into a beautiful strength, and the full range of your voice becomes available to you. Your voice has the potential to express your present, your past, your total experience, your agony and your ecstasy.

Granted, you cannot always let people know everything about you – sometimes you're better off putting up a mask. But be aware that it's when the mask comes down that you truly connect and people really listen to you. You can find some other good strategies for becoming more authentic in my book, *Butterflies and Sweaty Palms: 25 Sure-fire Ways to Speak and Present with Confidence* (Crown House Publishing, 2012).

Think of a time when you felt most fully yourself, whether it was with a person or people you love to be with, or in a place that's special to you, or doing some activity that you love to do. As you remember that time, ask yourself:

✔ What am I feeling?

✔ What am I most aware of?

✔ Where is my focus?

✔ What is true of me as I relive the time when I felt most fully myself?

As you answer these questions internally, you re-access a way of being that frees your body and mind and grounds you. When you speak from this way of being, your voice is clear, open, confident – and ultimately influential.

Return to this practice from time to time, and gradually try to build up awareness of how being real feels for you, so that you can recognise more easily when you are and when you are not.

Developing a voice that suits you

As you develop an awareness of when you're authentic and when you're less so (see the preceding section), you can practise more often speaking without a mask.

For example, if you're angry, expressing that anger in your voice may not be in your best interest – but wearing a mask of pleasantness or subjugation may be equally unhelpful. You want to find a way to bring some of the *energy* of your anger into how you speak without actually getting angry. You can bring the energy in by acknowledging that all emotion is energy, and using the energetic qualities of an angry voice without feeling angry. That way, you sound more honest and others are more likely to respect you for it.

When I worked with local politicians, I discovered that many of them dreaded public meetings where local agitated residents turned up to hurl insults at them. John worked with me on various strategies for dealing with such situations, and later told me this story. He was at a public meeting in a small town. Midway through his explanation of the reasons for certain road works, a heavy-set man got to his feet and yelled loudly, 'You couldn't care less, could you?! This is going to damage our trade!' Quick as a flash and with a similar volume and energy, John replied, 'Yes, it is! But very little, in fact, and not for long.' He then explained that the council had looked at the impact throughout the county, and that scheme was the one with the least impact. His voice remained strong but became calmer. The honest response with similar energy took the wind out of the man's sails, and he sat down with no more to add.

One way to get to know your voice is to *feel* it inside. Do the following practice with a friend, if you can. If you do it alone, answer yourself out loud or write down your musings on paper or in a journal.

1. **Reflect on your voice's different tones as you access different feelings.**

   What does your voice feel like when you speak with impatience or a sense of urgency, compared to when you speak with worry or concern? Think of some other feelings and try out the tone of voice for each.

2. **For each feeling, reflect on where inside your voice emanates and where you feel it vibrate.**

3. **Think about what feelings you hear most often in your voice.**

   What message does your voice mostly communicate? Urgency, worry, concern, control, excitement, impatience?

   What voices do you allow yourself? Confident, playful, stern, angry, sad, gentle, empathetic? Reflect on these voices and choose your favourites.

4. **Now ask yourself which sounds you *don't* allow yourself?**

   Silly, strong, peaceful, assertive, tender, angry, joyful? Imagine allowing any missing feelings space to express themselves. What that would be like?

5. **What new voice will you give expression to now?** Find a poem you love and read it in a new voice. That is your voice too.

If you can't think of a favourite poem, try speaking the words of the ancient Sufi poet Rumi. Here he invites you to welcome the energies of all your feelings:

> This being human is a guest house.
> Every morning a new arrival.
> A joy, a depression, a meanness,
> some momentary awareness comes
> as an unexpected visitor.
> Welcome and entertain them all!

Trusting in the Moment

The sidebar 'Stanley Kunitz's last poetry reading' describes the powerful connection that is created when a speaker connects directly 'from his soul to yours', without vanity, pretence or role playing. For that to happen, the speaker needs to stay present and trust in the moment. This requires him or her to let go of tight control and be willing not to know exactly what is going to happen from moment to moment. That can be scary! But it gives you an incomparable sense of freedom and self confidence that transmits directly and powerfully to listeners. When you speak like that, people love the fact that you're completely yourself and at ease in your own skin.

At an international coaching conference a few years ago, the keynote speaker was the coach and author Tim Gallwey. Other speakers on the day had delivered polished presentations with carefully crafted slides and notes. Even the official who introduced Gallwey had prepared a spiel for the occasion. Tim, however, came onto to the stage without ceremony and with the appearance of having nothing prepared. He thanked the official, then looked out at the 800 or so coaches who had come to listen to him. After a decent pause he remarked quietly, 'There's usually a blinding light in my eyes . . . you're very colourful!' He paused again. 'It feels quite intimate . . . I hope we can keep this intimate.' He did indeed keep it intimate. For the audience, his presentation felt natural and spontaneous. He thought and breathed, speaking in the moment, creating something special and irreplaceable in which he was himself and connected with those people, in that place at that time. It was a memorable occasion.

Letting it happen

People who like cats often say it's because they're so much themselves. You never see a cat acting self-consciously, or trying too hard. If you watch a cat focused on catching a bird, everything about the experience is graceful. Its stillness is active and alert, and when it leaps for the bird the action is fluid and effortless.

Stanley Kunitz's last poetry reading

In her excellent book, *Saved by a Poem: The Transformative Power of Words* (Hay House, 2009), Kim Rosen tells of visiting the poet Stanley Kunitz for tea in his apartment a few days before he died at the age of 100. At their meeting he read her one of his poems, 'King of the River'.

Kunitz was a man of generosity and compassion who focused in his work on speaking the truth as he understood it. As he read the poem, Kim heard that truth in the voice. She described it as a 'direct transmission from his soul to yours'. Nothing was hidden. The voice was old and wavering; there was hesitation; you sensed currents of feeling of that moment at the end of life. But you heard his openness and the great vitality of his wise inner being.

The experience was intensely moving and demonstrated how much more powerful transparency is in the voice than any so-called vocal skill. Kim Rosen confesses that every time she hears that poem now, it exists for her in the old man's unforgettable and inspiring voice.

The cat is a great model for you as a speaker. Its energy is entirely absorbed in the now and nothing presents effort. You find this quality in great musicians and dancers. However physically demanding the piece, the artist's face reveals complete and effortless absorption in the activity. It makes you want to watch and listen; it draws you in.

You can be like a cat when you remind yourself of certain things:

✔ Focus on what you're doing.

✔ Stay in the present.

✔ Enjoy what you're doing.

✔ Be alert for whatever happens.

Enjoying uncertainty

When you're alert for whatever happens, you've relinquished that all too human desire for life to be predictable. Life isn't predictable. The only thing to be sure of is . . . uncertainty! After you can fully grasp this truth, you can do anything.

The great Polish theatre director, Jerzy Grotowski, told his students it was better not to think but to act. He encouraged them to let their performance grow spontaneously and organically and assured them that if they did, the result would always be more beautiful than anything calculated.

You don't need any preconceived idea of how you should sound. Think and feel before you breathe, then just let your voice happen.

When you speak, the sound waves dissipate on the air. Even if you say exactly the same words a second time, you have to recreate them. When history was told in stories, everyone accepted that each old story was new in the telling. Musicians accept that each playing of a familiar piece is a new story. So even if you're reading a written speech, each reading is a new utterance and therefore different from anything you've spoken before. Whatever you say is a meeting between the words you speak and you, your personality and life story.

People who enjoy public speaking revel in the fact that, even when they're repeating something they've said before, they're creating words afresh. They never get bored and love to play with saying things a bit differently each time. Each time, what they say is heard like something new.

Play a game of creating something new from old. Your task is to tell a story strongly and convincingly, using the same words – but in different ways. Here is the story:

> Mary Mary quite contrary,
> How does your garden grow?
> 'With silver bells and cockle shells
> And pretty maids all in a row.'

Tell this story in the following ways:

- ✔ Electrified with the energy of disbelief and condemnation
- ✔ Inflated with the energy of pride or superiority
- ✔ Infused with the energy of huge empathy and concern

Trust yourself and take a few risks. Enjoy the game! Sometimes people find themselves unable to do this practice because they say, 'It isn't me. I'm not a proud person or I never condemn' Yes, you are – and yes, you can! It's all you, limited only by your imagination.

Having a Voice in the World

Music connoisseurs sometimes say that Beethoven found his true voice in his final quartets or that Mozart found his true voice in his final Requiem. They describe that moment in a composer's creative life when echoes of other composers become fully assimilated, and their sound is at last uniquely their own.

This moment happens for you when you use all the possibilities of your voice. 'Be yourself, everyone else is taken', says Oscar Wilde. When at last you're able to free your voice of its blocks and inhibitions, the true you emerges, and other people begin to listen to what you have to say. In the act of speaking, you give voice to what is truly you.

Becoming you is to tune into your inner voice and express what is in you – to sing your own life song, not anyone else's; to find your voice in all senses of the phrase.

The following sections offer some ideas for sharing your true voice with others near and far.

Giving yourself the green light

Someone who worked for a charity in conflict zones wrote after one of my workshops, 'I found my voice! I felt like this course allowed me to look at me, rather than the technical side of making presentations. I can apply so much of this to all areas of my life!'

Finding your own voice can be facilitated by learning technical voice skills, but it also requires your consent. You've passion inside you, but people cannot hear passion in your voice without your permission, and that requires the courage to allow yourself to be seen in your voice.

You don't actually need to think of expressing passion, you just need to believe that whatever you express is okay.

Marissa was so scared when she gave her presentation at my workshop in London that she was shaking. 'Just allow yourself to shake,' I suggested. She looked at me as if I were mad. 'No, really,' I urged. 'Do it deliberately.' So she did. She shook her shoulders and arms, then gradually her legs too, and she continued to speak. At one moment, her voice wavered with emotion, and it seemed that she would break down, but she continued to shake and speak, and gradually her voice found its strength and the shaking stopped. When she had finished, Marissa made a gesture of triumph with both arms in the air and shouted: 'I found my voice!'

Becoming eloquent

You're used to hearing articulate voices in the media, but they're becoming increasingly predictable *versions* of reality. Listening to adverts, the voices fit the images, but they're bland and non-personal. It's the same with most chat shows and documentaries, the voice fits, but you can change it for another similar voice and not notice much difference.

I watched a programme on building new homes last year. This year a similar programme was born on another channel, and the new presenter's intonation identical to the person's on the earlier programme. What is happening? More and more people are performing like stereotypes, becoming *cartoons* of themselves.

True eloquence is not the same as being articulate. True eloquence is about allowing you to be you, to express freely and be heard – not only your ideas but your emotions and inner energy. When you trust yourself to do that, you have a direct line into others' lives. Your voice is alive and is able to move others by creating sympathetic vibrations deep inside their hearts. You create harmony between yourself and others like music.

Being rather than doing

If you're like most people, your first instinct on being asked to speak is probably to ask yourself panic-struck, 'What do I say?' But the better question is, 'How can I just be me?' Finding your voice is more about being than doing.

If you're able to stand in the moment, present to your feelings, then the words come. Your voice resonates freely and you speak to the hearts of your audience. This ideal is indeed an *if*, but here are some suggestions that can help you to just be:

- **Breathe.** As you take a good breath, you're able to think. Chapter 4 abounds with activities to get you in touch with your breath.

- **Accept that this time is this time.** What happens right now happens. You'll have other times.

- **Accept that the way you're feeling at this moment is absolutely okay.** It is as it is, and you're sufficient. Repeat to yourself, 'I am enough.'

If you produce the voice that you think is expected in a particular situation, if you care too much about what others think, or aim to create an impression or fear to express your own truth, you will not find your own voice. That's a shame for you – and society is the poorer for it as well. The world needs voices that are forthright and honest in order to truly communicate with each other. A voice of truth ringing with conviction moves people in a way that consciously created voices cannot. The voice of truth constantly varies second by second, reflecting your strength, confidence, warmth, friendliness and sincerity. The speaker is no longer delivering something prepared earlier; instead the words move through, starting from deep inside. This is the voice that changes the world.

Part IV
Beating the Voice Gremlins

The 5th Wave   By Rich Tennant

"The Ventriloquists Society has asked me to give the keynote address and I'm just afraid my lips will move."

In this part . . .

*P*acked together in this part you find all the scary bits – your fears of speaking and other emotional blocks that sabotage your voice – and you discover how to send them firmly on their way. You learn how to turn your accent into a blessing and modify the bits you don't like. You get to the core of hesitation and stuttering and replace the stop reflex with a smooth following-through. You're ready to step out into the public arena with confidence!

Chapter 11

Stopping Vocal Sabotage

- -

In This Chapter

▶ Appreciating how emotions affect your voice

▶ Overcoming emotional blocks

▶ Stopping vocal gremlins with new habits

- -

*W*hat gets in the way of you having a great voice – even more basically, what gets in the way of you expressing yourself and communicating your message?

Your voice's gremlins – such as squeakiness, breathiness or mumbling – come in various guises and stem from various causes, including fear, heavy-handed control, trying too hard and other issues such as health and age. Some more subtle gremlins such as having two distinct voices for different parts of life, or deliberately hiding your feelings through your voice, result in people taking you the wrong way. Your voice's gremlins are nearly always connected to your emotions, which is exactly where I begin this chapter.

You may not realise that emotions are affecting your voice because often vocal sabotage develops into an unconscious habit. Over time, an under-performing or problematic voice feels part of who you are. Fortunately, as I explore throughout this chapter, you can examine old habits and choose to replace them with new, more effective ones.

Examining the Impact of Emotions on Your Voice

Any emotion that creates tension cuts off access to your breath, which is the life in your voice. The most frequent unhelpful emotion that negatively impacts your voice is fear or anxiety, but all kinds of emotional overload and conflicting emotions can play roles in weakening your voice.

During your life various emotion-laden factors have affected your voice, moulding it to fit in with your family and environment or to protect you in various ways. As a result, your voice no longer works entirely spontaneously.

Now, you probably don't *want* your voice to be completely spontaneous. Imagine life if you blurted out the first thing that came into your head all the time! But if your instincts to protect yourself are over-developed, you deprive your communication of spontaneity and, in the extreme, can destroy every vestige of authentic life in what you say.

Guarding yourself affects your voice in different ways.

- ✔ I had an acquaintance who even took a moment to react when someone stepped on his toe; instead of an immediate 'ouch!' he responded after a fraction of a second with a controlled, 'I say, that was a bit . . . uncomfortable.'

- ✔ A bullying teacher gave Tom a difficult time at school, but when Tom cried he suffered an almost worse fate at the hands of teasing classmates. So Tom learned not to react. Whenever people said anything hurtful or insulting, he gave no sign that their words had an effect. This strategy worked as self-defence, but as an adult he had lost the ability to react spontaneously to people. In consequence, his voice was flat and boring.

  The work Tom and I did together helped him to free his body of tensions he'd been holding for years. At the same time, he built up his inner confidence, which enabled him to be more open in showing emotions. As a result of these paired approaches, his voice became freer and stronger.

- ✔ As a young child, Jessie feared the sharp admonitions of her grandmother and learned to speak pleasantly and politely, regardless of how she felt. As a result, her voice had a light unsubstantial quality completely at odds with her role as HR director of an international pharmaceutical company.

  An important factor that helped Jessie find her voice was getting in touch with her inner strength, and allowing it to underpin her voice. As her voice became more robust, she noticed that people treated her with more respect and other directors listened to her opinion in meetings more. See Chapter 10 for how to express inner qualities in your voice.

To protect yourself, you may mumble or gabble, speak in a monotonous tone or tail off. Perhaps you sound aggressive or artificial or have a piercing, screeching, heavily nasal or whining voice, that's not a match to your personality.

Whatever your specific vocal gremlins, take the time to examine your fears and anxieties first, as I explore in the following sections.

Fighting Fear through Movement

Feeling nervous when you speak – common as the experience is – can sabotage you in all sorts of ways. Nervousness can:

- ✔ **Affect your body language:** You fidget, shuffle your feet, put your hands up to your face or chew your lips in your general discomfort.

- ✔ **Cause you to lose focus:** You forget what you have to say, muddle your argument or skip important points.

- ✔ **Make your body contract:** You hug yourself, grip your hands tightly together, narrow your shoulders and shrink into yourself. As a result, your voice/sounds tight and constricted.

- ✔ **Make you want to run away or be swallowed up:** You may mumble or rush through your words in your desperation to flee the scene.

- ✔ **Prevent you from looking at the people you're talking to:** You stare at your feet or the ceiling and lose connection with your listeners.

You can find descriptions of many of these behaviours – as well as ways to make effective adjustments to them – in the excellent *Body Language For Dummies* by Elizabeth Kuhnke (Wiley).

When your mind creates tension in your body, it tightens your voice. The effect of fear on your voice is more subtle than on your body, but even more devastating. You may feel that everything is shrinking into your throat. Your shoulders go up and in, as does your chest. Your breath seems to contract into your throat.

On the other hand, the effect of fear may be a general shakiness – wobbling knees, trembling hands, churning stomach and pounding heart. But in the area of your throat, you're still stuck because fear is preventing the free flow of your breath. And with your breath not doing its job properly, other more delicate muscles step into the breach to control the breath and your throat tenses to push the voice out. This take-over by muscles wrong for the job spells disaster for your vocal folds, and, as the tightness affects other parts of your body, it's a disaster for body resonance too.

The best remedy for your body's fear responses is to reverse the contraction. Imagine yourself expanding instead of contracting – you immediately feel more confident. When speakers make expansive gestures, they're doing more than emphasising a point; they're opening their bodies to a feeling of confidence.

Actually, your feeling *about* the fear, more than the fear itself, is what creates the biggest problem for your voice. Your judgement that fear is not okay is what sabotages you. Your inner critic clamps down and blocks you. Riding the feelings of shaky nervousness is easier than unblocking rigidity created by controlling self-criticism. Allowing yourself to feel shaky isn't as bad as it may seem – in fact, movement can be positively helpful, as the following practice shows.

Address your fear – as well as your unhelpful, judgemental feelings about fear – with the following activity:

1. **Imagine yourself on a beach with a big sea wave of fear fast approaching.**

   If you just stand immobile on the shore like King Canute and tell the wave to go back, the sea doesn't take a blind bit of notice and the waves of fear keep coming.

2. **Rather than standing still as that wave of fear approaches, become a wind surfer.**

   You can *ride* the wave and let it take you where you want to go.

   The solution to working with your fear is *movement*. Shakiness is only another form of energy. Focus on the feeling of going with your energy rather than blocking it.

3. **Before you speak, engage in energetic activity.**

   Walk about. Shake out your body. Give yourself a workout. Accept all the nervous movements in your body and exaggerate them into broader movements.

   Launching into words is much easier when you're active beforehand; your brain works better as well.

Breathing is motion too – as well as the main secret of remaining calm. When you feel tense, you may forget to breathe, which amplifies your anxiety. (No wonder you feel like you're in a life-or-death situation!) Next time you feel anxious, breathe. Tell yourself that fear is the same as excitement because the upward movement of excitement encourages you to breathe.

Listening to people's breathing tells you a lot about their state of mind – and gives you insight into what can happen with your own voice. Become more aware of people's breath as you listen to them. Train your ear, and hear when the muscles that support the breath stop working and the throat is unhelpfully getting involved in producing the sound. Listen to the reduced quality and power of the sound; listen for tightness and the voice being starved of air.

I write in depth about how to deal with performance fear in my book, *Butterflies and Sweaty Palms: How to Speak and Present with Confidence* (Crown House Publishing, 2012).

Pouring Calm on Squeakiness and Shrillness

Squeakiness in your voice is one of the first results of fear. If you're suffering from a pounding heart, sweating, trembling and struggling to breathe, your throat tightens and your voice comes out higher. It's almost instantaneous; fear produces adrenaline and in a micro-second the adrenaline affects your vocal apparatus, making you sound shrill. Then when you hear those high sounds, you get concerned about *them,* and the tension increases even more and your voice goes higher still – a vicious circle!

Constriction in your throat cuts your body in two. Below, you have your powerful breathing apparatus and resonating cavities that make you sound adult and authoritative, but they're unable to come into play. Above, you have your head, and the tension in your tongue and palate means that this resonance gets over-played. Your voice sounds high and thin.

You can hear when the pressure is on from voice tones. The British Chancellor of the Exchequer George Osborne is sometimes criticised for his strangled high-pitched voice when matters get tense. Hillary Clinton was attacked in her earlier political career for being shrill. One journalist even talked about her 'you're stepping on my foot' tone!

One of the most surprising high voices in public life is that of football celebrity David Beckham. The magazine *Vanity Fair* likened it to 'wind chimes that tinkle constantly in the background'. In his sporting life he understands brilliantly how to be in his body, yet vocally he cuts off all the energy from below his neck. He has grown in competence and confidence as he has matured, but his voice hasn't updated itself from his shy early days.

Fear is not the only reason for a squeaky voice. Sometimes deeper resonance is avoided because of a desire to be ladylike, chaste or intellectual. I explore these issues later in the section 'Making Effort Easy'.

In order to free your throat and speak at a more adult pitch, relax and keep breathing. Remind yourself that your voice almost never sounds as high as you think it does. If you fear that you're becoming squeaky, take a few moments to release your shoulders and neck, and free up your face, brow, jaw and tongue. Then breathe slowly and gently in and out through your nose, feeling the connection between your breath and your whole body. You find many other ideas for relaxing in Chapter 5.

Mitigating Mumbling

Some tension and vocal blocks arise from a lack of trust in yourself – a strange state of affairs indeed. You want to be heard but at the same time you fear to be heard. You half hope that you're invisible and inaudible, and that some part of you imagines that if you speak timidly people will forgive you any mistakes. As a result:

- ✔ You sound as if you're starting to speak but then pulling the plug at the last minute. You begin to say something, but your breath slumps and your words die away. Or you launch into a thought but then slip off it and don't finish. Or you start a word but don't get to the end of it.

- ✔ Alternatively, you sound muffled and full of air. You produce only half a voice because part of your air is making your vocal cords vibrate while the other part is just coming out as whispering.

- ✔ Your body language also sets you up for failure. You hunch your shoulders, slouch and gaze on the ground. You lock your knees and your arms. Your jaw becomes rigid. Your stance declares you closed and blocked – just like the sounds you're producing.

Mumbling doesn't attract sympathy. When you're semi-audible, people get irritated. Their negative reactions then increase your lack of trust in yourself. So round you go again.

Hugh Grant has made a comedic art form of the bumbling, mumbling Englishman in films such as *Notting Hill*. Watch out for when he bumps into something mumbling an apology, or shows shyness by mumbling a greeting.

Counteract the tendency to mumble by speaking out in a safe setting with a friend. Put energy into your words by sharing the reading of a poem. You can use a favourite poem or the following verse by Victorian poet Felicia Hemans. Invest your reading with all the drama and determination you can – however, you must take it in turns word by word; one person reads the words in italics and the other the words in non-italics. Work together to make the poem flow.

The *boy* stood *on* the *burning* deck
Whence all *but* he *had* fled;
The flame *that* lit *the* battle's *wreck*
Shone *round* him *o'er* the *dead.*
Yet *beautiful* and *bright* he *stood,*
As *born* to *rule* the *storm;*
A *creature* of *heroic* blood,
A proud, *though* child-like *form.*

Make each word you speak stronger and more passionate than the previous word that your partner spoke. Point or strike the air with your hand to add energy to each word if you want.

After you and your partner read through the poem successfully, read out the lines alone, investing them with the same level of energy as you did as a duo.

Controlling Gabbling and Jabbering

Fear often causes you to gabble or jabber. The shortage of air that goes with anxiety makes you rush to get through the words before your breath runs out. As a result, you can hear the sound tail off as you run out of air.

Children also gabble when their talking can't keep up with their ideas. Sometimes this way of talking hardens into a habit that persists in adulthood. Listen to the teenage delinquent character Vicky Pollard in the TV series *Little Britain* for a virtuoso comic performance of gabbling.

You may think that gabbling is a big issue to deal with, but it's not really. The main thing is to *decide* to slow down. So do that now, and read exceedingly slowly the following wartime passage by Sir Winston Churchill.

Churchill wasn't a born speaker. He had to discover how to speak clearly and powerfully – as you're doing now. Pretend that you're Churchill himself, with all his gravitas. I've laid the lines out like poetry (as he did himself). Take your time to read each line; they're short so breathing shouldn't present a problem. Take a good breath as you read each line, then look up steadily and speak using lots of breath. Slow words, slow breath – the voice of authority!

We can see before us
the difficult and dangerous onward path
which we must tread. . .

We feel around us
the upsurge of all the enslaved
countries of Europe. . .

> We are marching in company
> with the vast majority of mankind,
> all trending, bearing,
> forging, steadily forward
> towards a final goal, which though distant,
> can already be plainly seen.

Get someone to listen to you and comment. You'll probably find that what seems slow to you, is easy and comfortable to listen to.

Untying Your Tongue

Virgil wrote 'My voice stuck in my throat' in *The Aeneid* more than 2,000 years ago – so this section isn't dealing with a new phenomenon!

In common with mumbling (see the previous section 'Mitigating mumbling'), getting tongue-tied has a push-pull impulse. You want to speak and yet you fear to speak; you want to be heard and yet you fear to be heard. In a tug of war, when opposing forces are even, movement ceases. The system seizes up.

If this sounds familiar, at least you're in good company:

- ✔ Gandhi, who eventually spoke powerfully to nations across the globe, was shy as a young man. He recalls that the first time he cross-examined a witness as a young lawyer, his head reeled and he couldn't get a single word out. He was completely unable to continue.

- ✔ Iain Duncan Smith, former leader of the British Conservative Party, struggled to speak up and was famous for his 'frog in the throat'. He became known as the 'quiet man', and the opposition taunted him by raising their fingers to their lips to ask for silence whenever he spoke.

Sometimes you become blocked through expecting too much of yourself. You're just about to pipe up in a meeting when an inner voice tells you that you don't know enough, aren't interesting, or people are going to scorn what you say. Then someone else fills the moment. Again you wait for a gap in the conversation and, when it arrives, the same happens again. Your sabotaging thoughts grip the muscles around your throat, and you seize up. All too soon the subject thread has moved on and the comment you wanted to make is no longer relevant. This process is a pretty effective way to sabotage yourself!

As in preceding sections in this chapter, breath can come to your rescue. The moment you see your opportunity to speak, take a large breath, maybe raising your hand a little to gain attention at the same time. A big breath is somehow energising and helps you think clearly and set your intent. Having taking the breath, breathe out the air into energetic words. If you block yourself at this point, you're going to look strange as you deflate all that air. Speaking is the more graceful exit from the situation!

If talking isn't something you do much, make sure you practise to oil the wheels, so that you get used to speaking 'mistakes and all'. First, choose safe settings in which to practise. Talk *anywhere*. Make a comment to the person at the supermarket checkout. Talk about the weather when someone else is in the lift. Then graduate to other opportunities. Enrol in an adult education speaking class. Join a committee and speak at meetings. Find an amateur dramatic society to join. Pat yourself on the back every time you speak up.

Practise making good mistakes and you get your voice moving. The practice is as much to do with forgiving and recovering from mistakes as with speaking up. After you give yourself permission to make mistakes, you improve like wild fire.

Loosening Heavy-handed Control

Many people see hiding all fear and doubt while putting their best foot forward as a strength. Some control their movements so rigidly that their mouth scarcely moves. 'Stiff upper lip' is a phrase you may associate with the Victorian or Edwardian era. You can almost hear Lady Prudence Fairfax say under her breath, 'Not in front of the servants, my dear.'

Even today, the Queen's English is still characterised by a stiff upper lip and minimum movement of the mouth. Queen Elizabeth II herself provides an example of someone who speaks in this way. Some upper-class speakers from New York and the East Coast speak with minimal mouth movement too.

Physically, a stiff upper lip is just what it says: your top lip doesn't move, so your lower lip and jaw has to do all the work. The jaw isn't nearly as responsive as lips or tongue, so the voice lacks nuance. Some people lock their lips half open, almost like a ventriloquist!

This style of speaking feels like control, but in fact tightness is not control. Your taut lips and face have no flexibility, and inadequate air deprives the sound of life. Your sound becomes unvarying, either metallic or tediously plummy. Sound has been civilised but has lost its heart in the process.

The simple solution for a stiff upper lip is to shake it out – which means letting all Edwardian decorum go. Shake your shoulders, waist, bottom and legs vigorously and blow a few raspberries with your lips. Come alive! See Chapter 6 for activities to further loosen your lips, jaw and tongue.

Letting Down the Mask of Control

If you're used to hiding your emotions from the world, your whole face may have become an impassive screen that reveals nothing of the planning and thinking you're doing behind it. It may look like sophisticated cool but it's also a front masking fear of emotion.

Many people worry that if they allow themselves to feel, they're going to fall into a bottomless pit, never to emerge again. The trouble, in terms of your voice, is that in pushing your feelings down, you're repressing your vitality and constricting your expression. You may have heard a public speaker who performs in this deadpan way. They look solemn and formal, but their performance is lifeless.

If you reveal none of the life in you, you're like a robot! You may feel stronger that way, but in keeping your emotions and vulnerability hidden you sacrifice the energy and variety in your voice. When instead you risk revealing yourself, you connect more powerfully and come across much more strongly.

Take a risk. Allow other people glimpses of what you're truly feeling. You're much more likely to build a connection when someone can at least glimpse your personality, passions and, yes, feelings.

Avoiding Droning On

If you experience fear but force control onto your speaking, you may indeed use your strong abdominal and inter-costal muscles, but you lose the finer flexibility of tiny muscles stimulated by your thoughts that give life to your voice. In the process, you lose the lightness of your upper voice and sound forceful but monotonous.

Monotonous voices result from several different restrictions and over-compensations:

- ✔ Gordon Brown, a former prime minister of the UK, was often criticised for his dull delivery. He kept his emotions locked; his mouth moved little and his face revealed nothing of what was going on inside. His voice seemed stuck on the same low pitch, permitting him a narrow range of emotion between solemnity and dogged determination.

- ✔ John Major, another former British prime minister, had a habit of ramming the back of his tongue up against the root of his mouth, which made his voice sound strangulated.

> ✔ Kenneth Williams, who appeared in many *Carry On* films, provides a comic example of forcing sound through the nose, which gave his voice its characteristic hard nasal quality.

Droning voices probably hold some responsibility for the UK being named the world's most boring nation in a survey by VisitBritain of 25,000 people from 35 countries in 2006. A good reason, if you're British, to work on your voice!

The effective response to each of these snore-inducing habits is to relax around the mouth and throat (see Chapter 5), and breathe well. Not taking yourself so seriously is also an excellent strategy, as that relaxes you and energises your voice!

Making Effort Easy

Some people associate success with effort, but performing at your best can never be about trying hard as too much conscious effort makes you tense.

You may have heard some people speak and just felt uncomfortable or irritated as you listened. Perhaps you found yourself not trusting them. You may be picking up on a lack of ease caused by their trying too hard. Ironically, people often become most tense and sound most patronising at the very moments when they're trying their hardest to be understanding or tactful. If you think about anything you struggled to pick up in the past, you're likely to find that tension got in the way of your success. When a child tries hard to balance when riding a bicycle for the first time, the result is inevitably to fall off. When he gets the idea and relaxes, he can balance well.

Similarly, if you're too anxious to communicate or try too hard to convey a certain impression, people see it in your body. You lean forward; your shoulders rise and stiffen, and your jaw locks. The more effort you put into getting things right, the more tense you become.

Let go of insistence on a certain result and you sound better. You also look more at ease and enjoy speaking much more. All that effort you wasted in trying can now go to into thinking, feeling and being.

Physically and vocally, *releasing*, *opening up* and *extending* are the magic words for voice. *Gripping*, *closing down* and *contracting* are the gremlins!

Letting go of approval

One aspect of trying too hard is a desire to please people, which does strange things to your voice. If you're eager for approval, you tend to breathe only in your upper chest, and your voice becomes higher and more pinched – just as it does in response to fear (see the earlier section 'Pouring Calm on Squeakiness and Shrillness').

Listen to Jane Horrocks playing the shy little heroine in *Little Voice* (1998). When she's not mimicking great night club performances, her character's voice has a complete absence of any lower sounds. It's all 'little girl' head tones that say, 'Please like me! Don't bite me – I'm not worth the bother!'

If you've spent much of your life appeasing people, your muscles may set your mouth in a permanent tight smile – a smile that may not show in your eyes. You find this upwards lift in the mouth with people who believe others expect them to be a happy part of a happy family, church or care system. A desire to please may be an effort to get approval through being a good person. In hiding whole chunks of the 'not so nice' parts of yourself, you can end up speaking with an insipid pleasant voice lacking interesting lower tones.

If you allow people to see only a limited part of who you are, they also hear only a restricted range of your voice. If the whole of you shows up, the whole voice does too – in all its variety and splendour!

People who seek to please usually create a short hiatus between breathing and talking to allow them time to hide any 'negative' emotion they may be feeling and adjust to pleasantness. This effort cuts off the connection between thinking and feeling from the sound. You hear a tightly edited version of their instinctive response. This manner of responding can be so ingrained that people don't realise what they're doing, but the shallow voice with limited resonance gives the game away.

If you suspect that you may speak in a high, over-pleasant voice, try this test. Count from 1 to 10 with your hand resting on your chest. You should feel some body vibration under your hand. If you speak with a shallow pleasing voice, you don't feel that vibration. Chapter 9 provides help with resonating your voice in your chest, adding more interest and colour to your sound.

Dropping self-consciousness

As soon as you become too concerned with the effect you want to create, whether an attempt to be a particular way or create a particular response, you fall prey to self-consciousness. Self-consciousness, in being aware of itself, is always artificial, and listeners can hear the mental effort in your voice. Self-consciousness can manifest itself as:

- ✔ Vocal tension, which inhibits much of your voice's natural resonance.
- ✔ Overly careful enunciation and emphasis.
- ✔ Pasting of expression onto your words.
- ✔ A lack of natural rhythm and flow.

Unfortunately, your listeners may interpret your self-consciousness as condescension or arrogance instead of awkwardness. Self-consciousness certainly blocks your ability to move or inspire your audience.

Self-consciousness can feel like a ball and chain you drag behind you and have no idea how to cure. Don't despair! As you gradually gain in confidence as a speaker, you naturally lose your self-consciousness by realising that you're fine just as you are. Give yourself permission to make mistakes. No one ever became a 'natural master' of anything without making mistakes.

Sending Other Vocal Gremlins Packing

Various other issues arise for the voice because of how you use it. The topics I cover in this section may have emotional components, but the root of the problem is often one of less-than-ideal technique.

You know your body needs looking after. You don't lift weights that are too heavy. If you overdo it in the gym or on the squash court, you expect to be stiff and take time to recuperate. Your voice gets tired too.

Although it's pretty resilient, your voice does need tender loving care from time to time. If you've yelled your head off at a football game or been to a noisy party, don't go out the next day to give a public address for three hours! Vocal fatigue is common among people who use their voices a lot, such as teachers and actors. Your main defence against vocal fatigue is to discover how to produce your voice properly – as you're finding out in this book!

So if you have to talk against loud noise, ask for a microphone. If your voice feels tired, be especially careful not to force it, and pause when you can.

In this book, I don't talk about voice disorders that may need medical intervention. If you have serious concerns, read Chapter 19 and the Appendix for suggestions about where to turn for voice help. You can largely put the following gremlins right yourself with a little practice and effort.

Paying heed to your health

Watch out for signs that your voice isn't working properly:

- A sore throat, or soreness when you try to speak.
- Hoarseness.
- Sudden breaks in your voice pitch from low to high, or high to low.
- Your voice stuck on one pitch.

In the days before most of today's advanced diagnostic tools and tests, doctors diagnosed patients partly on what they heard in their voices. While a vocal coach should never replace your doctor, serious physical injuries and all manner of health problems cause changes in your voice.

Emotional trauma affects the voice and can even cause the sufferer to lose the ability to speak entirely. The poet Maya Angelou was unable to speak for five years after a traumatic incident at the age of seven. Help directed only at the physical problem wasn't the answer. After she recovered from the trauma and gave her inner self permission to communicate, her voice came back.

Your voice is closely linked to your emotions, your psyche and your health. Think of all three as a system and work on them all.

Keeping your voice young

It's official: talking is good for you. The therapists certainly say so, and the voice coach does too! If you don't use your voice, you lose it. People who live alone and seldom speak with others unfortunately find their voices become rusty, and they struggle to communicate. If that happens to you, you may be tempted to throw in the towel and blame old age, but you don't need to – your voice simply needs regular exercise!

Of course, life does inflict wear and tear on your voice, especially if you smoke, drink or frequent noisy places – or did these activities regularly or excessively in the past.

The typical symptoms of an old voice aren't attributable just to age. A voice usually wobbles or wavers because of insufficient breath. It gets high and whiny because of tension, sometimes associated with loss of confidence. This tension can happen at the age of 25 as easily as at 80. The quality of your voice has much to do with your physical fitness.

The voice of those who develop the ability to sing or speak well often gets richer and more expressive with age. If you want to keep your speaking voice toned and young:

- ✔ Breathe deeply and well.
- ✔ Keep your breathing apparatus practised and toned throughout your life. Chapter 4 gets you started.
- ✔ Use the correct muscles to support your breathing and other correct muscles to vary the voice tone. (See Chapter 9.)
- ✔ Practise relaxing all the muscles around the shoulders, throat and face, so you do not force your voice. (See Chapter 5.)
- ✔ Produce your voice with lots of mental energy and minimum physical effort so it serves you well.
- ✔ Avoid micro-adjusting how your speak constantly, according to what your ears (often inaccurately) tell you.
- ✔ Have a strong intention to connect with your listener or audience. (See Chapter 10.)

Starting smoothly

A common vocal misuse happens when the onset of sound is an aggressive hammering against the vocal folds, called a *glottal attack*. You can experience it yourself if you say the word 'everyone' giving a hard bang on the first 'e', or 'apple' banging the 'a'.

A violent glottal attack can seriously damage your voice if allowed to continue. A forced *onset* – the act of commencing sound after taking a breath – makes the two vocal folds bash together and in time can cause swellings, called *nodules*, on the folds, which cause hoarseness, reduced range, pain and finally, serious damage to the fold themselves.

Discover this new, glottal-friendly way of speaking now. Take a breath and begin to breathe out through your open mouth. As you continue to breathe out, turn your breath gently into the sound 'aah'. Feel comfortable and relaxed. There is no hiatus between breath and sound, therefore no glottal attack that stops the sound. Do the same again and slide the out-breath into a gentle contented comment such as, 'Ah, this is easy'. Here you *turn* breath into sound with no hiatus. Then start the sound with the same gentle onset without expelling air first. Get used to this way of launching into sound.

Softening a nasal voice

Some actors have instantly recognisable nasal voices: Michael Caine and Kenneth Williams, star of the *Carry On* films, are just two examples.

Many actors, especially in the past, were trained with exercises to focus the sound in their nose and front of the face. Back before the general use of microphones, speaking in the mask was an important skill to carry your voice to the back of the theatre. See Chapter 9 for much more on resonance.

Nasal resonance as a useful part of your head timbre is not the same as pushing the sound heavily into the nose, which strains your voice and sounds dominating and unpleasant. Harmful nasal speaking happens when you use the back of your tongue and the hard palate to control the air instead of the breathing muscles around your diaphragm. The tongue bunches up at the opening to your throat and pushes the sound up into your nose. The sound you make then is loud, grating and monotone. This way of producing your voice is tiring because you're forcing it, and it can easily damage your voice.

First of all, open your mouth wider when you speak to free yourself up inside your mouth. Feel that you're about to yawn. Adopt the smooth onset from breath into speaking that I describe earlier in 'Starting smoothly'. Then discover how to breathe better using your abdominal muscles; you can find useful information about breathing in Chapter 4.

Matching Sound and Meaning

Human beings are complex creatures who use their voices to tell truths and half-truths, to win people over, hide feelings, create impressions, fantasise or just make things up. People have hundreds of ways of confusing, pretending and defending with their voice. Most of these ways are unconscious, or having started consciously, have become unconscious over time. If you want to express the full power of your voice, your meaning and voice tone need to match. The following sections describe various ways that people's voice tone suggests something at odds with their thoughts and feelings.

Sometimes, without any deceit on your part, the sound of your voice suggests something that you don't intend.

- ✔ 'People get the wrong idea from my voice!' Sandra wailed when she came to me for voice coaching. 'What can I do about it?' Sandra's voice was breathy, and men often misinterpreted her breathiness as sexiness. Through coaching she learned how to co-ordinate her breath and vocal cords so that air didn't escape. In the process, she discovered that she had a wide range of expression that she'd never utilised before. She could still speak breathily if she wanted to but wasn't any longer caught in the trap of creating an impression she didn't mean.

- ✔ In the 2008 US presidential race, people sometimes said that John McCain sounded depressed because his voice was low and lacked light and shade. I'm guessing he intended to sound statesmanlike!

In addition to giving a message that isn't intended, a voice that doesn't fit can be surprising – even off-putting.

- ✔ I first saw the young British actor Carey Mulligan in the film *Pride and Prejudice*. She has a sweet heart-shaped face and looks far younger than her years. I scarcely believed my ears to hear her rich deep tones when she spoke. That was a pleasant surprise.

- ✔ When I asked the 16-stone herculean man at the counter in my local bookshop about a recent publication, his high, overly melodic answer almost made me take a step backwards in shock. Something wasn't right with this picture!

Your voice needs to fit you. Look for voice coaching if:

- ✔ You speak the language of love in the tones of a robot.

- ✔ Your confident work presentation comes out in the voice of a child.

- ✔ You issue military instructions from a 6-foot frame in a squeaky voice.

- ✔ You're determined yet sound like someone who's just lost a running race, a job and a pet – all in the same day!

When you can vary your voice, you have many choices in how you speak and interact with others. Other people stop being confused and their response is more under your control.

Coming out from behind your voice

Your voice has the powerful potential to convey your feelings to other people when you speak, but you don't want to let others know what you are feeling on *every* occasion. Sometimes you decide to hide your feelings by adopting a voice that is bland and pleasant or dull and inexpressive. However, if you get into the habit of using that insipid voice all the time, other people are going to feel that they're not getting the real 'you' in conversations.

Sarah remembers being at a family party when she was small. An uncle she didn't know rushed up to her, picked her up and kissed her noisily on both cheeks. The moment he put her down, she shouted, 'I don't like you!' Her mother reprimanded her quietly and urgently, then later explained that you can't always say exactly what you think. 'You have to be tactful,' she said. 'Is tactful pretending?' asked the bright young Sarah. Her mother looked a bit taken aback. 'Er, yes, it's sort of pretending,' she admitted.

Growing older, you get used to being tactful, and often have good reasons for doing so. However, a disjuncture can grow between what you think and feel – and how you express it. Your voice can become conventional and less expressive.

Are any of the following familiar to you?

- ✔ Do you sometimes hold back the first thing that comes into your head in order not to offend?
- ✔ Have you praised someone for something you thought poor in order to provide encouragement?
- ✔ Have you ever said 'no' when you meant 'yes' in order to save yourself from embarrassment?
- ✔ Have you been upset with someone and assured the person with a smile that it didn't matter?
- ✔ Have you spoken pleasantly to someone when you're actually angry?

If the answer to any of these questions is yes, of course you've been thinking or feeling one thing and saying another. If you do this often, you're likely to reach a point where you don't even know that you're giving double messages any more. But you may give away clues in your body language and voice that show you're not all of a piece.

One of the nastiest characters in the Harry Potter stories is Dolores Umbridge, the lady from the Ministry of Magic who becomes headmistress of Hogwarts. When Harry first meets Umbridge in the film *Harry Potter and the Order of the Phoenix* (2007), she's wearing a fluffy pink cardigan with a black velvet bow on her head. She's cruel and ruthless, but the actor Imelda Staunton gives her voice the fluffy pink and velvet qualities of sweet saccharin.

Vocal variation across cultures

Communication is more than words. In particular, everyone makes assumptions based on other people's tone of voice — and sometimes you get things wrong. It happens particularly easily when communicating across cultures.

I was asked to coach a social worker who some considered aggressive in the workplace. When I met and spoke with Aman, who came originally from the Punjab, I was impressed by her conscientious approach and caring attitude. However, her voice had a tone and rhythm that made every sentence sound like a command. Moreover, she didn't use traditional English roundabout language conventions such as, 'I wonder if. . .', 'I don't know if you might. . .' or 'Could I possibly. . .', which soften conversations. She sounded rigid and domineering because she was using the vocal tones and customs of her birth language. When Aman found out how to speak lightly in head tones and softly in deeper tones (see Chapter 9), she was able to use her voice to express what was already inside her but previously not audible to others.

People sometimes joke that England and the USA are divided by a common language. You can actually say the same of voice tone *wherever* English is spoken. A Chinese speaker uses silence more and a Western listener thinks that he has nothing to say. An American speaks with energy and an Asian thinks she lacks deference. The possibilities of misunderstanding tone are legend.

Having a voice free enough to tune in with another person's way of speaking is a sure-fire way to begin 'speaking the same language'. You meet various ways of 'tuning-in' in Chapter 15.

If you deliberately *produce* your voice tones in a particular way rather than allowing your thoughts and feelings to create the sounds, your conscious efforts make you sound predictable. You can never reproduce the subtlety of natural expression consciously. When Miss Umbridge gets furious, you'd expect angry voice tones to come from the chest and lower in her body, but she continues to produce her sugary voice up in the mouth with a tight throat.

Your voice is more influential when connected with your real thoughts. The sounds you produce have more depth and subtlety when you're 'all of a piece', and not fighting yourself internally – by looking friendly when you feel furious for example!

You may feel stronger by forcing your voice to tell a particular story to convince your listeners, but often vulnerability is your strength – you just sound more *real* and therefore more convincing. See Chapter 10 for more on releasing your authentic voice.

Acknowledging your emotions

Scott was complaining to me about another work colleague with whom he'd recently fallen out. He complained that he'd made every effort to make peace but his teammate refused to listen. When I asked him what efforts he'd made to patch things up, he replied in exasperation, 'You may well ask! I stopped him after lunch and insisted that everything was okay. I assured him it really doesn't matter and I'm fine! He just didn't believe me.' His voice was sharp with a metallic edge. 'So, you're not angry about it?' I prompted. 'No, I'm *not* angry!' Now, he was almost shouting. His real feelings were obvious in his sound, but he was completely unaware of showing anger.

Watch out for emotions leaking into the sound without the speaker's knowledge. Here are a few examples to listen for:

- ✔ Someone says sharply, 'Go away!' yet there's a shade of yearning in his voice that tells you of loneliness.

- ✔ 'I'm fine,' someone responds to your query, and the slight fall in pitch after the high sound at the end makes your heart sink and realise that he is not fine at all.

- ✔ 'Sure, I'd love to,' she says, the 'sure' tailing off on a high sound, and the final 'to' dropping away. Sure? I don't think so!

If your words and your voice tone are at odds with each other, people are likely to believe your voice tone rather than your words. The sounds you create give a more accurate picture of what is really going on inside you than any explanations or protestations you may choose to give. On most occasions, instead of hiding your feelings half-successfully, aim to acknowledge them in a controlled way. One possible response when you are angry for example is to say, 'It's true that I'm not happy about . . . what I want is . . .'. If your feelings are going to leak out anyway, use them to your advantage!

Using all your voices

Some people have a voice that never varies. 'I call a spade a spade,' they say. 'Take me as you find me.' Others, however, have different voices for different people, and this is particularly marked when dealing with authority. People use a particular light head tone unconsciously whenever they feel intimidated. It makes them sound like a timid child as they nod and answer, 'Yes, yes; yes that's fine; yes I will; okay I'll do that; yes of course, right away.'

Glenna wanted to be taken more seriously at work. She spoke all the time in a light compliant voice. When we worked on projection as a group, her voice remained high and feeble. During a break, I noticed her with a man and two young children outside the venue. The little boy wandered off towards the road, and I heard her yell loudly in a full voice, 'Greg! Come here!'

In conversation later, I mentioned the episode and asked if she were willing to recreate in her mind the situation when her son ran towards the road. She went back to her memory of the incident and realised that she breathed differently to raise her voice and that her breath arose from a totally different energy. 'So, if you were to tap into that energy to say something at work, how would that be?' I asked. She hesitated and confessed that the difference in energy was so enormous that she couldn't imagine coming anywhere near it at work. 'So, add just a tiny bit of that energy,' I suggested. When she did that, she took a much better breath and was able to produce firmer sounds.

Later, she reported that the experience had made her conscious of how different she was at work and at home. 'I now realise how pathetic I've sounded!' she said. 'I've been leaving half of me behind. But no more!'

Often, you don't need to struggle to *learn* how to produce your voice differently. Many people use their voices differently in different contexts. All you need to do is make a connection with a voice you use in another part of life and adopt that voice in a new context where you need it. When Glenna imagined shouting at her children in the workplace, she was able to summon the energy and vocal power she needed. It had been there all the time!

Find an area of your life where your voice is most full and free, whether out with mates, at home with a partner or chatting to your best friend. Get to know *that* voice. Then you can use it anywhere!

Chapter 12

Putting the Accent on Accents

In This Chapter

▶ Examining the pros and cons of accents

▶ Addressing aspects of class and education

▶ Developing the best of your accent

▶ Choosing to change

*Y*ou may be turning to this chapter because you hate your accent or sense that people don't quite accept you because of your accent. The first words I'm tempted to say on the subject – before you can even jump in and disagree! – are that you can speak influentially and well in any accent. The most important features of good communication – clarity, volume, energy and emotional content such as determination, excitement, love, enthusiasm and seriousness – are found in voices of every accent. These aspects influence listeners, far more than a particular accent.

Everyone has an accent. A voice without an accent doesn't exist. Some people speak like you and some other people don't. What is often called Received Pronunciation or BBC English is just a southern English accent that came to prominence and became associated with class. Standard American is as much an accent as the notable pronunciations of native speakers of New Orleans or Texas; it just became associated with television and film and acquired a currency that other accents lacked.

This chapter isn't about how to 'do' different accents – that task would require a thick book of its own. English has innumerable different accents and is unusual in its geographical scope going as far as the Caribbean, Hong Kong, India, Australia, New Zealand and numerous other countries – it literally spans the globe. With such a spread, variations in the way English-speakers speak English is unsurprising!

This isn't to say that accents are a trouble-free zone! Accents can cause problems. In this chapter, you find out what to do if yours is proving a challenge.

Received Pronunciation

Received Pronunciation is just another English accent, but one that gained a lot of prestige through being associated historically with people of intelligence and breeding. What started as a regional dialect became a social one. It came to prominence as the accent of London and the court in the 18th century and went on to acquire tremendous prestige as the 19th century wore on. It was the accent of members of the English ruling and privileged classes and was spoken in public schools such as Winchester, Eton and Harrow; and the universities of Oxford and Cambridge.

The accent was initially the preserve of only a small minority but became accepted as correct English. Using it was a way of suggesting to other people that you belonged to a certain social class and had enjoyed a prestigious public school education, As a result, people who didn't naturally speak in this way became eager to acquire the accent. Public schools still influence children's accents today; after seven formative years boarding in the enclosed school environment, most pupils leave those schools with the upper-class accent of their peers.

Daniel Jones produced an English Pronouncing Dictionary in 1917 in which he first called this accent Standard Pronunciation, Standard Southern English Pronunciation and Public School Pronunciation before settling in a later edition for Received Pronunciation. His dictionary remained the accepted authority on pronunciation for most of the 20th century.

The main factor maintaining the accent's pre-eminence was the emergence in 1922 of the BBC, which became the broadcasting authority in the UK. See the sidebar 'This is the BBC . . .' for details.

Investigating Accents – and Responding to What Really Matters

Your accent is made up of many different parts – your pronunciation of vowels and consonants, word stress and the intonation and rhythm of your sentences. The word 'accent' is sometimes used interchangeably with 'dialect'. A dialect includes accent, but contains fundamental idiosyncrasies of vocabulary that can make it more like a different language. (I'm not concerned with dialect in this chapter.) Many people fret or complain about their accents, but what genuinely matters about your accent? The four main ways in which accents matter are:

✓ **Being understood:** This element is the most important. If people find you intelligible, your accent probably doesn't cause a problem – or at least matters much less. See the next section 'Increasing understanding' for more on this essential topic.

  ✔ **Sounding pleasant:** The actual sounds of an accent can be more or less pleasant and people's preferences affect the way they respond to you. In the section 'Toning down and tuning up your accent', you find several minor vocal adjustments that make you more pleasant to listen to.

  ✔ **Belonging:** Accents show where you belong and allow you to be accepted by a particular group and taken in a particular way. An accent can also distinguish you from members of other groups. See the later section 'Fitting in' later for more.

  ✔ **Being judged intellectually or culturally:** People often use your accent to make judgements about your intelligence or class. You can avoid this, as I discuss in the section 'It's a class act'.

You *can* entirely change your accent, and many people have done so (see the later section 'Changing Your Accent'). A much easier path, however, is to identify features of your accent that you dislike or which cause you problems and then modify just certain elements to create a different impression from the one you create at present. That's my approach in the following sections.

Increasing understanding

Basically, the most important feature of speaking in any accent is for *people to understand what you say*.

You can easily jump to the conclusion that people despise your accent when all that's happening is that they can't understand you. You've probably had the experience yourself of speaking to someone you can't understand properly, and the effort you have to make stifles any real communication. In the end, you just want to slip away and end the embarrassment.

British singer Cheryl Cole, a judge on the panel of the talent show *The X Factor*, who enjoyed great popular success in the UK, was unable to connect with American audiences when she joined the US version of *The X Factor*. Viewers struggled with her British Geordie accent and didn't make the effort to tune in to her way of speaking. After just a few programmes, she was pulled. People in England enjoyed her feisty regional accent because they understood her easily; in the US, her way of speaking was just too different and too difficult for people to interpret.

English speakers are famous for not understanding 'foreigners'. One of the reasons for confusion is that English contains many similar sounding words with different meanings that can be genuinely confusing, especially when someone pronounces familiar words in an unfamiliar way.

What can you do to help people to distinguish among the many sounds that are similar and understand you more easily? I recommend that you focus on the following three strategies:

- ✔ **If your accent isn't familiar to your listeners, *slow down*!** This recommendation is obvious but so important. Slowing down not only gives your listeners more time to make sense of what you say, but also makes it easier to distinguish the separate words in your sentences.

  When you speak quickly, everything runs together, and listeners struggle to interpret how the sounds divide into words. If, for example, you're ordering a bottle of oil, you need to communicate that you're talking about a *bottle* and about *oil*. If you say quickly, 'A bo'llo'oil', those details disappear!

- ✔ **Take care with consonants.** English is a consonant-based language; these sounds matter for understanding. If people struggle to understand you, try putting in a few more consonants.

  In addition to consonant practice in Chapter 6, say the following words and pronounce every consonant clearly:

  > **comfortable:** *com-f-t-bl*, not *com'table* or *com'ferble* – four syllables, not three (in English pronunciation)

  > **finished:** not *finish'* (hear the strong final 'd')

  > **world:** not *worl'*

  > **jumped:** not *jum't*

  > **curtain:** not *cur'in*

  Of course, pronunciation varies from region to region, and you may not pronounce the above words in exactly this way. However, as a general rule, guard against leaving out consonants that help people to understand a word.

  Consonants also bring your voice forward and make your voice clearer, rather than trapping the sound at the back of your throat. Compare for example the clear tones of John Kennedy with the guttural sounds of Arnold Schwarzenegger to hear the difference.

- ✔ **Be as consistent in your accent as possible.** English speakers understand sounds in context, and whether you speak with a Yorkshire accent or a Kentucky one, listeners gradually tune into an accents particular patterns of sound.

  For example, whatever your accent, the word 'sleep' must rhyme with 'peep' and 'leap', and the word 'slip' must rhyme with 'pip' and 'lip'. People understand you if your accent is consistent but get utterly confused if you switch from one to another. For example, if you say 'slip' when you mean 'sleep' and then pronounce 'leap' in the traditional way, your speech becomes really confusing.

The ascent of new accents

A hundred years ago, someone who lived in Hampshire would be able to tell that someone came from the next door county of Dorset just by his or her accent. Populations didn't move around so much and every part of the small islands of the UK had a distinctive accent.

Australia provides a good example of what happens to accents. The first colonists in New South Wales included many Irish and Cockneys, as well as people from other parts of the British Isles who spoke in a variety of accents. The colonists' children, on the other hand, created a new dialect that was based on an amalgam of all the different sounds they heard; this dialect is the basis of the New South Wales accent of today with its strong traces of the Irish lilt and Cockney chirpiness. As new groupings occur everywhere, they create new accents. The popularity of hip-hop for instance, based on sounds introduced by Jamaican immigrants in the UK, influenced the accents of large numbers of young people in the UK. British state schools are a great melting pot of accents and are creating new generations whose accent is different from their parents.

Toning down and tuning up your accent

Quite apart from ease of understanding, some accents just *sound* more pleasant than others. Plenty of pitfalls exist, as you can read in the following sections, but you can quite easily avoid most of them by modifying your accent just a little.

Playing with pitch

The English East London and Essex accents favour flat wide vowels so you get more of the 'ee' sounds, which produce the typical chirpy accent we associate with Cockneys like Bert in *Mary Poppins* – friendly, yes, but lacking in gravitas. Compare these sounds with the typical sounds of the British establishment, with the long rounded vowels of 'How now brown cow'. The inner mouth shape and darker vowels create much deeper sounds that sound more authoritative.

Blow air through your lips in an 'oo' shape. Now blow through your lips in an 'ee' shape. You will find that the pitch is different. 'Oo' produces a lower air sound than 'ee'.

Darken your sounds a little by opening your mouth more long-ways, and people may take you more seriously! Many politicians have taken this step.

Opening your mouth

Other accents use different mouth shapes. The upper class accent of South Kensington and other exclusive parts of London uses only a tiny portion of tongue and lips and the lips are kept tight. This tightness produces a restricted high sound from the head and neck that can sound almost disapproving. It's a physical feature of the famous English 'stiff upper lip'. Members of the British royal family, for example, move their mouth and jaw little.

Listen to the voice of Queen Elizabeth, particularly in older recordings. She moves her mouth scarcely at all. As a result, her voice is small and tight and sounds highly controlled. Listen out for the signature upper-class words spoken with an almost closed mouth: *orff* for 'off' and *Edwaahrdian* for 'Edwardian'.

If you open your mouth a little more – without strain – you seem more relaxed. If your mouth is 'buttoned up', people are more likely to find you tense and unapproachable.

Emphasising strongly

The strong emphasis of southern English creates an impression of certainty. The Welsh accent on the other hand, influenced by the soft consonants and elisions and particular intonations of the Welsh language, has a musical ring to it. The softness of Welsh makes its speakers sound less forceful than their English equivalents – though probably more poetic and musical!

If you want to sound definite, use stronger emphasis. See Chapter 8 for more on effective emphasis.

Softening nasal sounds

Some accents with insistent nasal sounds have acquired especially poor reputations.

- ✔ The sharp tones of New York and New Jersey, which catch the sound in the back of tongue and soft palate, can be hard to listen to.

- ✔ Brummie (the local Birmingham accent) has been described pejoratively as 'a nasal drone that suggests despondency'. In a Bath Spa University survey of voices in 2008, people judged speakers with a Brummy accent as the least intelligent of all English speakers. Popular British comics such as Jasper Carrott and Lenny Henry have added to the impression that Brummie is an accent not to be taken seriously. The tone is nasal and thick, and uninformed people assume that the people who speak it are thick too.

  Accents go in and out of fashion. Studies made of the rhymes and vocabulary used in plays by Shakespeare suggest that he spoke the local West Midland dialect of the Birmingham area.

If you want people to enjoy listening to you, avoid bunching up your tongue and pushing the sound into your nose. You find more about how avoid pushing your sound in Chapter 11.

Minding your speed

All over the world, people in cities talk fast while country people speak slower. The widely held assumption is that, with regard to speech, slow equals stupid. This stereotype may be part of why some consider people with the British West Country accent or the drawl of the American South to be slow in mind as well as speech. Even Chaucer, writing *The Canterbury Tales* back in the 14th century, makes fun of a slow northern accent in the Reeve's tale and insinuates that he is stupid: 'And therefore is I come ar ye', says the reeve – 'This is why I've come'.

If you speak with a brisk pace, people find you more alert and intelligent than someone who speaks slowly with long pauses. Just don't rush and lose your clarity in the process!

Ending strongly

English people used to the falling cadences of Received Pronunciation sometimes make the mistake of not taking Australians and New Zealanders seriously because their high endings sound informal and questioning. This pattern of speech is also found in parts of the US, Canada, South Africa and elsewhere. Ending on a higher tone sounds friendly and inclusive and is especially popular among young people, including in the UK, but this practice can make you sound uncertain, as if you're seeking constant reassurance from your listener.

End your statements firmly on a low pitch if you want to sound definite and authoritative.

Avoiding gagging on the glottal stop

Many accents favour the *glottal stop,* which takes the place of a consonant such as 't'. For example, instead of 'cattle' they say *ca'ill,* or *fli'* instead of 'flight'. This casual pronunciation is okay for simple words where the listener can guess the ending but can seriously get in the way of understanding in more complex sentences, such as 'E dinna fi a lo'o ba'ills' (a Scottish version of 'he doesn't fight a lot of battles').

Try to put a few more consonants in your sentences if your listener doesn't share your accent. The extra effort on your part makes for better understanding!

Some accents have characteristics that create cross-cultural misunderstandings. For example, Indian speakers can be considered too direct just because they speak with direct strong intonation with little pitch variation. Germans are accused of sounding bossy because of their language's strong emphasis patterns. Most Americans speak fast and loud, which gives the impression of energy, youth or arrogance. Chinese, for whom soft low voices denote gravitas, can be mistaken as feeble or passive.

When you listen to English speakers from different cultures or non-native speakers, make allowances for different intonation, and don't jump to conclusions about speakers from their accents. When you speak yourself, a slight adjustment to your accent to lean a little towards the character of theirs can make them feel an easier connection with you.

Fitting in

The way you speak is your badge of belonging. English, in particular, is highly efficient at immediately categorising you. The region you come from, the cultural and economic group you're part of, your education and your age all tell other people where you belong.

Many groups of young people have their own ways of speaking, which include accent and vocabulary, to differentiate themselves from other groups. Children in schools acquire a homogenous accent. A new metropolitan accent has grown up among the young in major cities in the UK and elsewhere. Societies that are more laid back have a looser way of speaking. Societies that are more formal and regulated have a more clipped way of speaking.

Most British people are happy to belong to a particular area of Britain and to announce it in the way they speak. In a recent study of 5,000 people by the *Journal of Socio-linguistics,* 70 per cent of respondents said they were proud of their regional accents. Even in the past, when received pronunciation had more prestige than today, someone from Yorkshire never spoke in Received Pronunciation because doing so would have distanced him socially from neighbours.

The accent of your community is part of your identity. Furthermore, your way of speaking tells other people where you *don't* belong, and people are quick to make assumptions based on accent.

If you want to fit in, being able to modify your accent, even slightly, to match the rest of your group can be a useful skill. Modification tends to happen naturally when there's rapport between you. If the other person speaks slowly, for instance, you probably find yourself naturally slowing down as well to match their pace. Many people find that, without their even meaning to, their accent begins to approximate to that of the other person. Look at Chapter 15 for more hints on how to tune in to other people's way of speaking to create better connections.

The English broadcaster Melvin Bragg confessed that in his youth he acquired three different accents for different contexts of his life. He came from Cumbria so naturally spoke with the regional accent. His town, Withan, had a particular dialect for insiders that included Romany, the gypsy language. At his Grammar School, and later at university and working with the BBC, he spoke Received Pronunciation, the accent of the BBC. Having three accents happened naturally to fit into the different contexts of his life.

Multiple accents are common in other languages too. For example, most Austrians, who speak a particular dialect of German, happily switch to 'hochdeutsch' (High German) to be better understood by foreigners. Italians too, who are in general immensely proud of the dialect of their birthplace, speak in a more Tuscan accent to be better understood. For them, the shift is a matter of facilitating communication and lacks the baggage of prestige and class.

It's a class act

The playwright George Bernard Shaw claimed in his preface to *Pygmalian* (which is the basis for the musical *My Fair Lady*) that 'an English man only has to open his mouth and someone despises him'.

In the UK, especially, accent is closely associated with class. For much of the last century, the accent of the public schools, Oxford and Cambridge universities and the BBC was considered the only acceptable one for people of culture and intellect – and people all over Britain aspired to speak in that way.

A regional accent used to mean working class to most people, so the only way to improve your status was to acquire the 'correct' accent. Elocution was your passport out of the gutter. Here are a few notable examples:

- ✔ Internationally famous hairdresser Vidal Sassoon was born in the East End of London. When his father left his mother penniless, he spent much of his early years in an orphanage. When Sassoon decided that he wanted to become an apprentice hairdresser, he was told that he would never get a job in Mayfair with his Cockney accent. So he worked on his elocution, going frequently to the theatre to hear 'posh' English and tune his ear. Only when he was able to speak with an 'educated' accent was he offered a job in a salon.

- ✔ Margaret Thatcher had no trace of her childhood Lincolnshire accent by the time she left Oxford University.

- ✔ A school student asked Cherie Blair why she didn't have a Liverpool accent (as she was brought up there). She confessed that she changed her accent while studying law at university.

✔ The comedian Linda Smith was uncompromising in her comment on accents. She claimed that in films the hero always had a southern English educated accent. Watching a film, if someone had a cockney accent, she said, 'As soon as they said, "Fancy a brew up skip" you knew they were going to be dead in the next frame, that they were basically surplus to requirements.'

You still get British politicians who go for the Received Pronunciation accent in order to fit in. For many, their accent shifts naturally when they mix with other students at universities such as Oxford or Cambridge. The UK MP and former Minister Patricia Hewitt, for example, is Australian, but has acquired an accent quite similar to that of Margaret Thatcher, whether by natural blending or by design, to fit in with other members of parliament.

Although changing your accent can seem like the pathway to power, popularity or riches, many people find a deliberately acquired accent patronising because the final effect isn't quite authentic.

In any case, you no longer need to acquire a whole new accent in order to fit in. Instead of prescribing specific accents, the following sections take a slightly different tack.

'This is the BBC . . . '

The first General Manager of the BBC, Lord Reith, accepted Received Pronunciation as a standard for broadcasting because he considered it the mostly widely understood accent. A Scot himself, he maintained that it was a 'non-accent' and wouldn't irritate people like a posh accent would. Reading the news on the BBC emphasised truth and formality. Reith even had radio news readers wear dinner jackets when on air!

He established an advisory committee on pronunciation, which included, apart from the dictionary expert Daniel Jones (see the 'The beginning of Received Pronunciation'), the playwright George Bernard Shaw, the actor Forbes Robinson and later Alistair Cook (of *Letter from America* fame). This group used to vote on pronunciation!

After the war, as opportunities opened up to people from different backgrounds, most considered the sounds of the BBC the only way to speak to gain advancement, so people made great efforts to modify regional accents. The subtle message, reinforced in schools, was that Received Pronunciation was the standard for correct English, and that therefore all other accents and dialects were wrong.

Even though a standard was established in the early days of the BBC, pronunciation has steadily changed through the years and early broadcasts now sound extremely old-fashioned. Listen to news bulletins, or famous speeches – King Edward VIII's abdication speech or King George VI's wartime speeches for instance – to hear how different the accents are from today. Compare also Queen Elizabeth as a young woman and today, and even Margaret Thatcher at the beginning and end of her career.

Celebrating regional accents

Received Pronunciation used to stand as an emblem of truth (see the sidebar 'Received Pronunciation'), but that has changed in the UK. The barriers began to come down back in the Second World War, when Wilf Pickles was employed to read the BBC news because his Yorkshire accent couldn't easily be imitated by the Germans. Then the Beatles made the Liverpool accent popular, and bit by bit English has become less formal with a decline in the popularity of formal 'BBC-speak'.

Regional accents have come into their own in broadcasting. In the UK, regional speakers began to supply weather forecasts and gardening advice. (No one minded a bit of rural west country when talking about planting onions.) Then DJs wanted to sound younger, and John Peel swapped his English public school accent for one with traces of Liverpudlian in order to be able to talk with authority about the Beatles on Dallas radio. Certain Scottish accents came into vogue in the belief that Scottish people somehow sounded more truthful than English speakers. Irish became popular too, though not northern Irish at first. Then anchors of popular programmes wanted to sound like their fans, and the Essex accents of Jonathan Ross and others were imitated.

As the population moved into cities, urban accents became more popular and rural accents drained away. At the same time, young people began to feel that their regional accents no longer presented barriers to getting the jobs they wanted.

Demographic and social changes have imperceptibly changed pronunciation year by year until the norm is different from 50 years ago. One of the main influences has been of the colloquial East London accent often called Estuary English.

Listen to everyday speech in the media, and note recent differences:

- ✔ 'Y' endings have become much stronger. Brits now say *happee* instead of *happi*.

- ✔ You hear the sound *ch* instead of *t* in 'Tuesday', 'duke' and 'reduce'.

- ✔ The vowel *oo* has become flatter. People no longer say *spoo-oon* but *spune*.

- ✔ Brits have lost a lot of 't's. Most people say *take i'* instead of 'take it', and *tha's ri'* instead of 'that's right'.

- ✔ Lots of people now lose the 'l' in 'milk' and say *mi-ook* instead, and *appo'* instead of 'apple'.

Standard American

Standard American, the American equivalent of British Received Pronunciation, also acquired its credibility through radio and television. The accent is sometimes referred to as 'television English' or the 'newscaster accent'. It's also widely heard in films, television series and advertising. Just as Received Pronunciation originates from the south of England and the capital, so Standard American is broadly the accent of the mid-west. The news anchors Walter Cronkite and Dan Rather are excellent examples of this accent in broadcasting.

Most Americans are unlikely to give accent the close scrutiny it attracts in the UK, and this attitude reflects the country's more egalitarian history. However, stereotypical assumptions still exist around strong southern accents and the typical accents of rural areas of the US.

While, in the UK, media accents are moving fast away from 'posh', US listeners still have respect for the measured tones and clarity of English broadcasters such as Alistair Cooke and Stephen Fry, and Standard American, in part, reflects these qualities.

The strong message of all these changes is that you're free to *choose* how you want to speak. The increased popularity of regional accents is good news for everyone. Don't worry that your accent is unacceptable. Concentrate instead on making sure that you're easily understood and getting your message across. And enjoy the increased variety and colour that different accents offer to our language and expression.

Dimming posh's appeal

In contrast to the rise of regional accents, various recent factors have given 'posh' accents a bad press:

- ✔ In the economic downturn in the 1970s, Margaret Thatcher's clipped accent and upper-class demeanour became associated with privilege; large segments of the population ended up trusting those who spoke with a similar accent less.

- ✔ Advertising research discovered that people heard regional accents as more honest and reliable. Scottish became the accent for the honest banker, Yorkshire for a person to trust!

- ✔ As Received Pronunciation or Standard American pronunciation has an air of authority about it (think Walter Cronkite), the more common-sounding estuary English is more in tune with our less authoritarian times. People no longer submit easily to being told how to think and what to do!

✔ More and more in Hollywood films, it was the 'baddies' who had the posh (often British) accents. In the *Harry Potter* films, the main evil characters such as Voldemort and Dolores Umbridge have upper-class accents.

✔ For Oxbridge-educated politicians in Britain, dumbing down your accent became important for connecting with crucial marginal constituencies. See the sidebar 'Tony Blair's political accent' for a great example of this phenomenon.

If you want to hold public office and appeal to a wide cross-section of people, you'll do better to adopt a colloquial accent than to strive to speak like a product of private education. Most politicians now attempt to show that they're ordinary in the way they speak (as well as extraordinary as politicians and human beings, of course!).

Politicians and public figures who wish to appeal to a wide audience are neutralising their accents to hide their roots and sound more inclusive. Listen to the voices of Barack Obama, David Cameron, Oprah Winfrey and others. Pinning them down in terms of race, education, culture and more is becoming increasingly difficult.

Tony Blair's political accent

Tony Blair's speech after the death of Princess Diana was an important moment in British politics because he seemed to speak for everyone and struck a chord with the masses when he spoke of her as 'the people's princess'. Blair, educated at public school, adapted his accent to sound more a man of the people. Since then, many others in politics have followed his lead in sounding less posh. Blair achieved the change by:

✔ Speaking in short staccato phrases with little pauses in between.

✔ Pronouncing certain words less clearly, for example, dropping the 'l' at the end of words like 'people' and shortening words like 'government' to 'govmund'.

✔ Ending some phrases and sentences high, giving a questioning effect and an air of humility.

✔ Adding tags such as 'you know' at the end of phrases, to sound more like your friend in the pub.

✔ Consciously using the glottal stop, which instinctively happens when you're choked with emotion.

When Blair was less trusted as a politician later in his career, people became suspect of these features of his accent, but it was something he did instinctively to connect with a particular audience.

These trends offer you some useful tips for the way you speak:

- ✔ Feel free to be natural and colloquial in your speech, including your accent.

- ✔ Even on formal occasions, you can dispense with a special formal voice and style; it sounds stilted today.

- ✔ Focus on being understood easily, pronouncing clearly, speaking at a steady pace, and emphasising firmly; and enjoy your accent.

- ✔ If you want to appeal to the widest audience, modify your accent just a little to be more neutral.

Joining a shrinking, ever-changing world

Accents are currently in the melting pot. Film and television have shrunk the world, and as a result people in every English-speaking country are hearing the same accents.

While establishment voices flavoured with traces of strong English cadences still appear throughout the UK, US and Australia, other commonly recognised accents are developing. For example, listen to younger generation broadcasters around the world, and you find that their accents have more in common with each other than with the region or country they come from, including relatively high pitches, fast urban pace, wide pitch variations – a kind of swooping from high to low and back again, a lack of really low notes and extremely strong emphasis.

The energy in such voices is great, but is empty technique unless linked to the message the broadcasters are trying to convey. The best broadcasters employ energy and variety purposefully to underline their points, not as a catch-all technique.

When you speak, use the techniques you discover in this book as means to an end – to express your full meaning. A single vocal technique, albeit a lively energetic one, can't serve for all expression. Use your *whole* vocal toolkit; if you do, you'll communicate powerfully with people.

Changing Your Accent

As I assert in the preceding sections, accents matter much less today than in your parents' time. If you're clear and people can understand you, your accent is *not* the most essential aspect of your voice.

Far more important are sounding alive and interested, showing your feelings and passions in your voice, connecting well with people and empathising with your listeners. The sounds of the emotions and of your inner energy can come across in all accents. Usually your accent only jars with people if you fail to respond to a mood or atmosphere. If you connect well with others, your voice naturally adapts itself to tune in with them. For example, if the conversation is quiet, you moderate your voice; if the subject is serious, your tone takes on gravity; if you're having fun, your voice is lighter and more buoyant. Chapter 15 gives you hints on how to make all these shifts.

Aim to 'fit in' with others vocally in conversation by matching their tone, volume and so on. If you do this, accent no longer matters in 99 per cent of cases.

If you still desire to change your accent, read on.

Wanting to change

Often, all you need in order to change your accent is to *want* to change. Consider the following experiences:

- ✔ The television presenter Joan Bakewell, a grammar school girl from Cheshire, recounts being teased mercilessly by other girls at Cambridge – who had been educated at the top public schools – because of the way she pronounced certain words. She says that after one attack she disappeared into the bathroom and re-emerged with the 'plum in your mouth' accent ready formed. Her simple desire to sound like her peers was sufficient for her to be able to do it. Of course, she also had a good ear, which enabled her to pick up the distinguishing features of the new accent immediately.

- ✔ As a young woman, I taught clarinet at a state school down the Old Kent Road in London. This area is a part of London that used to be deprived – the road features on the London Monopoly board game as the most down-at-heel real estate in London! On my first morning, I realised that I wouldn't last a day in that environment with my cut-glass Surrey accent, and by the end of the day I was matching the east London accent of my pupils pretty well and feeling more in tune. Needs must!

- ✔ A while ago, a family I know moved to the north of England from the southern counties. The parents didn't want their young son to lose his educated accent so they insisted on good pronunciation at home. But he was teased about his posh accent by other children at the local primary school. So, almost immediately, he picked up the vernacular and began to speak in two dialects, one at school and one at home. For the child, having dual dialects was a life-saving strategy.

This strategy can help you too. All you need is a strong desire to fit in with the accent of the people you're speaking to. You need to listen too; if you never listen to other people, you'll never tune in to the way they speak!

Changing through osmosis

For most people, the easiest way to modify your accent is to spend as much time as you can with people who speak in the accent you want to acquire and to speak it yourself as much as you can.

When the American actor Renée Zellweger got the main role in the film *Bridget Jones,* she spent 14 weeks working incognito as a secretary at a publishers in Kensington in London, speaking all the time with an English accent to carry out the deception. She was so successful that at one point one of the girls in the office told her how much she looked like the 'woman in *Jerry Maguire'* (another film she had acted in), without ever suspecting that she was other than a publicity assistant. She reported that during those weeks she went from acute self-consciousness to feeling that she was truly living the role.

Like Renée Zellweger, get into your role. For example, when I was learning Italian, I found that using my hands like my Italian friends and drinking a glass of Chianti really helped the flow of the language! You'll never sound like the chirpy Essex presenter Jonathan Ross (if that's the accent you want) if you stand formally and rigidly like Prince Charles. Adopt the physiology and get in the mood! And practise every moment that you can.

Few people live in a new region or country and keep their own accents untouched unless they have strong motivation to do so. Osmosis always plays its part. Most people accommodate to the sounds of people around them, certainly sufficiently for friends in their former area to notice how their accents have changed when they meet up again. Don't worry though. Congratulate yourself on your ability to tune in, and rest assured that you haven't lost your original accent for good – you can easily 'tune-out' of the new accent again!

Using a coach

A common way to change your accent is to hire a voice coach, a practice that's happening more and more in business, politics and the theatre. The general public reckons that acquiring a convincing new accent is a major challenge, but as in the anecdotes earlier in the section 'Wanting to change' demonstrate, some people do it successfully with little trouble.

Don't attempt to memorise specific pronunciations one by one: you never get to the end of an accent if you go about practising it in this manner! Rather, absorb an accent as a whole. If you want to work with a coach to change your accent, make sure that you do everything you can to take on the world of that accent – with lots of conversation and getting the overall feel of what speaking as part of the new community is like.

The actor Meryl Streep, renowned for her ability to pick up accents, tells a story of how *not* to do it. She once had a coach to help her with the Irish accent. This coach constantly told her little things she was doing wrong, and asked for a bit more emphasis for one specific word, a little more lilt for another and a string of niggling pronunciation details. She says that the result was that she lost confidence, forgot her lines, missed cues – and 'completely forgot the reason for the existence of my character'.

Instead, whether she is becoming Danish (*Out of Africa*), English (Margaret Thatcher in *The Iron Lady*), Italian (*The Bridges of Madison County*), US mid-western (*A Prairie Home Companion*) or Australian (*A Cry in the Dark*) she *lives* the accent, a bit like Renee Zellweger. For *Sophie's Choice,* for example, she went to the lengths of learning the Polish language for four months in order to get a feel for the physical movements required to speak Polish, which helped her to produce a convincing Polish accent in English. But even more than her vocal prowess, Streep lives the character in its entirety with all the person's mannerisms, gestures, and energy – everything that contributes to the whole. Her genius is a matter of tuning-in rather than a bounty of technique. When asked how she reproduces different accents, Meryl Streep apparently replied simply, 'I listen'. Good advice!

Getting the Best of All Worlds: In Praise of Accents

As communication becomes easier, more instant and worldwide, accents are becoming more homogenous. Any popular craze that sweeps the world influences accents enormously. A whole generation of young people picked up the questioning cadence of Australia through watching the TV soap *Neighbours* several times a week. The swoopy cadences of young presenters with their exaggerated emphasis and extreme highs and lows of pitch pop up on television from Los Angeles to London to Sydney. Young executives in the City of London regularly drop the final 't's from words, an unheard practice just 50 years ago.

Communication's rapid and constant change means that you have less to worry about in terms of your accent. The idea of a 'correct' accent has disappeared. A regional accent is no longer the block to advancement it used to be. You can concentrate on communicating with people and enjoy the individuality of your way of speaking.

Your accent is part of your story and continues to be as you live in different places and meet different people. To the acute ear, your accent comes through regardless of your efforts to change it. Every time you speak, you offer a thousand clues to your roots and your journey. Even if you've spent a lifetime away from the village of your birth, someone from that village can probably hear something familiar in the way you speak, particularly when you're under pressure or feeling strongly emotional. It's like a fingerprint. So enjoy it!

By all means lose the worst qualities of your accent, but keep its unique music – this music is part of who you are.

Chapter 13

Conquering Hesitation and Stuttering

*I*n 2010, the popular and critical response to the film *The King's Speech* brought stuttering into the public gaze. (See the sidebar 'Stuttering – a king's story'.)

If you stutter – or *stammer* as people in the UK more frequently call it – you know what a painful and difficult condition it is. I devote a whole chapter to stuttering because the condition causes a high degree of anxiety and embarrassment, and yet has often been misunderstood as a purely physical voice production problem. In reality, stuttering is likely to involve the stutterer's beliefs, perceptions and intentions as much as his or her physical responses. To become fluent, you need to address the problem on all these levels, as I explain in later sections.

This chapter addresses the full range of hesitations from an occasional stumble to a full-blown stutter. Whatever the degree of hesitation, you can do a lot yourself to improve your fluency. I also suggest where you can look for professional help.

Stuttering – a king's story

The popular film *The King's Speech* (2010) tells the story of King George VI of England's battle with stuttering when he came to the throne after the sensational abdication of his brother Edward VIII. A practically unknown speech trainer, Lionel Logue, who had previously worked with shell-shocked soldiers, helped the King – affectionately known as Bertie – beat his lifelong impediment and find his voice.

The story captures the public imagination regardless of where you're from, because Colin Firth in his award-winning performance as Bertie leads to you feel the King's pain, shame and powerlessness towards his condition. When he triumphantly delivers a powerful wartime address to the nation through the new medium of radio, you share the thrill of his victory as well.

Logue – brilliantly portrayed in the film by Geoffrey Rush – used methods that were relatively controversial and untested in the 1930s but are now recognised as effective strategies for combating stuttering.

Hesitating: Realising that Everyone Stumbles

Hesitancy in speech covers a range of different situations, from the occasional slight trip over a word to a full-scale stammer that cripples daily communication. Do you experience any of these milder stumbles?

- ✔ Starting hesitantly if you're uncertain how to answer a question or what to say next.

- ✔ Interjecting an 'er' or 'um' before you find the words that you want to say.

- ✔ Hesitating when you're confused, embarrassed, emotionally upset or overwhelmed.

- ✔ Tripping over your words in your rush to express an idea because your brain works faster than your lips.

- ✔ Leapfrogging from one idea to another in a jerky way because you've so many ideas in your mind.

- ✔ Hesitating due to shakiness from old age or a physical disability such as Parkinson's.

Everyone experiences vocal hiccups at times. Most people don't even notice when they hesitate now and then – but for people who stutter, any stumble can be hell on earth.

If you know that your speech is hesitant and want to do something about it, take the following first steps:

✔ Think more clearly.

✔ Slow down your speech and speak with more emphasis.

✔ Master good breathing.

I cover the first two bullets in the following sections, but I want to highlight the last point briefly. Much hesitation is entirely due to poor breathing. If you develop the ability to breathe better, launching into speech is easier, your words flow more easily and you don't snatch tiny breaths or intersperse 'ers' and 'ums' into your speech. Refer to Chapter 4 for more about effective breathing.

Thinking clearly

Don't be insulted by my next comment! You can avoid much hesitancy just by knowing what you want to say. I'm not suggesting that you don't know *how* to think, but you may not be getting yourself in the right state for good thinking or allowing sufficient time for it.

If you speak before you're ready, you're heading for a cropper. As Abraham Lincoln said, it's 'better to remain silent and be thought a fool than to speak out and remove all doubt.' Yet many people start speaking before they're ready. As soon as someone asks a question or looks at them expectantly, they feel a tension that they can only relieve by launching straight into words. Ironically, though they speak immediately in order to look confident, they usually produce the opposite result.

When you hear people start every sentence with an 'erm' and then slot in an 'um' a few words later, they're probably searching to bring something out from their minds, and because their thoughts do not come quickly enough, they feel they must make sound anyway. In these situations, the mind – not the voice – is creating the hesitation.

Give yourself thinking space. Not only do you speak better, you look more confident when you take your time. Clarity starts with clear thoughts. If your mind is all over the place, you're going to sound muddy. Of course, you don't need to plan in detail the exact words you're going to use, but you do need to think and feel as you breathe in before speaking in order to clarify each thought.

The following activity shows you how to clarify your thinking and, in the process, better focus your speaking. Write a short speech or refer to one you've already written. Then:

1. **Select a sentence or a short section from the piece and read it out loud.**

2. **After you read your statement, imagine someone asking you, 'What did you just say?'**

3. **Look up from your text and give a shorter, simpler version in your own words.**

   If your simpler version is still quite long, repeat the question, 'What did you just say?' and simplify your simpler version yet further.

   For example, in a coaching session Sunish read the following long sentence:

   The regulator for energy companies put simple tariffs and clearer bills at the centre of proposals for a root and branch overhaul of the energy market this afternoon as it warned that deliberately confusing systems is creating a lack of competition in the market, which is certainly indicated by soaring profit margins, which have risen at least 8 per cent on average for consumers in the past six months in spite of opposition.

   In answering the question, 'What did you just say?' Sunish had to think of the main points without reading them and then say them in his own words. This task simplified his statement substantially. I then prompted him, 'What's most important about what you said?' and he simplified even more. After a couple of trial attempts, he came up with this shorter version:

   Fuel bills have risen significantly this year. The regulator suggests that clearer tariffs will increase competition by allowing customers to make easier comparisons.

When you express the main points in your own words, you gain ownership of your material, and most importantly, you *think and speak*, rather than read out words that you crafted earlier. The process hones your thinking and forces to you focus on only the most essential information.

1. **Read through to yourself a five-minute speech until you're familiar with it.**

2. **Look up from the text, and summarise the entire speech in no more than five sentences.**

3. **Test out your summary by having a friend ask you about your speech.**

   Reply out loud: 'It's about . . . ' and share your summary. Remember: five sentences max!

Structure your response

The following activity enables you to clarify your thoughts and speak with confidence. Being creative in the exercise is more important that getting things right, so just have a go. At first you may feel nervous or even intimidated, but after a few rounds your confidence in your ability to respond to questions – even tricky or technical ones – will grow.

Practise with another person. Person A thinks of a subject and asks Person B an open-ended question about it. Person B takes a second or two to consider, then replies with a phrase that introduces and *provides a structure* to what he or she is going to say next.

For example:

Person A: What do you think of wind power?

Person B: (short pause to breathe in and think) I think there are three important points to think about here (Structure = 3 points). The first is . . . , secondly . . . ; and finally, I think it's important to consider . . . .

Or Person B can reply as follows:

Person B: I think there's a strong argument for – and a strong argument against (structure = for and against). An important factor in favour of wind power is . . . . On the other hand, there's a strong argument against that . . . . On balance, I'd say . . . .

Then switch roles; this time Person B thinks of a subject and asks a question about it. For other statement structures, look at Chapter 14.

Try the process several times with the same speech; you should find that the summary becomes increasingly succinct with repetition.

This activity is great practice prior to networking events or meeting new people. Imagine how great you can feel when you're able to respond fluently and concisely the next time someone asks you, 'And what do you do?'

Slowing down and using emphasis

One of the best ways to think more clearly is to convince yourself that you've no need to hurry. The following tips are sure-fire ways to steady your pace without sacrificing your passion.

- ✔ **Take time on the in-breath.** A full breath helps you to slow down and helps your thinking too. Big breath equals big thought. Lots of inadequate tiny breaths on the other hand interrupt your thinking pattern and scatter your thoughts.

- ✔ **Know where you're going energetically.** Have a strong intention to reach the end of your thought and feel this intention in the way you breathe out, using your air to move towards the end of your sentence. When you do this, you're less likely to pepper your speech with 'ums' and 'ahs'. Refer to Chapter 4 for more about following through with your breath.

✔ **Pause.** Listeners enjoy a pause – if only more speakers realised this fact! Without breaks, everything runs together, whereas a pause allows you to punctuate your thoughts and think new ones. Just as the comma and the full stop on a page help the meaning of a written sentence, so a short or longer pause in speaking helps your listeners to make sense of what you have to say.

✔ **Use language that prepares and explains.** Some words and phrases have the purpose of *signposting* where you're going.

In a meeting, instead of offering the main thrust of your thought in your opening words – before people even have a chance to tune in – first provide an introduction to your idea. Use words such as, 'I'd like to add something here', or 'I have an idea I think we should consider'. Short, simple phrases like these let people prepare themselves for what's to follow.

✔ **Use emphasis.** Emphasise the words that are most important for the meaning of the sentence.

Read the following sentence, placing strong emphasis on the italicised words

Emphasising your *main points*
helps you to *slow down*,
to speak with *understanding*,
and to sound *clear* and *confident*.

When you speak a sentence with strong emphasis, you find that you do indeed slow down and sound clear and confident – and that any hesitancy disappears. Whether reading or speaking off the cuff, remind yourself to emphasise strongly, and you find that your delivery becomes better paced and your meaning clearer. (You can find more about using emphasis effectively in Chapter 8.)

Practise reading with emphasis. Read out loud a piece of text from a newspaper. Decide which words are most important for the meaning, and mark them by underlining or highlighting. Then read the text again, emphasising heavily the words you marked.

Discovering the Roots of Stuttering

Stuttering is of a different order from mere hesitation. A person who stutters knows for sure that they have a stutter. Most adults who stutter have struggled with fluency for a long time and find stuttering painful and distressing. They constantly block on particular consonants, struggling to get those sounds out, and often attempting an initial consonant several times without success, producing the typical stutter. This block can also feel like a physical lump in the throat, preventing a stutterer from getting a word out.

ANECDOTE

Fluency tactics of the famous

King George VI isn't the only famous stutterer who found a way to deal with his problem. Many famous people have found remarkable individual ways to overcome or cope with fluency problems.

✔ **Rowan Atkinson**, the comedian best known for his creations Blackadder and Mr Bean, was bullied at school for his appearance and stutter, and still admits to stuttering if he is nervous. However, he discovered that if he played a character other than himself, his stuttering entirely disappeared. You can *just* notice a trace in the deliberate way in which he pronounces words such as 'Bob' in *Blackadder*.

✔ **Aneurin Bevan**, a contemporary of Churchill, and famous for the establishment of the UK National Health Service, also stammered as a child. When he won a college place sponsored by the South Wales Miners' Federation, he forced himself to speak in public as often as possible. He found that he was able to speak most fluently when his passions were highly aroused. He was adept at substituting words to avoid problem sounds and built up a remarkable vocabulary as a result.

✔ **Sir Winston Churchill** grew up with a stutter and continued stuttering into adulthood when he got excited or emotional. As a young man, he gave the condition a positive spin when he wrote, 'Sometimes a slight and not unpleasing stammer or impediment has been of some assistance in securing the attention of the audience.' However, he worked hard to avoid stuttering. His strategy was to put great effort into preparing his speeches word by word weeks in advance, and even into studying responses to possible objections. His speeches are masterpieces of language and design,

and he memorised them, then spoke them slowly and deliberately with gravitas.

✔ **Scatman John,** the jazz musician, had a severe stammer throughout an emotionally traumatic childhood and into adulthood. 'Playing the piano gave me a way to speak,' he claimed. His album *Scatman* begins with a song about stuttering. He claimed that scatting turned his biggest problem into his biggest asset. He shows in a spectacular lyric such as 'Ski-ba-bop-ba-dop-bop-do-be-scu-bid-da-babadebadobaoebdoidan-mbnobbnbnbmbnmnbnbnbmnaoambibao-ibbambma-Bop!' how the strong beat of music completely eliminated his stuttering when he performed.

✔ **James Earl Jones**, an actor with a wonderful deep voice that he used as Darth Vader, had a stutter so bad that he barely spoke to anyone from the age of 5 to the age of 13. He remembers reading his lesson at Sunday school and having all the children behind him falling on the floor with laughter. He is thankful to a high school teacher for discovering his love for writing poetry and getting him to prove that he had written a poem himself by reciting it in front of the class from memory. Gradually, he began to build his confidence. He is now fluent whenever he plays a role, though he still stutters sometimes when speaking spontaneously.

✔ **Marilyn Monroe** admitted to stuttering at times, though not when she was acting. Some film experts say that her famously breathy way of speaking was a way of treating her stuttering; it kept the breath flowing and she used exaggerated mouth movements. Her way of speaking was certainly part of her charm!

Stuttering is very common – 750,000 people stammer in the UK, more than 3 million in the US and an estimated 70 million worldwide. Medical and voice experts have looked into remedies for years.

Recently, specialists have made rapid advances in curing the condition after recognising that stuttering isn't so much a voice problem as a systematic communication problem. For too long experts treated the physical vocal symptoms in isolation, but when you look further into the whole context and examine the causes, you discover an interlocking system of mental and physical causes including behaviours, emotions, perceptions and beliefs that have to be unpicked before you can finally speak fluently.

Getting stuck with the label of 'stutterer'

Stuttering is nearly always triggered by fear at an early age. It's often triggered when children fear they can't fulfil the expectations of authority figures, particularly in reference to speaking. George V, for example, used to show impatience when his son Bertie (King George VI) stumbled, and would bark at him, 'Get it out!' Sometimes, children are frightened by scary kids at school and find their hesitant responses are then ridiculed, exacerbating their fears.

Stuttering only really becomes a problem when you get the label. What starts off as common stumbling develops into something bigger through criticism or ridicule. Sometimes, in spite of excellent intentions, sending a child to a therapist can suggest to the child that something is wrong with him or her. The child then assumes that they have a problem and that the problem has a label: 'stuttering'. They then identify themselves as 'a stutterer'.

If you have a child who hesitates badly, of course you want to seek help from a professional. Be aware though that over-concern on your part, especially when the child is young, can exacerbate the problem. Be happy to accept hesitation in your young child; this hesitation is probably a sign that your child's early language skills are unable to keep up with a bright enquiring intelligence. Given encouragement, your child should soon acquire fluency.

Stuttering becomes a fully-fledged disability when children come to understand that not only is something wrong with their speech, but also that something must be abnormal about *them* in order to create the problem. They internalise and take responsibility for the problem, creating more fear in the process.

After you take on board that you're 'a stutterer', you set yourself up for an intolerable situation in which you think in impossible never-ending circles:

✔ I have to speak, but I can't speak.

✔ I have to stop stuttering, but in trying to stop, I block.

✔ I want to speak, but if I do, I block, so I don't want to speak.

Pip stuttered from early childhood and knew that it disturbed and irritated his parents. At secondary school, he was unable to give his name to his teacher in front of the class on the first day and the other children instantly labelled him stupid. He vividly remembers the agony of reading aloud in English class. He used to work out in advance how many lines each child would be asked to read and, therefore, which lines he was likely to have to recite. He then scoured the lines for tricky consonants before deciding whether to brave it or ask to be excused and leave the room just before his turn. When he became a civil engineer, he became extremely skilled at finding alternative words for ones that were hard to say. Thus, every day of his life, he used his intelligence to mask his difficulties. When he finally discovered ways to avoid blocking and began speaking fluently, he always told people that he was grateful for his former disability. 'I put in hundreds of hours on creative thinking,' he said. 'It certainly taught me to think laterally about problems!'

Creating what you fear most

Putting your attention on what you don't want is a great way to confuse your unconscious mind; every time you think about what you don't want, you create a mental image of the very thing you fear, which then gets larger and larger as a mental block in the mind and becomes ever more likely to happen.

Almost everything that happens in communication with others confirms a stutterer's conviction that something is wrong with them: a teacher doesn't understand properly what a hesitant child is saying and avoids contact; other children don't bother to stop and listen and then don't invite the child to play.

When George VI started as a Royal Navy cadet at Dartmouth, his tutor asked him a simple question: what is half of a half? Bertie was unable to pronounce 'q' for 'quarter' and so froze. The class sniggered and the tutor resorted to sarcasm. In such ways, Bertie came to believe that he was stupid.

If you struggle with stuttering, you may begin to see life through the eyes of 'a stutterer' and doubt your ability in all areas. You sense that you cannot relate to others. You decide that something about you as a person is unacceptable. You become everything you fear most.

If you regard stuttering as the kind of stumbling that everyone does from time to time, it has no power. But stuttering becomes embedded when you make *meaning* of your tendency to stumble, when you allow it to become a fully-fledged abnormality that extends to every part of your life. You come to believe that you're weird or different, that you haven't any friends and that you've no chance of any success in any aspect of your life.

This interpretation of what stuttering means becomes a downward spiral that constantly lowers your self-esteem, feeding on itself in the process. However, you *can* respond differently, as I show in the following section.

Changing Your Focus

Fluency comes when you stop fixating on stuttering. Because thinking about *not* stuttering only intensifies your stuttering; you have to get your mind to pay attention to something – anything – other than the specific words and sounds coming from your mouth.

The following sections cover various ways that you can shift your focus from stuttering to other more useful topics.

Seeking out times when you are fluent

A few years ago, help for people who stutter always focused on attempting to cure the physical manifestations of stuttering. But this approach ignored an important fact. *Nearly all people who stutter have occasions when they don't.*

You most likely stutter when you're acutely aware of other people's expectations and feel under pressure. Perhaps you feel that someone's waiting impatiently for an answer, or you feel a sense of urgency in a phone call, or maybe a conversation is making you tense, or you have to speak in public or to an authority. On these occasions, you get self-conscious and go into 'fear mode'.

If you don't stutter in particular circumstances, then you already know how to speak fluently. So the obvious starting point to look for clues on how to speak fluently is to investigate those times where you're *already* fluent.

Make a list of every occasion when you *don't* stutter – including where, when, how, with whom. The following scenarios may jog your memory. Do you stutter when:

- ✔ You're talking inside your head?
- ✔ You speak out loud at times when you're alone?

> ✔ You talk to your cat or dog?
>
> ✔ You're with close friends?
>
> ✔ It's so noisy you can't hear yourself?
>
> ✔ You feel completely comfortable?

Play the part of a detective and examine these occasions closely. Ask yourself, what are the factors in each situation that allow me to speak fluently? Write down anything useful that comes to mind.

Pretending to be someone else

Some people stutter when they feel self-conscious, but become fluent when they're released from the straitjacket of being themselves and can pretend that they're someone else.

Examples of actors who stutter in private life but not when playing a part abound. I mention Rowan Atkinson, James Earl Jones and Marilyn Monroe in the sidebar 'Fluency tactics of the famous', and other stars include Nicole Kidman, Emily Blunt, Bruce Willis and Anthony Hopkins; numerous public figures are much less fluent in interview than on stage.

Watch online unedited video clips of your favourite celebrities or public figures being interviewed. You quickly see that these larger than life figures are people too – who speak with pauses, hesitations and ordinary verbal mis-steps.

Alan Badmington, a former stutterer who won the international oratory championship at the World Congress for People Who Stutter in 2004, encountered countless difficulties in his former career as a police officer. Yet he recalls playing the part of Goldilocks in a pantomime he wrote himself for a Christmas party, and having no problem with stuttering whatsoever. Badmington's Goldilocks was assertive and spoke fluently; whereas Badmington as himself was shy and reserved – and stuttered. His problem was one of identity not fluency.

In a similar way, parents of children who stutter often note that when their children have their teddies talk, the stutter disappears. Of course, if teddy makes a mistake, that reflects badly on teddy, not the child! The phenomenon is similar to the actor in a role: when it's not 'me', there's no stutter.

1. **Choose a celebrity figure or character who you admire as a communicator.**

2. **Step into that person's shoes.**

   Pretend to be that person. Stand, move, gesticulate, adopt the expressions and even try to think and feel and breathe like the person. Take your time to get into being the other person.

3. **Speak as that person speaks.**

Make the kind of comments the person makes. If you like, imagine that you're that person in interview, and tell the interviewer about your latest project, about how you became famous, or about what you're looking forward to. The more you can make the pretence real, the easier it becomes to speak.

When you next need to speak as yourself, notice what elements of this practice you can take into your own speaking, without having to adopt a different persona in his or her entirety.

Singing

The speech therapist Lionel Logue got King George VI to sing phrases that he was having difficulty speaking, and the King found that he was fluent in song. Before his coronation speech, Logue even encouraged the King to take singing lessons.

Singing has various things going for it from the point of view of people who stutter:

✔ When a person who stutters sings, rhythm takes precedence over fluency and consonant sounds. As soon as rhythm takes the attention over everything else, blocking is released.

✔ Breathing also takes place rhythmically. Sound follows breath directly, with no hiatus. You breathe within the rhythm of the music and break into song within the rhythm.

✔ You've no time to worry about the initial beat because the next beat comes hard on its heels. If you have rhythm in your veins, you'll find it quite hard to sing un-rhythmically. The pulse of rhythm is such a strong impulse within you that it overcomes any impulse to block.

Quite a few professional singers stutter. The singer and song writer Carly Simon turned to song for release when she felt blocked at the age of eight. The operatic baritone Robert Merrill was probably offered singing lessons in the first place as a child because he stuttered. Scatman John had an almost superhuman fluency in rhythm.

ANECDOTE

The young English singer-songwriter Gareth Gates first appeared on the scene as a petrified contestant in the first series of the UK TV talent show *Pop Idol* in 2001. He went on to become runner-up, sell more than 3.5 million records in the UK alone and become a popular live performer in musical theatre. In his audition, he was unable to pronounce his name and had to tell the panel from the outset that he had a stuttering problem. There was something extraordinary in watching the young man go from embarrassing blocking straight into fluent song. For him, rhythm was the difference between disability and talent.

A similar effect of unlocking happened in 2011, when the English National Ballet commissioned Roehampton University to conduct research into the effects of dancing for Parkinson's sufferers. Researchers noticed remarkable results from patients moving to rhythm and music.

1. **Find a song with a catchy tune you know well.** 'When the Saints Go Marching In' has a good strong rhythm ideal for this purpose.

2. **Sing the song with plenty of gusto, beating out the rhythm with your foot.** Don't worry about getting it perfect; strong rhythm and enthusiastic energy are all that's needed.

3. **Get the rhythm going again with your foot, but this time *say* the words in rhythm instead of singing them.** Again, strong rhythm and enthusiasm are the only requirements.

4. **Sing the first line of the tune in silence to a good beat, and for the second line, instead of the song lyrics, launch into a spoken comment.**

   (Line 1 sung in silence): 'O when the saints go marching in, o when the saints go marching in.'

   (Line 2 starting when the tune starts, but with spoken words) 'I want to tell you all a story.'

Getting it out with bad language

Many people who stutter admit that they never stutter when they swear. In swearing, you utilise two important factors for fluency:

✔ When you swear, you're already breaking a barrier – you've already moved beyond the powerful inhibitor of caring what others think. In a memorable scene in *The King's Speech*, Logue deliberately provokes the King to swear.

Incidentally, there's an interesting correlation between the favourite initial consonants for swear words and the consonants that people who stutter find hard to say – 'f', 'c' and 'b' for instance!

✔ The powerful emotion that makes you swear carries you straight from breath into language. The emotion of anger is more powerful than the inhibitor of fear, so you don't block.

Go to Chapter 7 for examples of Shakespearean insults to practice loudly without offending your neighbours. Notice the strong mental energy you can bring to the insults and try using similar energy for other strong (but acceptable!) comments such as, *Go for it! Now or never!* and *Seize the day!*

Being among friends

Many people who normally stutter find that they're fluent when they feel comfortable among friends and family or with pets. Similarly, many children easily talk to their toys or an invisible friend. Lewis Carroll (Charles Dodgson) stammered in the company of adults but not with young girls because he felt more comfortable with them.

When you're among friends, anxiety is low, and other energies, such as trust, curiosity and connection, come into play. You're completely absorbed in interacting with others and don't have time to focus on how you're performing. You're no longer involved in a test; you're in a relationship.

In a scene late in *The King's Speech*, Logue encourages King George VI before his broadcast to the nation to speak just to him as a friend. In fact, the whole of his coaching has been about promoting the idea of a friendship between equals.

Gentle support and friendship is the idea behind the Speaking Circles International program (www.speakingcircles.com), founded in 1989 by Lee Glickstein. Glickstein was a shy child from Brooklyn, who suffered agonies of self-consciousness that escalated into bad stage fright. Yet, he had a secret desire to be a stand-up comedian. He now observes that fear seems to be most extreme among the very people who are drawn to be in the limelight and points to Winston Churchill as a prime example. Glickstein believes that it's possible that children who stutter or suffer badly from shyness are protecting their gifts for communicating behind symptoms. (In my own work, I notice too often for chance, that people who are most hesitant at public speaking in the beginning are often those who have the potential to speak with the greatest passion and energy.) In Glickstein's current work, he gets groups to focus on the quality of relationship between speaker and audience and to foster a warm connection.

Look at Chapter 15 for tips on tuning in to other people. You find that as you focus on the other person instead of on yourself, fears of non-fluency melt away.

Avoiding self-judgement

Blocking doesn't become a firm habit in the initial phase of frequent stumbling. As I describe in the earlier section 'Discovering the Roots of Stuttering', blocking happens when people who stutter become self-critical and have feelings *about* what they feel. This blocking is one of the reasons that someone who is hesitant often finds speaking off the cuff easier, whereas waiting in a line of people to do a self-introduction can be sheer hell – too much time to build up self-consciousness and self-criticism!

In *The King's Speech,* Lionel Logue's first act with King George VI is to prove to him that the King can speak fluently by asking him to read a passage out loud while wearing earphones blaring out loud music. Bertie can read this passage fluently because he is unable to hear himself and criticise his hesitations.

Alan Badmington acquired a device that blocked out the sound of his voice by emitting a loud buzzing sound every time he spoke. He wore the device every day for about 20 years, and it allowed him to speak adequately in front of groups. Although it achieved the purpose of preventing him from hearing himself, the device also created unpleasant side effects such as headaches. He eventually found more holistic remedies such as those described in this chapter. The device's success however shows that when self-criticism is absent, stuttering doesn't happen. Any work you can do on thinking positively and quietening your critical inner voice will bear fruit in terms of your fluency. You may like to start with a few ideas from *Confidence For Dummies* by Kate Burton and Brinley Platts (Wiley), which contains a wealth of useful material.

Changing Your Thinking

People who stutter and their speech therapists have in the past tended to aim towards an outcome of non-stuttering by treating the *symptoms* – as if being physically fluent were the cure to everything. This approach aims in the wrong direction. Given that people who stutter can at times speak fluently, their problems are not solely physical. Becoming fluent requires you to look wider.

The best book I have read on overcoming stuttering is *I Have a Voice: How to Stop Stuttering* (Crown House Publishing, 2011) by Bob G Bodenhamer. This important book takes the fruits of Bodenhamer's own practice and research, plus the latest thinking on the subject to provide a pathway to success that can be adapted to the individual. Although you can work on many of his processes on your own, you need to work with a professional on some of the processes he describes. An experienced neuro-linguistic programming (NLP) practitioner specialised in voice work can help.

In Bodenhamer's view, success depends on realising that you have the capacity to change your *thinking* about stuttering – a powerful process that I outline in the following sections.

Challenging your feelings

Stuttering has a physical effect – a lump or block in your throat, jaw, neck or chest. But the physical effect is caused by emotional fears – of not meeting expectations, of not being smart enough or fast enough, of others' judgements, of stuttering itself and of the ensuing disaster.

Stuttering may feel like a physical problem but the place to start to find a remedy is with the *feelings* that give rise to the blocking.

Feelings aren't simple; they're a complex package with layers of feelings and feelings about those feelings. Generally, for stutterers, in the first layer are anxiety, self-consciousness, hopelessness and helplessness; in the second line are anger, frustration and resentment *about* the first feelings. These secondary feelings can be even stronger than the primary emotions.

A simple emotional trigger on its own can fire off the whole show, like the master fuse on a fireworks display, causing you to block. Trouble may start with someone staring at you, waiting for an answer. This situation creates self-consciousness in you, which triggers anxiety, which makes you feel helpless, and then you start feeling angry and frustrated with yourself . . . off goes the fuse and you stutter.

The stress of your condition gives you tunnel vision, so that stuttering becomes the be all and end all, with no before and after, and no limit to its scope. You begin to catastrophise and attach powerful meaning to small moments:

Trigger	Meaning
I stutter.	Something is profoundly wrong with me, and I am a bad person.
I just slipped.	I've always stuttered and I always will at all times and in all places. I must always try to play safe.
I feel nervous just now.	In all places, I will always stutter and make a fool of myself.
People didn't get what I said.	I haven't got friends, no one likes me, I'm rejected and alone for all time. I can't ever assert myself.
I feel nervous.	All my feelings create problems for me. It isn't safe to have strong feelings about anything ever.

The remedy is to challenge these beliefs one by one. Take the following steps:

1. **Challenge the all-consuming importance of fluency.**

   Remind yourself that your life is more than fluency. There is more to life than consciousness of self.

2. **Challenge your low self-worth.**

   Stuttering does not mean that you're also stupid or worthless or completely inadequate as a human being. Remind yourself that you're an intelligent, capable and worthwhile person.

3. **Challenge your thinking about relationships.**

   Stuttering does not prevent excellent relationships. Plenty of people who stutter have good friends.

4. **Challenge your dependence on the good opinion of others.**

   Develop your internal reference so that you don't depend on others so much for your sense of well-being. Start noticing what is working well in your life – all those small successes and happy moments.

5. **Challenge your hopelessness.**

   Success is possible; many have achieved it. Start to believe in your fluency. You're not powerless.

6. **Challenge your feeling about stress.**

   It's okay to make mistakes. In fact it's impossible for any intelligent person not to! You're sometimes calm, so you know how to be calm. (Turn to Chapter 5 to get started.) You're not helpless.

Challenge these beliefs one by one. Working on some of them with a competent coach is a good move. The International Coach Federation has lists of qualified coaches, many of whom can help you with this kind of work (www.coachfederation.org).

Choosing your emotional state

Emotions lie right at the heart of the problem of stuttering. One great tool in your search for fluency is the realisation that you don't have to be stuck with negative feelings. You can change your emotional state at any given moment – as long as you:

- Know what state you're looking for.
- Know what it feels like to be in the state you want.

This activity helps you experience and then choose your emotional state:

1. **Discover your current emotional state.**

   Perhaps you feel panicky. Great. Feel that feeling.

2. **Take a big breath, and release air quite strongly, letting go of that feeling.**

   Shake your shoulders and body as well to change your state.

3. **Consider what state you would like instead – maybe calm.**

   Remember a time in a different context when you were in a state of calm.

4. **Recreate that state of calm.**

   See, hear and feel in the same way you saw, heard and felt when you were calm. Enter into that state of calmness, with calm breath, calm pictures, calm sounds, calm thoughts and calm feelings. Enjoy its quietness and peace. Get to know every feature and quality of being in this state so that you can return to it whenever you want.

5. **Run forward in your mind to a time when you're likely to feel panic.**

6. **Breathe in the state of calm that you now know well.**

   Remind yourself: calm breath, calm pictures, calm sounds, calm thoughts and calm feelings. Enjoy your new state.

Repeat this practice with other feelings you prefer instead of your current negative feelings. Try it with courage, determination, trust, relaxation and flow – or any state of your own choosing.

During Step 3, think of your emotional state when you're in conversation with friends or during another time when you're fluent. Get to know in your body and bones as well as your mind what this state feels like.

How you feel is a choice. You have the power to choose.

Speaking with passion

Many people who stutter employ a strategy of extreme caution when they speak, and go slowly, carefully choosing words that are easier to say. But sometimes the best remedies are counterintuitive, and passion is one of these. Allowing your passion free rein may seem risky, but doing so can be your salvation as a speaker (see the sidebar 'Passionate release').

ANECDOTE

Passionate release

Lloyd came to me with a stutter he had tried to fix with every strategy in the book for more than 20 years. He had considerable determination and energy and had recently been promoted to a senior position in his organisation. But he was worried about having to give more speeches in the higher profile role. I spent time with him doing various activities designed mainly to make him feel as much at ease as possible, yet his speech continued to be hesitant.

Lloyd told me that he had been invited to his first board meeting and was concerned about stuttering there. With deliberate provocation, I suggested that maybe his promotion didn't mean much and that there probably wasn't much point in his being on the board anyway. He strongly disagreed with me. 'What is the point then?' I asked somewhat disparagingly. 'What's so important that these people need

to know from you?' 'The point?!' he burst out. 'There's so much we could be doing!'

He proceeded to give me a passionate account of all the things he wanted to change – as well as why the changes would make a difference to the organisation and its people. His stuttering practically disappeared altogether, and where it remained it seemed a normal consequence of excitement.

Lloyd told me afterwards that in that moment of passion he experienced an 'aha' moment. He explained that he had always enjoyed speaking spontaneously more than speaking with a script, but had felt that he must prepare excessively to guard against stuttering errors. Whereas, by guarding himself *less* and allowing his passion free rein, the risk paid off and he became more fluent.

TIP

Take a risk. Allow yourself to be passionate about something outside yourself. The strong flow of passion carries your words along powerfully.

The power of passion can squash feelings of anxiety, as the British Labour politician Aneurin Bevan found. The son of a miner, he was a passionate fighter for workers' rights and against the British class system. He found fluency in passion. When he became passionate, his thoughts and emotions were focused entirely on something outside himself, and as a result his stammer disappeared.

George VI had a similar experience when he gave his most famous wartime address. Even as a severe stutterer, with Logue's support he found his genuine passion and it carried him through.

REMEMBER

Passion has energy and movement in it. Stuttering is the opposite. Your intention to speak instructs the diaphragm to lower to allow you to breathe, but at the same time your anxiety contracts the diaphragm upwards. Your opposing intentions cancel each other out and the result is a frozen diaphragm, unable to move in any direction. See Chapter 4 for more details on your diaphragm.

When you're passionate, you breathe in the passion, and its energy goes straight into expression with no pause between. Moreover, as passion is a whole-body emotion, you take a full strong breath using your diaphragm and lower muscles. This energy follows through into sound.

You don't have to wait for passion to come upon you. Activating your passion is something you can practise. Find body movements that have an energetic flow to them such as:

- ✓ Swinging your arm forwards in a big vertical circle up and above your head and then *down* again in a broad sweep past your thigh.

- ✓ Taking a big step forward and bending your leg as you *land*.

- ✓ Raising both arms together in front of you and then sweeping them *down* past your thighs curving outwards at the end, bending your knees when the arms reach their lowest point.

Now find something you want to say with passion, take a full passionate breath with the upward movement, and say your words with passion as the movement comes downwards strongly to its lowest point. If you like, start with just one word, like 'Wow!' or 'Yes!' Then try the movement with a sentence.

Focus your action on outcome and moving inexorably towards 'Wow!'– or whatever you want to say. There's no fixed position where in-breath finishes and out-breath/sound starts – the process is continuous, like the broad sweep of your swinging arm.

Try this practice saying something quite softly as well as loudly. The energy remains almost the same regardless of volume. You find other useful material on unlocking your voice in Chapter 11.

Expanding your frame

People who stutter often make their own experiences the sum total of everything. Change comes in expanding your *frame of reference*.

- ✓ Remind yourself that there's more of you than this stuttering. You're also a person who speaks fluently, has passions, determination and so on. You have flexibility.

- ✓ Integrate other people and their perceptions into your frame. Stop trying to read others' minds and really step into the shoes of others to check the truth.

- ✓ Step outside yourself and look at the situation from the moon. From that great distance, how important is hesitation really?

Using neuro-linguistic programming (NLP) techniques

In order for you to stutter, some physical stumbles connected with your emotions have influenced your perceptions and your beliefs, resulting in habitual responses that have lives of their own and feel out of your control. You'll find it positively affirming if you stutter to gain understanding of how you stutter instead of remaining confused and out of control.

Your responses are within your control, provided that you look beyond the physical blocking to the whole system that supports the stuttering behaviour. Try any and all the following (NLP) techniques to begin taking control of your responses:

Practitioners of NLP and associated disciplines have been particularly successful at looking at stuttering as a system and developing models that can help the stutterer. Every person who stutters is different, and therefore different models are more effective for different people.

- ✔ **Circle of Excellence** permits you to develop more resourceful states of mind, such as calm, control, flexibility, positivity and so on.

- ✔ **Perceptual Positions** encourage you to take different perspectives and open up from your tunnel vision to see matters in a clearer, more balanced way.

- ✔ **The Phobia Cure** allows you to dissociate from the fear-based elements of stuttering and therefore avoid falling into the 'black hole' of your feelings.

- ✔ **Positive By-Products** allows you to understand the positive motivations behind blocking behaviours, such as protecting yourself from hurt, gaining control, getting back at people in authority and so on. Seeing how stuttering served a purpose, you can find alternative and less harmful ways to achieve your intentions. Bob Bodenhamer explores this search and other NLP techniques in his book on stuttering mentioned earlier in this section.

- ✔ **Re-imprinting** involves going back to the point in childhood when stuttering began and establishing new beliefs at that point to take with you through life.

- ✔ **The Swish Pattern** interrupts your habit of stuttering at the very point at which you decide to block and puts in place a different, more useful habit.

You can find details about these techniques and many other useful resources in *Neuro-Linguistic Programming For Dummies* by Romilla Ready and Kate Burton (Wiley). Working with a trained NLP coach boosts the effectiveness of all the processes I introduce in this chapter.

Part V
Engaging with a Broader Public

The 5th Wave   By Rich Tennant

"Moses! Indoor voice! Indoor voice!"

In this part . . .

So you have to give a speech? Here you find useful know-how for presenting and public speaking. You discover the magic art of connection used by the greatest speakers. I introduce you to the particular talking skills needed in different jobs to help you in your professional life.

Chapter 14

Developing Your Public Voice

· ·

In This Chapter

▶ Preparing and sharing a speech

▶ Pitching your voice for politics

▶ Responding to tough questions

▶ Developing media skills

· ·

As soon as you move from talking to one person to addressing a group of any size, new dynamics come into play as you can no longer rely on direct cues from the other person that they're engaged. In a group, different members may react differently. Nor can you apply your natural conversational habits with the give and take of normal dialogue and one-to-one eye contact.

For some people, speaking in public is no big deal. They alternate happily from speaking to one person to addressing a group. But if you dread speaking in front of people, you may feel as if you're acting or showing off, and find yourself faltering in confidence.

From meetings and interviews to presenting, negotiating, selling or giving a wedding speech, you need to be able to cross the divide between communicating effectively with an audience of one or two, and a group. In the following sections, I guide you into the public arena and share all my best tips for connecting with groups.

Crossing from Private to Public

In spite of outward appearances, the most important aspects of speaking are the same whether you're communicating with one person or many. Basically, you need to have something to say, build a good connection with your listeners and be heard and understood. It's a matter of finding out how to do these things in a larger space with people further away.

One-to-one, you can spot minute changes in your listener's eyes as he or she expresses different feelings. But when your listeners are a dozen metres away – or half the world away on the other end of a teleconference – you miss those subtle variations.

When speaking to an audience, you have to use a few different skills for them to catch the nuances of what you want to get across. The best professional performers know how to connect strongly with an audience, and you can too.

Filling the space

Have you ever encountered someone famous in a context where you don't expect to see them – a well-known actor walking down a street for instance? And did you think, 'Oh, they were much smaller than I thought they were going to be!'? A good actor has the ability to 'grow' on stage.

I watched the legendary singer Placido Domingo in a documentary film prepare himself in the wings before going out to meet a vast audience in a Roman amphitheatre. He paced up and down for a few minutes, wringing his hands and looking quite agitated. Then he paused, composed himself, took a large breath and crossed over the threshold. As he crossed into the public space, he became huge in stature, graceful, and exuded confidence. He took a large breath with a strong sense of purpose to cross the threshold from private space to public space.

Follow Domingo's example. Take a big breath and fill yourself with expansive energy before you speak to an audience. You're more powerful than you may imagine. In a larger space, your audience needs to be more aware of you physically, so try the following:

- ✔ Make your movements slower and more definite. Make any gestures more obvious.

- ✔ Speak clearly, especially the ends of words and ends of sentences. In Chapter 6, I share ways to make your diction clear.

- ✔ Give lots of space to your words – slow down! See Chapter 7 for more on rhythm and pacing.

- ✔ Think of your voice waves spreading out from you and resonating in all directions and not just straight forward from your mouth. I explain more about resonance in Chapter 9.

Don't give in to the temptation to push your voice out in order to be heard. Doing so just makes you smaller and less effective. Besides, it's not good for your voice.

If you can, try out the room where you are to speak to a group before the event. Stand in the space and breathe in, imagining that you're breathing in the whole space from wall to wall. Breathe out, and imagine that your mouth is a spray can and your breath a steady stream of coloured paint with which you cover the walls. This activity gives you a physical sense of how much energy and breath you need to reach everyone who'll be sitting in that space. Then use the same amount of breath to practise speaking in the space for a few moments.

The improvisation teacher Keith Johnstone talks about the subject of status in his classic book on improvisation for actors, *Impro* (Routledge, 1987). High-status people dominate a group whereas low-status people shrink and look small. His descriptions of high and low status offer a few useful tips to follow if you want to command your space. The following table describes and contrasts high and low status, so you can be aware of what to avoid – as well as what to emulate! Try out his suggestions from both columns yourself while you speak. Exaggerate them for fun and see what happens!

High Status	*Low Status*
Keep head still and high.	Waggle head about.
Make your movements smooth.	Make jerky movements.
Hold eye contact for a second or so.	Glance briefly, then look away.
Take time to breathe deeply.	Grab short high breaths.
Use arms openly and freely.	Keep touching your face.
Imagine that you're on a hilltop with a view.	Imagine that you're cramped in a tunnel.
Speak in long smooth lines.	Speak in short bursts.

Stepping up your energy

As you move into larger spaces and bigger audiences, you need higher energy.

- ✔ Before you speak, get your energy moving by warming up: walk fast, shake your hands vigorously; energetically move all parts of your body.
- ✔ Imagine that you're about to run a race. Feel the physical energy vibrating inside you as you stand there ready to speak.
- ✔ As you breathe in, feel yourself grow in stature.
- ✔ Imagine that you're the centre of your world, and that everything you say spreads out from you through 360 degrees, powerfully and easily.

Now speak, and feel the sense of excitement and power.

You're speaking for yourself and to each individual in your audience; beyond that imagine that you're speaking to a wider universe. Know for sure that you're tall and confident enough to do that.

Acknowledging that you're still you

After reading the preceding sections, your fears may be telling you that you're *not* sufficiently tall, big, expanded or any of the rest of the things I describe. But speaking up doesn't require you to be something you're not. Often, people fear that speaking to a group demands some sort of exhibitionism that they lack. They get the idea that their job is to impress people. It isn't.

You don't need a special voice or manner – you can still be you. In fact, nothing is as convincing, moving and impressive as someone being him or herself.

But which 'you' are you going to choose? The 'you' that slouches bleary eyed to the bathroom on the morning after a night before; or the 'you' that is having a great time and enjoying yourself?

Think of an occasion when you're having a great time – laughing with friends, arguing pleasurably with someone, trekking in the hills. What represents *you* having a great time? Get to know the 'you' of those times by asking yourself the following:

✔ What am I feeling and thinking at that time?

✔ How am I standing, sitting or holding myself?

✔ How is my energy level?

That's the you I'm talking about – the best of you!

Return often to the feeling you have at these good times so that you get to know it and can recreate it when you want. Then, when you step in front of a group to speak, remember and recreate that good feeling. Even just a trace of that good feeling can make all the difference to how you look at your audience and how you embark on your speech.

Giving That Speech

In days before the printed word, people communicated almost entirely with their voices. Even a hundred years ago, children remembered texts by heart and recited them out loud in class. Now it's all Internet, Twitter and Facebook, and people don't get as much voice practice. Yet, voice still matters.

If you can speak successfully in public, you still have a big advantage when participating in presentations, roundtable talks, pitches, debates, campaigns, advocacy and more. Public speaking is a skill, and one that you can pick up, refine – and enjoy. Success starts with getting in the right frame of mind.

Dealing with nervousness

Nerves are the most common block in public speaking. Every public speaker at some time or another has to face stage fright, performance anxiety – whatever you call it. Following are some of my top suggestions to help you feel more comfortable when you speak to a group:

- ✔ **Realise that every speaker feels nervous at times, and nerves don't matter as long as they don't block you.** An audience isn't as aware of nerves as you are. As a seasoned veteran once advised the nervous beginner, 'It's fine to have butterflies – as long as they fly in formation!'

- ✔ **Get to know your audience, if you can.** Talk to people casually before you begin speaking, or at least hear the buzz of their chatter to get a feeling of their mood. Even if you're speaking to a group of people you know well, make time to get a sense of the current mood of the people you're about to speak to. See the later section 'Knowing why you're speaking' for more ways to figure out your audience. Chapter 15 features some useful ideas on connecting with your audience.

- ✔ **Have a route map for what you're going to say.** You don't have to know precisely, but have a general structure and know what matters to you. See the later section 'Deciding How to Prepare' for several ways to get ready to present important information.

- ✔ **Imagine success.** Paint a mental picture of you walking on confidently and speaking strongly and clearly. Hear the enthusiastic response of your listeners. Concentrate always on what you want – not what you don't want.

- ✔ **Relax.** Release tension from your shoulders, neck, facial muscles, arms, legs and stomach (see Chapter 5). Say to yourself before you begin, 'I am enough.' You are, indeed, enough.

My book on how to deal with your nerves – *Butterflies and Sweaty Palms: 25 Sure Fire Ways to Speak and Present with Confidence* (Crown House Publishing, 2012) – gives you lots of ideas for dealing with performance anxiety.

Knowing why you're speaking

A speech is never just about facts. You always need to know *why* you're speaking and *how* the audience will get what you want for them. This knowledge is the main key to sounding interesting and engaging any audience.

The first question to ask yourself is 'What am I actually trying to achieve?' or 'Why am I doing this?' Don't worry if the your answer is simple – it probably should be! For example, if you're to give a wedding speech, the answer may be, 'To make people laugh and feel good.'

If your first answer to the question doesn't satisfy you, probe further. Ask yourself the question again with reference to the answer you've just given: Continue until you arrive at an answer that's compelling. The final answer determines what you're there for, and also gives clues as to how to connect with the audience, so that they get from your speech what you want them to.

Before her conference speech, Amanda asked herself, 'What am I trying to achieve?' Looking over her brief, she came up with, 'To give information about my department.' Not very compelling, so she asked herself again, 'Why give information about my department?' For a moment, to her consternation, she had no answer to this. Then she realised it was, 'To show what fantastic work my team does.' Thinking further, she asked, 'Why show what fantastic work my team does?' and came up with, 'To build the morale and motivation of everyone.' Suddenly, with this statement, she was clear about what she was aiming at and about the reaction she wanted from her audience. She also felt an energy and excitement about giving her speech because her aim was in line with her thoughts and feelings on the subject.

To know why you're speaking, get to know the world of your listeners.

1. **Sit quietly for a moment, relax, think about your audience; in your mind,** *become* **a representative member of the audience.**

   Sit in the way they would sit and imagine that you're watching the speaker (that's you!). Hear what the audience has to say. Ask:

   • How is the presentation going for you as audience?

   • What are your thoughts about what you see and hear?

   • How do you feel as you watch and hear the speaker?

   • What is working well for you as you watch and listen?

   • What else do you need from the speaker?

2. **Break off from imagining by taking a big breath to clear yourself of those thoughts as an audience member.**

   Enter into your own skin again.

3. **Reflect on what you discovered.**

   What will you change as speaker in response to those discoveries?

Telling tales: Stories, anecdotes and metaphors

If you want your listeners to remember what you say, you can't just give them the facts. You need to engage their emotions.

A great way to engage their emotions is to tell a story. Whether you want to motivate, reassure, galvanise or inspire, a story will do it. Adults and children are all hardwired for stories.

I remember well the presentation given by Gina. She was extremely tense as she went through the various bulleted items on her demonstration with presentation software. I saw stiffness in her shoulders and awkward movements, and her voice was tightly controlled. That is, until she reached point number five – 'Field Experiments'. She suddenly laughed. 'Oh, I was involved in the experiments in Sweden. We had such an amazing time over there! Challenging too . . . I can't tell you how cold it was when we had to go out at night – but beautiful in winter too! And we got the results we were looking for. . . . ' Gina was suddenly immersed in her memory and switched to story mode. The differences were marked.

✔ She sounded genuine as she told a real story about real people.

✔ Her voice and body language became alive and animated.

✔ She was suddenly on the same wavelength as her audience, and they relaxed and began to enjoy themselves.

Afterwards, we remembered that part of Gina's presentation the most.

A great benefit about stories is that you don't tend to forget your next word – the story carries you along. You get to step away from your script or outline (see the following section 'Deciding How to Prepare') and speak casually yet compellingly.

You can purposefully make your key facts more interesting by turning them into stories – or by incorporating metaphors that have the liveliness of stories.

You can find stories and metaphors everywhere, in what you read, on television and in film, and in your everyday experiences. John watched his boss and thought how like a lion he looked, which gave him the idea of discussing people's characteristics in terms of animals in a speech. Celia was overtaken dangerously by a driver in a hurry who knocked his car on a traffic bollard in his effort to get ahead, which gave her an anecdote for her speech about whether the end justifies the means in business. Keep your eyes open, your curiosity aroused and a notepad at the ready and you'll soon have lots of effective and amusing stories and metaphors to use appropriately.

A finance director chose to make his point this way: 'We've been cruising happily down the river for a while, haven't we?' he asked his audience of insurance brokers. 'But then, the waves knocked half the paddles out of our hands just as we met the rapids. What a journey it's been the past six months! How we missed the large rocks, I'll never know. The giant wave of world events just hurtled us onwards. But the gorge widened a little, and we are paddling again, not as fast as before, but at least we are now in charge of our direction and see calm waters ahead.'

Deciding How to Prepare

You can prepare a speech in fine detail with hours of research, planning and practice and still meet the unexpected when you come to present your material to an audience.

Preparation is certainly useful and can make you feel more secure, but experience is even more valuable. You get better with more practice. The more spontaneous a speaker seems, the more hours of experience he or she has usually had.

When Barack Obama was a presidential candidate, he visited a school where he heard two eighth grade students give presentations. Obama told them he was impressed by their speaking, and then confessed that he himself had improved only with practice. 'I needed 15 months and some coaching before I was able to perform as well as they did,' he said. And some!

How you prepare for a presentation or a speech depends on your purpose, mode of delivery, the importance and type of occasion, the size of the audience, your time for preparation and your own preferences. However you decide to deliver your speech, stepping into your audience's shoes is a good first step to understanding what they hope to get from what you say.

Next, decide whether you're going to work from notes, read a full script, memorise it by heart, or at the opposite extreme, speak entirely off the cuff. I cover each option in the following sections.

Relying on notes

Speaking from notes is *not* reading full sentences. It means that you write down just headings and subheadings, key phrases to remind you of stories, and critical facts and figures that you need to remember.

You may be tempted to plump for notes when you give a speech and end up over-egging the notes in an effort to prevent yourself forgetting anything. *This approach doesn't work.* If you have too many words in your notes, you struggle to find the right place when you glance down for a cue, so your notes end up being useless. Or worse, you resort to reading them, which doesn't sound right as they weren't designed for reading aloud.

If you want to sound genuine and spontaneous, use notes rather than a full script. You use different parts of your brain to read and think, and using notes means that you have to think and compose your sentences on the spot, which comes across as more real. You create better contact with your audience too.

Design your notes in whatever way makes the information most accessible for *you*. Choose cards that don't shake and rustle rather than sheets of paper. I like to make the print larger than normal for easy reference. Other people use different-sized text for items of varying importance, and arrange the information on the page in ways that demarcate various sections more clearly. Some even mark the notes with highlighters to bring out particular points. Do whatever works for you.

Reading out loud

Speaking from notes is often not possible. Many political and business speeches must be read verbatim in order to:

- ✔ Ensure accuracy on important occasions.
- ✔ Release information at a specific time.
- ✔ Repeat details in official press releases and statements.

✔ Provide speakers opportunity to practise so their words are perfect and 'slip-proof'.

✔ Cut out nasty surprises – on the whole!

Despite the preceding benefits, few speakers can read a speech and sound genuinely authentic and interesting. Most people sound less spontaneous and less personal, and connect less well with their audience.

Reading out loud well takes special skill. Here are some of the essentials:

✔ Stay calm and breathe (see Chapters 4 and 5).

✔ Give what you say strong emphasis, just as you would in spontaneous speech. Most people emphasise much less strongly when they read a text. See Chapter 8 for more on effective emphasis.

✔ Practise your speech out loud, not in your head, to get the rhythm of the words and pause at the most appropriate moments.

✔ Say the text in different ways each time you practise in order to keep it fresh. It's all too easy to get into predictable patterns of speech that sound more tedious each time you practise. Play with altering your speed, rhythm, pitch and pauses each time you read the text, and new, better ways to express your message will emerge.

✔ Slow your speech down in order to give yourself plenty of time between looking up to speak and looking down to read the next piece of text.

✔ Think about what you're saying by following thoughts, not sentences. Use the written punctuation to move the thought from pause to pause.

✔ Look well ahead so that you can follow long thoughts. Even with a long thought, you've plenty of time to breathe and pause. Just keep the whole thought in your mind so that you keep moving and follow through.

The opposite of following a thought through is reading with expression – quite another thing. Reading with expression is reading where every time you come to an *interesting* word you give it *special* EXPRESSION, with added *emphasis* or raised **pitch** or other Significant but random *colouring* that doesn't add to the sense or direction of the thought. Don't be tempted to do that. It just sounds like amateur reading.

If you want examples of such 'expressive' voices, listen to certain commentators in the media who swoop up and down in a naive attempt to be varied and interesting. I heard a young news announcer recently announce the sudden death of a celebrity in the same chirpy up-down voice you would use to announce the winner of 'Pin the Tail on the Donkey' at a local fete.

Practice makes powerful

Churchill hated speaking off the cuff; 'speaking on unpinioned wing' as he called it. In his early days many of his speeches were disastrous, especially if he winged it. As a result, he composed his speeches carefully and then read them verbatim. He would walk up and down, dictating his speeches out loud to his secretary to get the natural flow of speech. She then typed up his words as she heard them, with a separate line after each natural pause. Churchill called this 'psalm form', and it helped him to follow the energy of spontaneous prose as he read.

When the War Cabinet was vacillating between war and compromise with the Nazis in 1940, Churchill prepared for a crucial speech in the House of Commons by rehearsing to his full cabinet. On that day, he admits that he felt 'physically sick' with nerves, but he put all his passion into a call against tyranny: 'We shall go on and we shall fight it out here or elsewhere and if at the last the long story is at an end it were better it should end, not through surrender but only when we are rolling senseless on the ground' ('when each of us lies choking in his own blood!' is what a supporter claims he actually said).

After this passionate outcry, members of the cabinet rose to their feet and thumped their approval on the table. He honed the speech and used it to take Parliament by storm a week later. By then, his words on fighting and surrender had turned into the immortal words the English still remember, 'We shall go on to the end . . . we shall fight on the seas and oceans . . . we shall never surrender.' His words transformed the mood of a nation and turned the tide of the war more surely than any guns.

Memorising and speaking by heart

A handful of politicians have used memory to good effect. A famous example in the US was Patrick Henry, who persuaded Virginia in 1775 to join in the American Revolution. Imploring delegates to join the independence movement, he delivered the speech without notes, his voice growing ever louder, ending with the immortal words, 'Give me Liberty, or give me Death!'

Memorising a speech by heart may be a choice for you, but it is an all-or-nothing choice. If you succeed, your impact can be tremendous. If you don't succeed, you crash like a diver belly-flopping into a muddy pool. Delivering a speech by heart doesn't achieve anything for you if it's just a matter of memorising it and then reciting it.

I watched a hopeful entrepreneur make his pitch from memory in the television programme *Dragons' Den,* in his bid to persuade the millionaire 'dragons' to invest in his business. He was very nervous and at a certain point his memory failed him. His only way of continuing was to return to the beginning of his spiel to pick up the memory trail again, a strategy he used twice! The 'Dragons' were left open-mouthed as he struggled to recite by rote his prepared text.

Yet, speaking from memory can be extraordinary:

✔ You can look at your audience and connect without papers or lecterns getting in the way.

✔ Memorising by heart, you can literally get to the *heart* of what you're saying, and enter right into the core of your message, including the feelings and energy that are a major part of it.

Aristotle says that the heart rather than the brain is where the action is. The ancient Greek orators believed that the seat of memory was the heart. Memorising in the head is only one stage of memory; memorising in the heart gives you deeper understanding and long-term recall.

Choose an occasion that is low risk for your first venture into the world of memory. Rather than memorising a string of words and phrases in an unbroken line – which is a sure recipe for disaster! – use the following meaning-based method:

1. **Memorise the headings of your speech in order, so that you have a skeleton structure.**

2. **Follow with the sub-topics in order under the headings.**

3. **Memorise the main elements of your headings and subheadings.**

4. **Note specific phrases that you want to say in particular ways, plus facts and figures that need to be accurate; slot them into your structure.**

During each step, practise until you know the material really well. Start with the ideas and the flow, move onto the important points to remember and finally, as the last thing, work on the actual words in your sentences, realising that the odd wrong word doesn't matter: getting the ideas across is most important.

Create memory links between each of the headings and subheadings. For example, the first heading in your speech is 'The Worldwide Situation'. At the end of that section, imagine the sun rising on the world for the first of your subheadings, which is 'The situation in China, the land of *the rising sun*'. You can invent various ways to connect your different sections.

Speaking off the cuff

Most people give their greatest attention to preparing formal speeches, but unscheduled moments are really important too. Think of the sudden invitation to say a few words, responses to questions after a speech or interruptions, the times when presentation software fails or something else goes wrong, or when you have to fill in a bit of time.

Churchill had a wonderful memory for words, and clearly David Cameron too, but neither enjoy speaking off the cuff as much. Other speakers love it and can talk spontaneously for ever. Many people fear these moments for the very reason that they're unpredictable.

Richard Nixon was quick on his feet and used the skill to good effect. During his run as Eisenhower's Vice President in 1952, he was accused of cheating with his political expenses fund. When the story broke, Nixon immediately flew to Los Angeles and gave an impromptu half-hour television address defending himself. During the speech, he declared that whatever happened, he intended to keep one gift, the black and white dog his children had given the name Checkers. The speech produced a flood of support for him from the public. He and Eisenhower were swept to victory a few weeks later.

Being quick on your feet is essential when you speak to a group, but it may be that you find the impromptu parts of speech making – the interruptions and questions, for instance – the most scary part.

Spontaneity is a key piece that can give you the confidence to cope in any situation. You may feel like you're in uncharted territory at the moment, but there are pointers to help you.

Imagine that you're at a meeting with your team and some clients. One of the clients suddenly asks a difficult question. Instead of answering it herself, the chair of the meeting looks at you and says, 'This is your province, isn't it? Would you like to say a few words?' You stand up (mentally appalled) and begin to speak, working from the following formula:

- ✔ Pause a moment. Take a big breath.
- ✔ As you take the breath, decide on the simplest of formats for your reply and tell your audience what structure you're going to use.

    For example, you can say, 'Yes, thank you, there are a couple of things I'd like to say on the subject.' (Saying this means that you have to think of at least two headings in your mind.). 'The first of these is . . . ' (your first heading), and you think of a couple of things to say under that heading. Then you don't dry up because you have your second heading, which you give similar treatment.

You can use choose among various formats to structure your 'spontaneous' response:

- ✔ **Big to small, global to personal:** Give the general context of the issue as you see it and then move to detail – for example, noting your own part in it or your own view on it.

- ✔ **Different perspectives:** Consider different points of view regarding an issue. For instance, consider the views of competitors, stakeholders and you yourself – and then reconcile the viewpoints at the end.

- ✔ **Newspaper reporter approach:** Think of *what* the issue is about, *how* it works and *why* it matters.

- ✔ **Past, present, future:** Talk about the cause or history of the issue, the current situation and the future of the issue in any order you choose.

- ✔ **Problem and solution:** Outline the problem, and offer one or more solutions to it.

I'm sure that you'll come up with various other structuring ideas. Just remember to tell your audience first *how* you're going to respond – and then go about responding in that manner. In this way, what seems like a free flow of language to your listeners is actually based on an internal structure that you quickly think of before you speak.

You may be speaking off the cuff, but you're never starting from scratch. Comedians become popular when they know so many jokes that they seem to have one for every occasion, and then they sound spontaneous. The more you can build up a repertoire to talk about, the more you appear spontaneous and at ease. Practice helps!

You don't have to know everything about everything. Confident off-the-cuff speakers are confident because they know that they can say *something* relevant, not because they know everything. If the subject seems huge, take a chunk that you're familiar with and talk about that, explaining what you're doing. For example, in response to, 'So tell us about communication in your organisation', you may say, 'It's a subject that has been at the top of the agenda this year . . . In my own department for instance, we set up . . . '

If you trust yourself, even just a little, everything is possible. Communication is never more powerful than when someone thinks and then speaks. As e. e. cummings said, 'Once we believe in ourselves we can risk curiosity, wonder, spontaneous delight or any experience that reveals the human spirit.'

Persuading Others with Inspiration from the Political Stage

The Greeks put forward the idea of the leadership of eloquent men, and, more than 2,000 years later, little has fundamentally changed. The populace still elects those who have the power of speech over those who don't, however talented or active they may be in other ways. Theodore Sorenson, speech writer to John Kennedy, declared simply that 'words are how the President governs'. Personal style and communication skills in this mass media age are ever more crucial.

In this section, I introduce you to some of the techniques that successful political leaders use to influence and inspire – techniques that you too can adopt for times when you want to be persuasive.

Choosing between hustings yell or fireside chat

Speaking styles have changed. Back in 1984, the leader of the National Union of Miners, Arthur Scargill, stood in the open during the miners' strike and yelled at his members, 'Get off yer knees and fight!', his voice ravaged by hours of shouting. Politicians still speak in the open, but the experience is more staged, and a microphone is nearly always at hand.

Voters mostly listen to politicians in the comfort of their own sitting rooms. Some speakers excel at the more intimate informal ways of connecting with people; others excel at the dramatic set piece. The truth is that in these days of mass media, politicians and leaders need both skills.

Intimate moments

To be successful in communicating one-to-one, you need to use everyday language and intonation. Some leaders take this style successfully into the public arena and give each listener the impression that they're being addressed personally.

In the Great Depression in the 1930s, US President Franklin Delano Roosevelt decided that he needed a way to address the population more directly, and the radio was at hand as the perfect medium. He began to make informal addresses, which became known as his 'fireside chats', and used them as a way to reassure the nation and persuade the public that he felt as it did. Listening to the radio at home, each person heard the president speak to them personally. Margaret Thatcher also cultivated a softer tone to speak to viewers at home. A BBC news report announced the change: 'The Conservative leader ditches a voice that could strip the paint off the door of No. 10 for something deeper and more resonant.'

To create a sense of intimacy yourself when you speak to a group:

✔ Be yourself; that is, be natural and at ease. Speak using personal informal language, with access to your natural sense of humour (Chapter 10).

✔ At the same time, be sure that the audience can hear you easily in a larger space, by:

   • Taking time to get everyone's attention before you start, so that you don't have to speak over-loudly.

   • Speaking with simple clear diction (Chapter 6).

   • Slowing down (Chapter 7).

   • Using emphasis effectively without necessarily speaking louder (Chapter 8).

Catching the sermon

In Chapter 8, I introduce some rhetorical tools to give your speeches dramatic impact. In this section, I cover oratory style that owes much of its power to the church. The influence of religious oratory on public speaking in the US goes way back through Abraham Lincoln, John F Kennedy and many others. Martin Luther King is a great example of an orator using skills that he picked up from church orators and evangelists. The political leader's language and tone when speaking in this mode almost suggests that his or her beliefs have something of church redemption about them.

The church oratorical tradition has several main features that you can listen for and try out yourself. When you speak in this manner, you:

✔ Lengthen many of the vowels and consonants, expanding them like long notes in music.

✔ Speak at a much slower pace, without gaps between words and phrases within each sentence. A commentator timed an opening sentence spoken by Barack Obama in an election speech and calculated that it took 30 seconds to deliver just 45 words – slow!

✔ Join your words smoothly, almost like singing a melody. You can find more about speaking on a flow of breath with joined up sounds in Chapter 4.

✔ Rise to a high note for an important point in the middle of the thought and finish low at the end of a sentence, like the rise and fall of a wave. See Chapter 8.

✔ At appropriate moments of suspense, insert expectant pauses that last and last. See Chapter 8 for more on how to use silence in speaking.

✔ Gather speed as you approach the climax of an idea, then slow down with smooth control as you reach the important point.

✔ Use words that echo those of evangelists. King proclaimed 'every valley shall be exalted, . . . the crooked places will be made straight, and the glory of the Lord shall be revealed . . . ' His phrases sound Biblical even though they aren't exact quotations.

All the preceding features are strongly present in King's 'I have a dream' speech. You can hear in recordings of this historical address how the huge crowd in the open air responds vocally to King's powerful delivery.

At election times, emotions run high. When people are emotional, passionate words and gestures work powerfully.

You may not experience many occasions when you want to deliver the highest-flown rhetoric yourself. But even on less formal occasions, you can mirror the use of emotional words employed by political giants. Choose words that aren't tied down to specifics, but have universal applications. Instead of details about a subject, use emotive generalisations that can apply to every member of your audience. It also helps the rhetoric if you can find a metaphor (but not a cliché!) – 'pour oil on troubled waters' rather than just 'make peace' for example.

1. **Find a factual sentence in a business paper, an advertisement or an article in a newspaper or online.**

2. **'Translate' the statement into an emotive generalisation for your audience.**

Here are a few examples:

Original statement: 'Less tax for specific sectors of the population.'
Translation: 'Rising tides of prosperity.'

Original statement: 'Measures to combat burglary in cities.'
Translation: 'Enjoying the still waters of peace.'

Original statement: 'Country facing economic down-turn.'
Translation: 'Gathering clouds and raging storms.'

You get the idea! With your new language, every member of your audience can make some connection to it, unlike when you include specifics.

Speaking in soundbites

In contrast to the sublime of church oratory stands the advertising-slogan quality of the soundbite – that one-liner that incorporates the essence of a speaker's message and becomes the phrase that everyone remembers. The world is speeding up and what everyone wants most, politicians especially, is for one brief comment to stick, to become immortal, like the following:

> 'Ask not what your country can do for you – ask what you can do for your country.' John F Kennedy

> 'The only thing we have to fear is – fear itself.' Franklin D Roosevelt

> 'The Lady's not for turning!' Margaret Thatcher

> Or the ultimate 'denied' soundbite by Tony Blair: 'Now is not the time for soundbites. I can feel the hand of history on my shoulder.'

Soundbites are getting shorter. A typical 1968 radio interview allowed a speaker about 42 seconds to deliver a soundbite. At present, speakers have less than five seconds to wow listeners with choice phrases. The influence of Twitter has made some commentators suggest that eight words is now the maximum!

The idea of the soundbite can be a useful for anyone seeking to persuade. Finding just the right phrase to express an idea succinctly makes people remember your words. If you notice that you tend to be wordy, get a speech down on paper, and then hone it down into something more pithy. Editing takes effort, but eventually memorable phrases emerge.

Get to recognise the difference between a soundbite and a cliché. A soundbite strikes people with a freshness; a new take on something everyone knows but hasn't been expressed in quite your way. A cliché is old and worn and adds nothing significant to the meaning of a sentence. Here's a whole paragraph-full of grim clichés to avoid:

> Basically, to be honest, the writing's on the wall, it's survival of the fittest, and at the end of the day lessons have been learned. The fact of the matter is, at this point in time, we're beginning to think outside the box.

Read and listen with curiosity, and pay attention to language. Whenever you hear a turn of phrase that strikes you as interesting and well-phrased, make a note of it, so that you can use it later. Listen too for the phrases that people repeat so often that you tire of them, and remind yourself to avoid them!

Connecting with your public

You want an audience to believe that you understand where they're coming from and that you're just like them in ways that matter. In order to connect, you must tune in to the mood of your audience. Do all the following to connect with a group:

- ✔ **Look on your audience as a group of your friends that you can interact with in a dialogue.**

- ✔ **Think of practical connections with the audience.** Comedians often start a show by asking where people come from and making funny comments about it.

  Be careful that the connections you utilise are positive and appropriate for your audience. A wealthy British politician made a speech in a bread-making factory and 'tuned in' by telling the factory workers that he had an electric bread maker at home. He found a subject in common, but completely missed the common touch!

- ✔ **Trust your beliefs and passions.** Advisors recommended that Al Gore not talk about global warming during his 2004 presidential campaign because they thought people didn't care about the topic. But voters found that Gore lacked passion, and Gore lost his bid for the presidency. A year or so later, when he spoke about his true passion, voters were much more attracted to him.

- ✔ **Be prepared to connect with any audience.** Some politicians, such as Margaret Thatcher, performed really well only in front of their own party. Pick up the energy of your audience and try to understand where they're coming from. If you do that, you're far less likely to attract antagonism.

Refer to Chapter 15 for more about tuning in to your audience.

The most skilful politicians are in tune with their times and say what other people want to say, had they the eloquence. Speaking to, for example, youth or the working class, without sounding patronising, requires you form genuine connections with others. King George VI and Queen Elizabeth II achieved it during the blitz. Ronald Reagan had the ability. Tony Blair in his earlier career had it too. His speech about 'the people's princess' after Princess Diana died was one of his moments (a good soundbite too!). New York Mayor Rudolph Giuliani in his passion and sadness spoke as a channel for the times in the aftermath of 9/11.

Oratory opposites

When you analyse great speeches, you find a fascinating combination of opposites. Seek out Martin Luther King's 'I have a dream' speech for a case study in opposing energies, perfectly balanced and blended.

✔ **The message is both personal and universal.**

Universal: 'With this faith we will be able to transform the jangling discords of our nation into a beautiful symphony of brotherhood.'

Personal: 'I have a dream that my four children will one day live in a nation where they will not be judged by the color of their skin but by the content of their character.'

✔ **You get a combination of formal and informal language.**

Formal: 'The rough places will be made plain, and the crooked places will be made straight, and the glory of the Lord shall be revealed.'

Informal: 'Little black boys and black girls will be able to join hands with little white boys and white girls.'

✔ **You get a mixture of abstract language and sensory language that you can see, touch or hear.**

Abstract language: injustice, oppression, freedom and justice

Sensory language: rough, red, jangling, snowcapped, curvaceous

✔ **Some of the verbs are in the passive tense and sound impersonal, and some are in an active tense and sound personal.**

Passive: 'Every valley shall be exalted, every hill and mountain shall be made low,'

Active: 'We will be able to hew out of the mountain of despair a stone of hope.'

King's deft combination of opposites allows you to connect in common cause with him, while at the same time be carried to emotional heights by grand language. It both builds trust and inspires.

Take a speech you wrote yourself, and start with one of the pairs of opposites. Cast your eye through the speech to see which alternative you use most often. For example, do you use more universal language or more personal forms of expression? If you use one considerably more than the other, consider what small adjustments you can make to your language to redress the balance. Follow the same process with the other pairs on the list.

In order to connect well with groups in all circumstances, do the following:

✔ Be curious and seek to understand before you seek to be understood. The more you see things from others' points of view, the easier it is for you to connect with them.

✔ Don't pretend to be anything you're not in your attempts to connect. Be yourself; you're more authentic that way.

Speaking to the Media

You certainly enter the world of the unpredictable when you speak to the media, and being interviewed can push people to extremes. Some people make a special effort and exaggerate theatrically; others put on the mask of imperturbability and sound like an offshore weather bulletin.

Your style of speaking has a big effect on how people respond to your actual words.

Some irrepressible young members of an Oxbridge acting group used to play a forfeits game when they were on tour. The challenge was to walk up to the barman and say something unspeakable in such a normal way as part of normal conversation that the barman would do a double-take and decide that he had misheard and ignore it. It was surprisingly easy to do. The tone of voice won out over the content almost every time.

Understanding the game

Interviewing someone – and being a good interviewee – is ultimately a game. Before going into a media interview, you need to understand what the interviewer wants when you're questioned. Otherwise, you may be put off by the interviewer's forcefulness and feel that you're antagonists. You aren't.

Interviewer and interviewee are actually in this together. The interviewer wants to create a good lively debate to catch the interest of viewers and probably wants to look good in the process. You, as interviewee, want much the same.

In order to sail through an interview:

- ✔ **Whatever you're asked, have something to say.** Interviewers are not always so skilful and may ask you a *closed question* that already contains the answer, as in, 'So you walked all the way to the South Pole? That must have been dangerous?' The answer is of course, 'Yes', or 'Yes, I walked all the way to the South Pole and it was very dangerous' but it's your part in the game to choose a way to expand on the question.

- ✔ **An interview is your opportunity to share your soundbites.** Prepare some good ones *before* you're interviewed! See 'Speaking in soundbites' earlier for more strategies.

- ✔ **Keep your cool.** The interviewer may annoy you, you may make mistakes, the sky may fall down – but keep your cool (or sense of humour).

✔ **Build your resilience and believe passionately that you deserve to be heard.** You may find when you're interviewed along with another person that the more pushy person gets to say most. You don't have to be that pushy person, but if you've started to say something, stand your ground and allow yourself to finish, even if you're interrupted – unless the interview has run out of time of course.

If you aren't naturally resilient, practise the body language power walk the next time you're in a busy street or train station to feel your power. Simply walk with a strong sense of intention, knowing that nothing can interrupt your walk or force you to step out of the way. Focus on your destination, not on other people's eyes, and just *know* that you can walk smoothly, easily and confidently through the crowd without hindrance. You may be pleasantly surprised at how easily you stride through the crowd. Other people get a sixth sense of your determination *before* there's any chance of bumping into you and slide out of your way.

Answering questions

Many speakers become anxious at question time because they don't know what to expect, and feel an obligation to have an answer to *everything*.

Remember that people ask questions for many different reasons, not all of which arise from a genuine desire to know the answer. Some people ask questions to hear the sound of their own voice, to be the centre of attention, to express an opinion or to challenge you. If you can anticipate the reason for the question, you're in a stronger position to answer it appropriately. For example, if someone asks a question that is actually an opinion in disguise, thank them for the question and congratulate them on their point of view – job done! The following suggestions apply to most situations where someone asks a question.

When answering questions in the presence of an audience:

✔ **Be at ease.** You don't have to know everything. You don't have to know this particular answer. Just trust that all will be well. Relax and breathe and show that you're comfortable – your sense of ease inspires more confidence than any answer you may give.

✔ **Show respect.** Whatever gets thrown at you, assume a positive intention behind the question and treat the questioner with respect.

✔ **Respond to both to interviewer and audience.** Keep your attention on both as you give your replies, so that you're not sucked into a particular theme with just one person.

Your answers to difficult questions can fall between two camps:

✔ On the one hand, you can answer the question and be led by the questioner into all sorts of tricky places you don't want to go.

✔ On the other, you can say what you always meant to say and end up frustrating your listeners by not answering the question.

Skilful politicians find the sweet spot between these extremes. They go *with* the question and then steer it elegantly in the direction they want.

The martial art of Aikido uses a similar technique of going *with* whatever happens. The attacker approaches the Aikidoist and, at the last moment, when the attacker no long has time to change the attack, the Aikidoist moves quickly in beside the attacker so that they're both going in the same direction. From this point, the Aikidoist is able to influence the proceedings and dispatch the attacker.

So, in responding to a tricky question, first get into step with your questioner by using an acknowledgement or a similar tone of voice, and then influence the direction of the argument. You never need to fear an attacking question or indeed any question; you just flow with it at the beginning and then you have time to take it somewhere without panic.

Listen to Track 36. Imagine that someone asks in a loud and angry tone, 'What are you going to do about it?' You pick up the urgency of the question (like the speed of the Aikido attack) and reply quickly in the same dynamic, 'You're right, a solution is urgent, (then gradually you reduce your pace) and what we have decided (now sounding more determined than urgent) is to put the plan into action in the north initially, to test the reaction. Then (lower, slower, with Churchillian gravitas), we'll review the situation.' You end up with a different energy from the beginning, taking the questioner to that new place with you.

After you get into the swing of answering questions in this way, you start to enjoy the real exchange that happens and go with the flow. Many people find that answering questions becomes the most enjoyable element of public speaking.

Chapter 15

Tuning In to Others

In This Chapter
▶ Connecting with other people
▶ Rediscovering your listening skills
▶ Leading and influencing with your voice
▶ Dancing in the moment

Cognitive psychology has a saying that the meaning of a communication is the response it elicits. This statement basically means that you may think, for example, that you're speaking in a friendly way to someone, but if the other person finds you patronising, then – *whatever your intention* – the received message is condescending, not friendly. Speaking well is pointless if what you say doesn't receive the response you want.

Your voice doesn't exist in isolation – it's a communication instrument to connect you with someone else. All the time you're speaking, you're connecting or not connecting. Even by your silence, you're communicating something.

So the skill of watching and listening to others, tuning in to their state of mind and then expressing that connection with your voice is the magic ingredient of great communicators. When you're able to connect with the general feeling of your listeners and then speak so that they feel that you understand them, the possibilities are huge – you can carry them with you and inspire them.

Your tone carries the main burden of your message, more than the actual words you speak. So how do you tune in and express the connection in your voice? In this chapter, I help you become aware of others' tunes, match your tune to theirs and then strategically play different notes to achieve even greater things.

Getting on the Same Wavelength

Connecting with others is always about finding similarity. The most obvious way that most people connect is to find a common subject matter to discuss. When you meet someone for the first time, you may fumble around at first, trying to find a subject that interests you both; but after you do, communication becomes easy.

Deeper commonalities, like your common sense of ethics and values or how you choose to live your lives, cause you to think, 'That's my kind of person.' You can discover these fundamentals through conversation, but you sense them instinctively in the vibration of the person – that is, in their internal energy. Tuning in is about matching your energy to that of the other person or people. It's like entering into their way of experiencing the world.

You can bring your energy closer to that of someone else in a multitude of ways – physically, mentally, emotionally and more. But in terms of sound, getting closer to someone else involves using your ability to modulate your voice tone, volume, speed, rhythm and other variables, in order to bring your voice closer to the energy of the other person.

Opening up

In order to tune into other people, you need to keep your eyes, ears and heart open. Here are the different components:

- ✓ **Start by becoming aware of your audience, whether one or many.** You have to look at them – not to stare, but to truly see them as a group of individuals.

- ✓ **Notice whether they're interested or indifferent, engaged or distracted.** Your awareness of these characteristics influences what you do and say next. Use all your senses. Over the phone, your listening skills need to be especially acute.

- ✓ **Listen not just to what they're saying, but *how* they're saying it.** Doing so enables you to enter into your audience's world and get a sense of how everything seems for them. Appreciating your audience's point of view affects how you decide to communicate.

- ✓ **Let yourself feel the connection viscerally.** Sense the mood and energy of your audience so that you can respond at the appropriate energy level. Go to Chapter 10 for more on working with energy.

Of course you don't always want to be in the same mood as your listeners – particularly if they're angry! However, by tuning into their energy – not their presenting attitude – you make an initial connection from which you can influence the exchange and take them potentially to a different energy and therefore a different mood. For example, if your listeners are loud and angry, speak with a firm energetic voice at first to make your initial connection with them. If they're apathetic, respond in a calmer quieter voice to match their lower energy.

Singing the same tune

In 1665, Dutch scientist Christian Huygens discovered the phenomenon of *entrainment*. Think of entrainment in terms of clocks: say you have a room containing several grandfather clocks and you start them off with their pendulums all swinging at different rates: if you return a day later, you find that the pendulums have all fallen into the same rate as each other. You find this phenomenon throughout nature. Fireflies flash their lights in entrainment with each other. Women who share a communal life – students in a flat for example – find their menstrual cycles synchronise.

Research shows that, like ticking clocks or flashing fireflies, people who get on well in conversation oscillate in rhythm with each other. Indeed, their brain waves are in entrainment. In terms of sound, entrainment is like making music together. Think about all the ways that people use musical language to describe getting along in conversation. You 'tune in'; you 'get on the same wave length'. You 'sing the same tune' from the 'same hymn sheet'. You 'share each other's beat' or are 'in harmony'.

To tune in to your audience, the most important voice skill you can acquire is flexibility. You can't tune in if you have only one tune! Different situations demand different tones. Thinking in this way, you begin to realise that speaking is less about having a beautiful voice as an end in itself; speaking is more about having the right voice for the occasion – or more accurately, the right voice for the particular *connection*.

You never lose out by matching vocal energy. You may worry that you're following rather than leading, or even giving up your own identity; but following is the beginning of leading. The greatest speakers can go with their audiences and then soon have them in the palm of their hand and lead them where they wish.

The American statesman Colin Powell has a reputation as a powerful speaker who knows how to touch audiences with his passion and enthusiasm. He once explained that he tries to put himself in the place of his audience and understand their culture, their hopes and fears and what is going on for them. When he spoke to nurses who had served in Vietnam, he imagined their world in the war and asked them, 'How much of your heart did you leave there? How often were you the mother for a kid asking for mom in the last few seconds of his life? How many 19-year-old sons did you lose?' When asked how he thought to say those words, he said that his speechwriters had prepared good drafts, but nothing really clicked until he read some of the poems written by these women describing their heartrending experiences. *Then* he found the connection. He said that when he spoke, he never wanted to lecture *to* his audience but always speak *with* them.

Get in tune with a partner by practising the following:

1. **Person A chooses a subject he or she has opinions about and begins a conversation.**

   Your topic need not be political or controversial – just something you have an opinion about, such as your favourite activity or sport.

2. **Person B joins in the conversation and after a short while begins to disagree with Person A, using a voice that is different from Person's A's.**

   Try speaking louder or softer, higher or lower, faster or slower than Person A.

3. **After a short while of disagreeing in a different tone, Person B continues to disagree but begins to vocally match Person A in terms of volume, pitch, speed and so on.**

4. **Review your conversation.**

   As Person A, did you find that using a different voice escalated your differences? Was it easier to get a proper debate going when your voices became similar? How did you feel as Person B?

5. **Reverse roles with Person B choosing the topic.**

Cymatics: Sound in visible form

Cymatics, the study of visible sound and vibration, provides extraordinary insights into the effects of voice and music. In its simplest form, you can experiment by sprinkling fine sand on a stretched membrane – a drum for instance. Play sounds and watch how the vibrations affect the sand.

✔ If you play a tuneful sound, such as a pure note at a fairly high pitch, the sand shifts into a geometric pattern and, as you raise the pitch, different patterns emerge. The patterns can be very beautiful and complex, similar to the patterns of snowflakes, transparent jellyfish or mandalas.

✔ If you play a harsh sound, such as crashing cymbals or even certain pop music, the sand becomes chaotic with no visible pattern emerging.

Your voice produces similar effects on a listener; a harmonious sound produces beautiful ordered patterns in your listener's brain; discordant unpleasant sound produces waves of chaos. Look up 'cymatics' on YouTube for some striking examples of the phenomenon.

Most people discover that when they tune in with their voices to the other person, they can no longer be adversaries, even though they're disagreeing with each other. Suddenly real debate becomes easy and natural.

Tuning in isn't about *agreeing* with the other person's view. You can happily disagree if you remain in harmony voice-wise. Bear this in mind if you want to mediate or help in situations of conflict.

Choosing to sing a different tune

If you're standing on a podium about to address an audience of several hundred, tuning in may not be at the top of your mind. In fact, you may be looking for ways to stand out, be special, have power and control, under the impression that a presenter 'ought' to be different. This feeling may make you overdo your energy in an effort to lift your audience out of indifference or apathy. But overdoing your energy often produces an unexpected result – you fail to build a connection, and your audience gives up and slumps more than before. If you neglect the response of your audience, they fail to tune in to you and listen properly.

The opposite of tuning in is when two people are just talking side by side with no real connection. Have you ever been in a conversation where you suspect that the other person is just marking time and thinking of what they want to say next instead of listening to you? The entire conversation becomes draining. George Bernard Shaw was very likely thinking of such a poor conversational companion when he complained, 'The trouble with her is that she lacks the power of conversation but not the power of speech.'

A humorous Video Arts training video I've often used (www.videoarts. com) features a young lady in some distress speaking to her boss about some personal emotional difficulties. While her boss is listening to her, he is busily engaged in rearranging his pens and papers and gives her no sign that he is hearing her words. The young lady eventually bursts into tears of frustration and rushes from the room. The boss is nonplussed by her departure and lists accurately everything she just said. He did indeed listen but didn't give any of the vocal and non-verbal signals to show that he was connecting with her.

Listening and understanding intellectually isn't enough. You need to sense what's going on emotionally as well, and respond with your voice tone to this aspect of the communication too.

Tone-deaf? Think again

Some children get the label 'tone deaf' when they're very young and grow up believing they lack the ear to 'tune in'. If this scenario sounds familiar, you may fear that you will always be condemned to 'sing a different tune' whether you're singing or speaking.

Unless they're deaf, children tune in naturally. However, most very young children have a limited range of five or six notes that they're able to sing. This range is the range of most nursery rhymes, (think 'Twinkle, Twinkle, Little Star' for example). If your voice as a child is naturally deeper than the norm, your natural pitch range lies below the notes of the songs, and you're unable to reach the notes that are easy for the other children to sing. If the tune were played in a lower key, you would be able to sing accurately and the

other children would have the problem. But the teacher, in ignorance, calls you a 'growler' and orders you to stop singing or to mouth the words silently. From then on, you believe that you have the disability 'tone deafness' and feel bad about your musical abilities.

Any vocal problems you're experiencing now probably have nothing to do with your listening skills or musicality.

However, learning music is a great way to work on your listening skills. You can develop your ability to sing in tune at any age by starting with a note in your own natural pitch range and gradually building up your range upwards and downwards tone by tone.

Moving into the Lead

Your tone of voice is a brilliant instrument for taking an audience your way. The process of leading begins with connecting with your audience (see the earlier section 'Getting on the Same Wavelength'). Influencing your audience is always easier when you and your listeners are already both travelling together at the same speed – or singing the same song.

Shifting subtly

Get connected by matching your voice – pitch, tone, volume, speed – to the other person's, and then gradually introduce something new into your voice for the other person to follow.

Practise the subtle art of influence on another person, preferably without them knowing what you're doing at the outset. (Tell them afterwards!)

1. **Invite your partner to talk about something that he or she is fed up about.** Any everyday annoyance such as price increases or traffic problems will work fine.

2. **Join in the conversation, using a similar tone of voice to your partner without feeling fed up yourself.** It doesn't matter whether you agree or disagree with your partner – though you may find agreeing easier at first. Just match the tone of voice, speed, pitch and so on.

3. **After talking in this manner for a few moments, begin to vary your voice a little.** Perhaps speak at a slightly higher pitch in a lighter tone, or speak a fraction louder or faster.

4. **Gradually, change your voice a little more, paying attention to how your partner naturally responds.** The trick is to make these changes gradually so that your partner doesn't notice the difference consciously. Move the conversation towards more positive things too.

Think of making the changes mentally and emotionally more than physically. For example, feel brighter and think from a less serious perspective to help produce the physical lightening in your tone.

Most people find that the 'fed up' person in this activity is unable to continue in the same mode as the tone changes. When you move to a different energy, your partner unconsciously moves too.

Influence can be very gentle. You only need to make minor changes in order to affect the other person's response considerably.

The most powerful way to lead another person with your voice is through your resonance (I explain resonance in much more detail in Chapter 9). Tune in to the other person, then influence them in different ways through your voice resonance. Again, make the changes mentally and emotionally and physical change follows.

- ✔ **Your brighter, higher head tone** lightens the mood and helps you move discussions to easier, less emotional-heavy topics.

- ✔ **Your firm chest voice** draws the conversation away from emotion and into facts, figures and practical suggestions.

- ✔ **Your gentler heart voice** shows that you empathise with your listener and encourages the listener to consider how they're feeling.

- ✔ **Your deep gut voice** encourages your listener to consider things of fundamental importance beyond current surface irritations.

Notice the effect on the other person when you introduce each of these different voice tones.

In this exercise with a partner, notice the different results you get when you ask the same question with different resonance. Alert your partner to the fact that you're going to ask the same question about his or her issue in different ways. Listen to Track 37 to hear me try out different resonances.

1. **Ask your partner to headline briefly an issue that matters to him or her (a work or relationship problem maybe).**

2. **After your partner talks for a few moments, ask, 'What's this about?' or 'What's this about really?' in a particular resonance (head, chest, heart or gut) and listen to the response.**

3. **Ask your partner to tell you again about this same issue that matters to them.**

4. **Ask once again 'What's this about?' or 'What's this about really?' – but use a different resonance.** Notice how your partner responds differently when you say the same words in a different tone.

5. **Continue asking your question, using difference resonance and noticing how the question stimulates a different feeling and response in the other person each time.**

6. **Review the experience with your partner.** Discuss the differences for each of you. How did introducing different resonances into your voice take your partner to different emotional and thinking states?

   If you're a coach, therapist or in a similar profession, this subtle skill of using resonance can be immensely useful to lead your client to a different relationship with their issue. If you're in any leadership role, this gentle skill comes in useful again and again. Your tone of voice isn't like a specific directive, but a subtle invitation to look at things from a different perspective.

Influencing via your audience's state of mind

One day a colleague told me about her experiences in a couple of meetings she attends every week. 'It's really strange,' she commented. 'In the first, we always have excellent debate, and people treat each other with respect. In the second, the atmosphere is antagonistic, and nothing's achieved.' When I asked my colleague about the leader of the first meeting, she described her as 'pretty ordinary' but added that she 'has a sense of calm about her. As soon as she begins to speak, everyone pays her close attention.'

When you invite others to join you in a particularly emotional space, rather than tell them to act a certain way, the power of attraction comes into play, and people want to join you. Your state of mind is contagious, and people become infected with it; *attracted* towards it. A peaceful state produces calm; a forceful state provokes force or aggression.

Rather than telling a group what she wanted, the calm team leader in the preceding example invited others to join her in her calm space through calm physicality and a calm voice. She wouldn't have been very effective if she just acted calm in isolation without being aware of the current state of her team. She needed first to tune into that (see 'Getting on the Same Wavelength' earlier), and then move towards her calm state.

You influence others by affecting their states of mind. Your own state of mind and the sounds that you make from that place have much greater power to influence than your actions and words.

Because your power to influence links to your audience's state of mind, you actually have plenty of flexibility in how you can affect an audience. Inspiration comes in every colour of the rainbow! If you go to listen to a motivational speaker such as Tony Robbins, you easily become swept along by the enormous energy in his voice. If you listen to recordings of Mahatma Gandhi, his slow gentle voice invites you into his world of peace. You hear it particularly strongly in his speeches in his mother tongue, Gujarati – even if you don't speak the language.

The neuro-linguistic programming (NLP) developer Robert Dilts introduced this practice to me. Try it with at least two other people, or more if you can; one of you is speaker and the others are the audience.

1. **Have one person act as speaker, who chooses a topic to speak about.** Choose a topic that you can speak easily about, for example a business topic, a favourite hobby or sport, or your travel experiences.

2. **As speaker, select a desired state that you want to lead your audience towards. Keep this choice to yourself.** Some desired states include: curious, excited, relaxed, playful.

3. **Members of the audience select their current state.** Some current states include: critical, bored, confused, suspicious. Don't let the speaker know which state you select.

4. **The speaker begins a short presentation while the audience enters into its chosen state of mind.**

   So if, for example, the audience choose to be critical, sit there listening and feeling critical. Take opportunities to ask questions or comment, and do it in a critical way.

5. **As speaker, tune into the starting state of the audience and then, very gradually, change your voice tone and lead the audience towards your desired state.**

   Your aim is to finish when the audience is clearly in the desired state. In any case, come to an end in about five or ten minutes. The audience should respond instinctively and naturally to the speaker's lead, and not hold onto the original state rigidly as if it's a competition they must win.

6. **After the presentation, reflect and discuss what worked well and what was less effective in leading the audience.**

When you tune into your audience's state of mind, focus on picking up their energy, not their mood. If the audience is in a bored mood, for example, you don't want to become bored yourself. But you can follow your audience's low energy and slow or flat way of speaking to get on its wavelength. Take plenty of time to tune-in to the current state before aiming to lead your audience somewhere different. If you're aware of noticeable variations in different parts of the audience, address each in turn. For example, (in a quiet lazy voice), 'Some of you may be feeling quite lethargic after that great lunch . . . ; and (in a more dynamic voice) some of you, I know, have been looking forward especially to this section of my talk.'

Negotiating

In negotiating, you start from fundamental differences and seek to move towards similarities and from there to resolution.

Speaking in the same tone as the other person or people in a negotiating situation encourages them to fall into step with you. You're not agreeing to the *content* of their arguments initially. You're going through the process of coming into a shared space, which you achieve through your voice, body language and general energy. Again, after you match the other people's energy, you can lead them in an exploration to discover what the two sides hold in common – you both want a resolution to your differences perhaps or you all want to come out of the situation with dignity.

Negotiation can be surprising and even counter-intuitive at times. When the other person comes out with a strong angry statement in a loud voice, your natural response may be to gently placate. Instead of reacting to the mood (anger), match the energy. Make your next words (just the first few) as strong and loud as the other person's, though not angry. Doing so brings you both into the same space, and from there you can lead the other party to quieter tones and hopefully more peaceful sentiments.

When negotiating, avoid using the word 'but', which emphasises disagreement. If you use 'and' instead before presenting your own point of view, the other party is likely to find your point of view less jarring. For example:

✔ I understand that you need to consult your people, **but** we're keen to move things along as fast as possible. (I contradict you.)

✔ I understand that you need to consult your people **and** we're keen to move things along as fast as possible. (I accept your view and add to it.)

When actors and presenters speak well, they drive their words towards the end of a thought or a sentence, keeping the momentum up till the end (see Chapter 8). In negotiating, move confidently towards your goal in a similar way. *Negotiating For Dummies* by Michael C. Donaldson (Wiley) gives you many more tips.

Listening Skilfully

The writer Natalie Goldberg quotes a Sufi singing master who advised, 'Singing is 90 per cent listening. You have to learn to listen.'

You may think that the skill of listening takes years to acquire, but actually young children are remarkable good at it – in some ways better than well-educated adults. Everyone hears emotion through the *amygdala*, a primitive area of the brain, before they become consciously aware of sensory input in the hippocampus. This process provides an instant barometer for truth and sincerity. But as the years pass, most people lose the acuity of their perceptions. Few people discuss – or even value – voice tone, and modern media is brimming with falsely bright and energetic voices.

When you lose your ability to listen well, you stop trusting your instinct with regard to what you hear. You lose a vital element of connection with people. Fortunately, you can recover your ability to listen better, as I explore in the following sections.

In Chapter 5, I introduce the concept of 'not too tight and not too loose' for effective voice production. If you try too hard, you become tight, and letting go entirely, you slump – neither of which is helpful. To speak in a lively way you need energy without trying too hard, and freedom without giving up. Exactly the same concept applies to listening. You hear best when you're relaxed; free but not slumped, awake but not tense. Then you can really hear with understanding. As e. e. cummings says: 'now the ears of my ears awake and now the eyes of my eyes are opened'.

Hearing behind the words

You lose the sharpness of your listening as you grow older partly because your education and culture encourage you to get too interested in words at the expense of sounds. You end up listening with your head to make logical sense and paying little attention to the emotional energy behind the words.

If you come back to sensing the *sounds* that people make when they speak, you're able to tap into a mine of information beyond what lies there in the superficial meaning of the words.

Listen to live radio or television. Instead of using your ears, tune in instead to your heart and *feel* what the person is telling you irrespective of the words. In fact, you can ignore the words – or even listen to a speaker using a language you don't know.

The skill of listening with your heart is often in hearing what is missing in the voice tone as well as what is present – especially in hearing what isn't being said in the words. After you try 'heart listening', you can also 'listen' with your gut, and tune into the depths of the other person's core feeling and instinct.

Tuning in to the *sounds* rather than the sense of the words gives you additional clues to the other person that enables you to connect better.

Spotting truth and lies

Tuning into sound helps you to spot deception. Human beings are adept at deceiving with the voice, often to protect themselves. One person barks in a hard voice that hides an insecure person inside. Another talks with silky smoothness, masking a master manipulator within. A third announces control and command, hiding chaos and indecision. A fourth announces 'I am telling the truth' while lying, or 'I trust our leader', hiding mistrust and fear. Look at Chapter 11 to explore more of these subterfuges and find out how to see through them.

At the same time, people never entirely succeed in their deceptions. Some tone always leaks out at least part of what is really going on. *Body Language For Dummies* by Elizabeth Kuhnke (Wiley) shows the many ways that humans give themselves away through their bodies. People give themselves away as much and more through their voices.

As you tune in to other people, use the following clues to help you look and listen for the truth – and spot deception. Something is probably amiss whenever:

- ✔ **The speaker's face and voice do not match up.** John McCain was accused of sarcasm and lack of credibility when he continually smiled without pleasure during the 2008 presidential campaign.

- ✔ **The speaker hesitates just before the words come out.** Listen for the slight glottal stop that tells you the person is guarding what they say or manipulating it to make it more acceptable.

- ✔ **The speaker's tone is flat.** You can hear how narrow the voice sounds, with greatly reduced range. Some lie detectors measure this feature!

- ✔ **The speaker's voice takes on a 'social' tone.** Listen for a tone that is pleasant-sounding but unconvincingly so – lacking deeper tones and without energy behind it.

> ✔ **The speaker's voice is rich and plummy without subtlety or nuance.** Notice the lack of variation in the sound and how *relentlessly* rich and plummy it sounds.

The telephone is a good place to practise your listening skills, as you've only the sounds to go on. The next time you get a call, listen particularly to the first few moments of speech from the other person. What do you pick up from those first sounds? Here are a few examples of my own:

Call No 1: After a short silence, I suddenly heard the warm rounded tones of a woman sounding almost like the friendly compere of a television show mid-flow through her piece. Too evenly warm and too soon! I put the phone down after five words: it was recorded tele-marketing.

Call No 2: As soon as I picked up the phone, the other person asked to speak to me by name in such a happy sounding energetic voice I instantly knew that it was a sales call. Even the happiest of my friends doesn't launch straight into such chirpiness before we've even connected properly.

Call No 3: I recognised the voice and knew it was a friend. She instantly asked how I was, yet the enthusiasm in her voice seemed fractionally too light in tone and lacking in substance. 'Everything okay with you?' I asked. 'Well, actually, since you ask, no!' she replied. The enthusiasm in the voice had indeed been put on to mask the fact that she was troubled.

Dancing in Harmony

Listening and responding go together. In conversation, the rhythm and tone pass to and fro from person to person. If you're speaking to a group, the response is more an energy of silence, a sense you pick up that the audience is going with your words or not. Even though you don't exchange words, the energetic flow is still there.

Only by listening do you know what to say next. Speaker and audience dance together.

When you watch professional dancers, one movement flows into the next, and one dancer signals a change in movement to the other while they're moving in step with each other. You see mutual understanding of energy, speed, rhythm – and a sense of flow.

When you speak, to one person or an audience, your influence comes from flow, not brute strength. The root meaning of the word 'influence' is actually 'flow together'. Even when the exchange is tough, you're most likely to gain the result you want through flexibility. To shift the metaphor from dance to something tougher, watch a boxing match and notice how light professional boxers – even heavyweights! – are on their feet. This is how you need to be too in order to respond to someone instant by instant.

Becoming aware of dancing skills you already have

You probably already know how to respond, moment by moment. Become aware of when you tune in naturally and speak within the conversational dance, and then apply these experiences to your more challenging conversations and presentations. Build on the flexibility you already have, and take it into situations where currently you don't have it. Notice how you already respond:

- **When interacting with a child:** Do you naturally match your voice to theirs?

- **When a friend tells you of a personal unhappiness:** Does your voice drop to the level of your friend's as you show empathy?

- **When someone you care about tells you in excitement about something wonderful that has happened:** Does your voice rise in enthusiasm as well?

- **When another person speaks with formality or solemnity:** Do you find that you respond with a lower more serious voice yourself?

You never sacrifice yourself by being flexible; on the contrary, you give yourself more options and therefore more power. A bendy willow tree is more resilient in a hurricane than a rigid old oak!

The main obstruction to the dance of connection is tension in you. Because your mind and body work together, this tension can be physical or mental. So clamping your shoulders, jaw or teeth, or constricting your breathing, thwarts your listening just like mentally shutting out another person. Opening up your body and mind enables you to receive another person's underlying message *and* respond with the whole of yourself.

Leading and being led

The exchange between speaker and speaker, or speaker and listeners, turns into a dance at the moment when you're no longer sure who's leading and who's being led. As you tune in to others and are able to influence them, so they also begin to influence you, and then the possibilities become exciting.

To get the idea of how this mutual influence works, get together with a friend:

1. **Put on some music that you like.**

2. **Stand facing each other, hold up your hands, palms facing outwards and join up palms.**

Connect your right hand to your friend's left, your left to your friend's right. Just touch gently.

3. **Begin moving your hands and arms slowly every which way, and your friend, keeping hands touching, follows the movement.**

4. **After half a minute or so, swap roles so that you're now following your friend.**

5. **After another half minute, change again and keep moving – but this time no one is in charge.**

   Both you and friend tune into the movement.

6. **After a couple of minutes, reflect on the differences you and your friend experienced.**

   Pay particular attention to the quality of the sensations when neither and both are leading at the same time.

Transferring this concept to conversations and speaking to groups, think in terms of flexibility *with* proactivity. You're neither pushy nor passive, but a flexible equal partner in a 'dance' that you and your friend are creating together.

Co-creating new dances

Sound works in the same manner as the dance. When you speak in harmony with others, extraordinary things become possible:

✔ **You can go to amazing places.** After conversation begins to flow – and this applies to presentations too if you're in harmony with your audience – your interaction takes off on a path of its own. Good conversation ebbs and flows, producing something new and extraordinary.

Seek out an online clip of a 'murmuration of starlings'. In this amazing phenomenon, great flocks of starlings – 20,000 to 30,000 birds – wheel in the evening skies. They form a single great dark shape in the sky that shifts and changes as one entity as each bird wheels, turns and swoops in harmony with the other birds. The shifting happens so fast that the individual birds have to be very sensitive and quick to respond to the movements around them.

✔ **You awaken creativity in yourself and others.** Together, you move beyond what is possible alone. Your interaction ceases to be just an exchange and becomes a joint enterprise. You discover that within the flow you create together. A remark of the other person awakens your creativity and you think thoughts that hadn't come to you before. In a group setting, you find that a question sparks your creativity and you give an answer that is new to all of you.

✔ **Your conversation adds up to more than the sum of the parts.** In dancing together in sound, you go to places you haven't been before and produce something the world hasn't seen before. Such exchanges create the unexpected. First, you experience the harmony of an exchange with its sense of ease. Then you begin to feel the buzz of the conversation as you experience its excitement and creativity. At this point, you can be surprised and delighted by what emerges.

You can find a wonderful short video available online of jazz violinist Karen Briggs improvising with another classically trained violinist during a concert by Yanni at the Acropolis. At the start you can hear two different techniques, two different traditions and two different characters. As they jam together, they spark each other off and begin to imitate each other, expanding on the imitations with more and more creativity. By the end, they're almost challenging each other with increasingly exciting variations – and clearly deriving immense excitement and joy out of the exchange. Their 'dance' leads each to give of their best and to tap the depths of their creativity. The result for the listener is something new and exciting.

Getting a team flowing

You can produce flow in a team by asking members to accept each other's comments and flow on from each other. If they're unused to such harmony(!), start by getting the whole team in a similar space by creating rules for the discussion. One way to do so is to use the *Thinking Hats* concept, a way of thinking pioneered by Edward De Bono.

For this activity, each of the 'hats' is a way of thinking. If you take one way of thinking at a time, you put the whole team in one space to discuss an issue. You decide a period of time for each 'hat', perhaps 15 minutes or so. De Bono's ways of thinking include:

✔ *White hat* – **Information only.** Just talk about facts and figures: the information available.

✔ *Red hat* – **Emotions.** Talk how you feel, gut reactions.

✔ *Black hat* – **Negatives.** Discuss flaws, barriers and potential hazards.

✔ *Yellow hat* – **Positives.** Talk about good points, benefits and things that will work.

✔ *Green hat* – **Creativity.** Explore new ideas.

✔ *Blue hat* – **Thinking about your thinking.** Step outside the discussion and review your processes.

Encourage each member of the team to speak on the topic – but only under the current rule. So, for example, in discussing a project, when the sunny 'positives' hat is on, everyone may discuss only the benefits and good points of the project. Listen to how the voices harmonise with each other in the chosen space and how the debate develops into something useful. You can find plenty of information about Edward De Bono on the Internet, including a great YouTube clip where he explains his system.

Inspiring others

The skill of tuning in is one of the main differences that marks out inspirational speakers from merely excellent ones. Many people learn how to speak well in terms of communicating with strong, clear and even beautiful voices, but few inspire.

This distinction is true in many different fields of communication. Many actors do an excellent job, but few make the hairs on the back of your neck stand up. Those who inhabit their role so fully that they cause you to suspend disbelief carry you along in their experience.

Every singer in the finals of the international Cardiff Singer of the World competition (www.bbc.co.uk/cardiffsinger) is at the top of his or her art with a glorious voice and great technique. But for the celebrated judges, vocal technique tends to be a given; they choose winners who know how to express something authentic from their inner selves, and in communicating that to the audience, sweep them up into a magical world.

For you to inspire others when you speak:

- ✔ Become happy with your voice technique so that you can vary your voice at will.

- ✔ Have something to say that is more than words, a message that affects your audience positively.

- ✔ Tune in more and more to your connection with the audience, so that you can feel that you're carrying them with you.

- ✔ Play your audience like a violin and lead them to wondrous places they can only dream of!

Chapter 16

Cultivating Your Professional Voice

In This Chapter

▶ Walking your talk as an inspiring leader

▶ Influencing others through tone and tenacity

▶ Optimising your voice for classrooms, courtrooms and consultations

*A*re you a lawyer, a teacher, a preacher, a youth leader or a sports coach? Do you work in sales or in a call centre or a fish market? Do you teach aerobics, swimming or dance? Are you a campaigner or an actor, an auction-eer, a hair stylist or a journalist? All very different jobs to be sure, but the one thing they have in common is *talking*; and some jobs require *a lot* of talk.

Apart from the sheer load you put on your voice if you have to talk a lot, 'talking jobs' call you to always want to be at your best. However you're feeling, you make the effort to 'come up to the mark'. As a result many people 'crank up' their voices artificially to an energetic pitch for each meeting, lesson or encounter. This practice may be okay if you're feeling relaxed; but if you're at all tense, this heightened state puts considerable strain on your voice. Unfortunately, few people in vocally demanding jobs have more than the most elementary voice training, so in this chapter I introduce strategies to maintain your voice in the peak of condition for several professions.

But first, I address an attribute that every great leader needs, whatever your position or profession – a voice that inspires and influences others.

Finding Your Voice as a Leader

You may hear the saying 'you need to walk your talk as a leader'. Whether you're leading a corporation, directing a medical team, managing a football team or being a parent, you must have vocal impact on others in order for them to see you as a leader.

Of all the different ways that you can demonstrate leadership, your voice has a disproportionate impact. Whatever skills and qualities your possess, without a strong voice you just don't come across as a leader. Other people are likely to recognise you as a leader only if you sound like one. You don't have to make drastic changes to sound convincing but you do need one or two vital new skills.

Ask yourself the following questions to make sure that you have the basics of the voice of a leader, if you want people to follow your lead:

- ✔ **Is your voice loud enough? Can you gain your listeners' attention when you need to?** Look at Chapter 7 for help in projection.

- ✔ **Is your voice too high?** Find out how to put more gravitas into your pitch in Chapter 9.

- ✔ **Do people sometimes struggle to understand you because you rush or mumble?** Find more about dealing with gabbling and mumbling in Chapter 11.

- ✔ **Is your accent hard to decipher?** I talk about clarity in Chapter 6, and cover accents in Chapter 12.

Being all of a piece

Congruence – being all of a piece, or walking your talk – is a crucial element of a leader's voice. Your impact is minimal if your voice doesn't match your personality, drive, creativity, values and energy. Impact is like the Red Arrows aeronautic team in flight formation: it works when all parts of you are travelling in the same direction.

Mark's employees were used to his standard Monday morning pep talks during which he got everyone together, put on a solemn air (which he scarcely felt himself) and urged them to put more effort into sales and stick to deadlines. Because these gatherings were the same every week, no one took a great deal of notice. The company limped along for years until its financial situation became critical. Mark had some grave news to impart to his employees, and they had to take the information seriously if he was to turn the company around. Mark brought the employees together and in his usual unconvincing solemn voice told them how important it was to pull up their socks in this grave situation. His voice sounded just the same as any other Monday, and the result was that, as usual, no one listened and the company seemed poised for extinction.

In desperation, Mark came to see me, and we worked on connecting his voice to his inner energy. His breakthrough came when he confessed how much the company mattered to him. I heard emotion in his voice – emotion he fought to keep out of his meetings because he believed that it showed weakness. But suppressing emotion made his voice sound inauthentic. The next time he spoke to his people, he allowed some of his feeling to show and thus stepped into his full impact. People came to him afterwards with messages of support, effectively turning the tide for the company.

A successful leader is all of a piece – in voice and in action. You sense someone at ease in his or her own skin, rather than someone who gives out mixed messages. If the situation is urgent, you *hear* urgency in the voice tone; if he is sympathetic, you hear compassion; if she is enthusiastic, you hear lightness in her voice.

In public life, *how* you perform is taken as the truth about *what* you can achieve. If you announce good financial results in a depressed voice, people take it to mean depressed results. If you perform an act of kindness and speak about it in a sharp voice, many people fail to recognise the kindness. In a sense you're a role model in your voice and non-verbal language for the values you espouse – voice and values need to match.

You meet some absurdities when voice and message don't match. A voice coach colleague told me of a finance director she worked with: every time he delivered his group's results to the city (in a stifled and timid sounding voice), the company's share price went down! As another example, I found myself attempting to promote the value of peace and calm with my young son by yelling at him, 'Stop shouting at your sister!'

Speaking with presence

In speaking about being all of a piece, the emphasis is on the word *being*. The words you use matter, but the voice you use to convey them, as it reflects your state of being, matters even more.

The very first US presidential debate, between John F Kennedy and Richard Nixon in 1960, shows how your state of mind and your presence affects your message. Nixon had fine words, but people saw fear in his pallor and awkwardness and heard it in his lack of smooth delivery. Kennedy looked and sounded a leader, he had the sense of presence; that won him the country's support.

Speaking with presence is about finding your purpose and entering fully into the state you need in order to be able to achieve your goal. (I discuss states in Chapter 10.) Every shift in your inner state shows in your voice. Knowing this fact – and how to utilise it – gives you valuable insights for leading others.

Bringing others along

If you're tense and panicky when you take a meeting, you transmit that state to others in the room in your tones – regardless of what you actually say. If you're calm and peaceful, then you transmit this state to the people around the table even if your actual words are challenging.

Take the time to tune into yourself before you speak. Find the state you want for others and then take a few breaths to fill yourself with that particular energy first. This technique works for any state you want to create, be it calm, enthusiasm, determination or reassurance.

As you tune into yourself, you're able tune into your voice as well. Before you speak to your audience, decide what sort of message you wish to deliver:

1. **Ask yourself 'Where do I wish to speak from?'**

    Chapter 9 explores the various emotional and physical places of resonance that you can speak from, including confidence and determination from your chest; lightness and enthusiasm from your head; feeling and empathy from your heart, and quiet instinct from your gut.

2. **Choose one place of resonance, and let your attention focus on that physical place in your body.**

3. **Take a breath and sense that you're breathing *into* the specific physical space and feel the unique resonance of that space.**

4. **Have the sense of speaking from that place in your body.**

    For example, tune into confidence and determination in your chest, or quiet instinct in your gut, and speak from there.

5. **Repeat the process for each of the four places in your body.**

Whatever state you enter into yourself, you can spread to other people after you connect with them. If you sound enthusiastic, they pick it up and feel motivated too. If you feel respect, they connect with it in your voice and respect you. Find more about motivation and influence in Chapter 15.

Your state doesn't require you to *do* anything, but rather to *be* present in a particular way. When you're present, you're just that: present in this moment here and now. The ability to be present in the moment is the basis for influencing others.

Changing state

In addition to using your voice to carry people with you, you can interrupt one state you've created and move to another state. When you want to break a mood or move onto a new section of a speech, simply change your tone of voice.

Checking out gender differences

Before the Second World War, men and women's lives were so different that people didn't expect to hear women often in a work or leadership context at all. In the latter half of the 20th century, as many more women entered the workplace, women's voices across the board dropped significantly in pitch. Today, even though much has changed and men's and women's vocal patterns have converged in many ways, gender still affects tone as significantly as any other factor.

In general, men can benefit from the following strategies:

✔ **Incorporate greater vocal variety.** Men's voices are frequently more monotone than women's; putting more variation into your voice makes you sound more interesting.

✔ **Express emotion in words and tone.** Many men shy away from sharing emotion – and unfortunately forfeit one of the most powerful ways of influencing people. I can understand if you're put off by an over-emotional speech, but don't leave out feeling altogether. Feeling is an extremely powerful influencer and motivator.

✔ **Make the most of your deeper tones but don't overdo it.** Low tones give male voices much of their impact and power – but don't force your voice to make it low. Gravitas doesn't come just from your tone of voice but from the whole impression you give, which includes strength of purpose, energy and command of your words.

✔ **Talk *to* your audiences rather than *at* them.** Perhaps this tendency goes back to early games for girls and for boys. Little girls more frequently play participative playground games like skipping or hide and seek where they take turns, while boys have competitions for the fastest and strongest and fight for individual possession of a ball. Whatever the reason for this difference, remember to include your audience and think in terms of a partnership.

Women can frequently benefit from the following:

✔ **Speak from your body, not just from your head.** You can't get away from it – listeners prefer lower voices. Listeners associate a deeper voice with more assertiveness and confidence.

✔ **Take your time.** Women have the reputation for talking more than men, but research shows that in meetings and classrooms, men talk more. Maybe for this reason, women sometimes feel that when they get the opportunity to speak they need to say it fast. Slowing down makes you easier to listen to and elevates the value of your contribution.

✔ **Use your emotional intelligence.** Make the most of skills such as supporting and sharing, rather than joining in a competitive game of aggressiveness.

'Never imitate the boys,' Christine Lagarde, first female head of the IMF, advises. 'Don't assume you'll be better heard because you shout louder, because you use slang, because you behave like the boys . . . Just be yourself.' Interestingly, Christine Lagarde speaks slowly in a measured way, but with a sense of grace rather than aggressiveness.

✔ **Make the most of your listening skills**. Your ability to listen well allows you to be quick on your feet in responses.

Experiment with your ability to change gear in a speech or presentation as follows:

1. **When you get to the end of your first theme, pause for a moment.** If you want, you can also move a step or two from your original standing position to emphasise a change in mood.

2. **As you pause and move, capture the mood you're moving to for your next point.** The next mood may be rational and organised for facts, enthusiastic for an anecdote, or collected and serious for an important point.

3. **Take a good breath, and announce the beginning of your next theme in a *different* tone of voice to establish the new mood.** You may use a strong confident tone to announce a factual section, an enthusiastic tone to tell an anecdote about yourself, a more solemn tone to introduce some grave news, and so on.

Whether or not you state the new theme in so many words, your tone of voice guides your listeners to notice the change of mood and make a shift to the different feel of your new section.

Practise interrupting people – not as a device you employ all the time, but as a useful tool to redirect the energy and emotion of discussions or debates at critical moments. For example, if someone is droning on in a particular tone of voice, interrupt the pattern and choose a different tone, speed, pitch or volume to break in with your own statement such as a supportive high-voiced statement such as, 'That's a great idea; it could work well!' Interrupting the pattern breaks the current mood, and people can turn their attention to you.

Talking tough

In leadership, you have moments when you must show resilience and step up to the mark, which can be challenging. As one man expressed to me in a coaching session, 'I know that I'm meant to be aggressive, hard-hitting and tough, but I'm not that sort of person – I just don't *sound* tough.'

You can be resilient without sacrificing your identity. Try any of the following ways when dealing with difficult times:

✔ **Build internal confidence.** Building your inner confidence is more important than developing your shouting skills! If your voice resonates from that place of certainty low in the body (see Chapter 9), even if you speak at a normal volume level, it captures attention.

Say to yourself, 'I have something to say. I will be heard.' Everyone senses when someone has inner confidence, and it makes people stop and listen. Be one of these people, starting now.

✔ **Claim your time and space.** Fill your space. Don't rush in, but take a full breath and pace what you say. Fill your physical space too, not standing cramped with shoulders hunched, but tall and free with open countenance and physiology, able to move as you want (See Chapter 5). Gaze on your audience or not; know that a cat can look at a king. You're not being arrogant; you're acknowledging that you've a right to be heard.

✔ **Use strong language.** I'm not recommending that you swear! But use language that sounds committed, without the qualifications and hesitations that sometimes pepper everyday speech.

Avoid all the ticks and tags – the 'erms' and 'ums', 'okay?' 'you know?' – that make you sound tentative. Avoid expressions of uncertainty such as, 'I was thinking . . . ', 'possibly', 'perhaps' and 'maybe'. End your sentences firmly, not rising at the end as if you're undecided.

✔ **Stay committed.** Keep up your energy right to the end of your thought, even if you're interrupted. If you drive the thought forward with energy and focus, you're less likely to be interrupted. If someone's comment side-tracks the issue, keep to your point without being distracted, and don't be afraid to use strong eye contact as you continue. At times, you must stand your ground.

✔ **Master the art of interrupting.** In meetings, you may prefer to wait for other people to 'finish their turns' before you speak. But meetings don't often work like that; most vocal interventions are made before the previous speaker finishes, so if you wait for someone to complete a statement, you can end up waiting for ever.

Interrupting is about being heard, so do it definitely, in a clearly audible voice. Just leave the most important part of your intervention until the following sentence. The first sentence gets people's attention; the second makes your point.

✔ **Play your own authentic game.** You don't have to pretend to be something you're not. You don't have to adopt a serious monotone 'sensible' voice. You don't have to pretend to be the archetypal leader.

Talking for a Living: Your Voice in Professional Situations

Apart from a need for power and resilience, each profession has its own intonation and melody. Discovering what allows you to make the most of your voice in your particular area of work is helpful, whether you're a corporate executive, teacher, police officer or therapist. Utilise the preventive measures and training techniques in the following sections if you've a vocally demanding job.

Building resilience

A professional voice needs to be strong – and you need to know how to use it well. Athletes know that if they *force* their bodies to do their will, they're very likely going to suffer injury, so they work on flexibility and elasticity as well as stamina. Similarly, your voice grows stronger as you use it correctly without force.

You find resources throughout this book to help you produce your voice well. Essential strategies for vocally demanding careers follow (along with cross-references for more information) include the following:

- ✔ Warm your voice up by exercising mouth and jaw and practising body relaxation to make sure that you're not tense before you use it heavily (see Chapters 5 and 6).

- ✔ Breathe low down and support your voice with your lower muscles, not your throat. Breathe in to recharge your energy (see Chapter 4).

- ✔ Release your throat, jaw and mouth so that the voice isn't constricted. Relax often – even for a moment or so – to release tension. Keeping your body generally mobile helps you release tension in your voice (see Chapter 5).

- ✔ Discover your natural pitch so you neither force your voice too low nor speak too high (see Chapter 3).

- ✔ Use different resonances to convey what you want to convey, rather than pushing all your sound from your throat (see Chapter 9).

- ✔ Use variety, so that you're not doing the same thing all the time with your voice and wearing out one part of it. Include pauses and silences and different rhythms (see Chapter 8).

- ✔ Realise that getting across your message to listeners is more of a mind challenge than a physical voice challenge (see Chapter 10).

- ✔ Pay attention to the needs of your voice more frequently, so that you become canny about its use, giving consideration to space and acoustics, room layout and calm environment. (I show you more about how to look after your voice in Chapter 19.)

An important element to building your voice's resilience is to know when to stop! The danger point is when your voice gets tired but you ignore it and keep going. You start to use muscles in your throat to push the sound out, which leads to further voice problems. As soon as you know that you're suffering from vocal fatigue, put into action as many strategies as you can to save your voice – talk less, use non-vocal ways to get others' attention, and so on. Do all that you can to take time off and let your voice recover.

Is your voice part of the problem in the classroom?

Your voice may be having an effect that you don't mean it to have. If any of the following is the case for you, you may want to look into developing your voice skills or working with a voice coach:

✔ Your voice sounds tense and strained. Students express their discomfort at having to listen to your voice by lack of confidence in you and by disruptive behaviour.

✔ You yell instead of talking, and in doing so create stress in the classroom, which manifests itself in bad behaviour.

✔ Your voice is weak, and students assume that you're a weak person and begin to take advantage of you.

✔ Your voice sounds patronising, so students harbour resentment against your tone and respond to you more aggressively than usual.

✔ Your voice is so monotone that students lose interest quickly. Or perhaps you mumble, talk too fast, hesitate, use over-complicated language – or any number of other ways that cause your students to lose interest. Whatever the specifics, they find other ways to entertain themselves.

Teaching and instructing others

Teaching is one of the most vocally demanding jobs. Period. Teachers may use their voices vigorously for up to nine hours a day in noisy and demanding circumstances. The vocal folds of a typical primary school teacher vibrate about two million times a day! As a teacher, your voice is your main tool, but it's vulnerable to over-use, and more than 50 per cent of teachers suffer voice disorders at some point during their working lives.

As a teacher, you're a professional speaker. Your voice is an essential part of your equipment, so you must develop your ability to use it well. As a teacher, you need:

✔ A well-supported voice with a firm flow of air that allows you to speak loudly and quietly with equal intensity and authority (turn to Chapter 4 for much more on breathing and vocal support).

✔ A flexible voice that varies speed, rhythm, volume and tone to create a variety of different effects.

✔ A good pitch range for expressing different emotions and inflections.

✔ A pleasing tone that draws in students and encourages them to pay attention.

✔ The ability to tune into your students' voices with your own voice tone to create connection (see Chapter 15).

✔ The ability to adapt your voice to different venues and circumstances – from the noisy corridor to the main hall, from one-to-one conversations to the whole school assembly.

Your voice is your magic weapon as a teacher. If yours is flexible, you can use it to restore order, change a mood, build connections and much more, as I explore in the following sections.

Controlling with your voice

A prime concern of many teachers and other people who talk for a living is having a voice that is loud enough. Indeed, one teacher told me that the only vocal quality you need as a teacher is to be loud! Yes, you need to be heard, so at times you need a way to speak above noise. To find out how to effectively *project* your voice, have a look at Chapter 7. However, speaking loudly is certainly not the same thing as having impact – and control isn't only about volume.

Young professionals Jay and Steve were talking about their teachers at school and remembering Mr. Baxter. They recalled how well everyone behaved during his lessons, even though he never raised his voice. As they talked about Mr. Baxter's ability to control a room full of potentially unruly students, they identified several factors. First, Mr. Baxter had a strong character and set of values, so students respected him. He established various habits in his students. When he entered the room, students were used to becoming quiet. He raised his hand to bring the room to order. The nearest students instantly became quiet, which made the rest notice and follow suit. Every now and then, Mr. Baxter spoke very softly, which required students to be very quiet to hear. These moments were always the most interesting so students enjoyed them. Finally, when Mr. Baxter did raise his voice, he only did so for about four words to get attention, and then almost instantly he brought his volume down and continued in a much quieter tone.

When you want to get the attention of a loud, large group, try the following (I demonstrate it in Track 38):

1. **Take a big breath and make a loud general announcement that leaves something unsaid.**

   For example: 'I have something I want to show you . . .'

2. **Say a second sentence getting quieter.**

   For example, 'There's a different way to do this that I think you'll find much easier . . .'

3. Become even quieter, getting into the main theme of what you want to say.

The class have reason to want to listen and have to be quiet in order to hear you.

The secret is in the decrescendo. You want to take down the room's noise level with you. As you get quieter, so do they. But you have to be at a level that is always audible for them. With practice, it works like a dream . . .

Keeping them interested with your voice

Any skills that make listening more interesting for the students are good to consider. You have to *use* your voice a lot, but at the same time they have to *hear* the same voice for long hours. Make it a good experience for them.

Variety is always good. In today's world, the visual world has become so entertaining that children are less practised in focusing on vocal sound. Varying your voice – as well as using visual clues, movement and music – helps students to focus better and understand what you're saying.

The basic art of voice is always to be heard and clearly understood. But beyond this, your voice presents a wonderful opportunity to connect in different ways – to entertain, excite, reassure, sympathise, make others laugh and more.

When your voice becomes truly expressive, you've many ways to keep the students engaged – and therefore less reason to have to use your voice for control. Try the following to get students to hang on to your every word.

✔ **Tell a story.** Most teachers in primary school are well aware of the power of stories, but teachers of older students sometimes forget that everyone, regardless of age, loves a good story. A story doesn't have to be long; it can be a simple anecdote of a couple of sentences: 'I tried this experiment once and this is what happened to me.'

Introduce stories or mini-anecdotes in various simple ways:

- Just find an example. Make a statement and follow up with an example of what you just said.

- Make a comparison. For example, if I explain that your breath should come out in a stream, I can then say, 'It's just like blowing the candles out on a cake.'

- Use a metaphor. You can tell students that they've lots of work to do – or you can talk about a train journey, where they go through a tunnel sometimes and then when they emerge, the scenery is different and more interesting . . .

- Find an opener that engages curiosity, such as, 'Guess what happened when . . . ', or 'Not many people know this but . . . '.

Stories are great devices for using your voice well. Most people are more expressive when they tell stories. You sound more personal and connect better with your audience. See Chapter 9 for more effective storytelling strategies.

✔ **Change the mood.** You can change the atmosphere in a classroom merely by how you speak. If you want more tranquillity, for example, quieten your voice and allow your rhythm to flow more. If you want to break the boredom, raise the pitch and increase the speed to waken everyone up. You have innumerable ways to influence the mood of your listeners, as I explore in Chapter 15.

✔ **Meet in their court.** Influence starts with joining your listeners before leading them to some different place. So tune in to the energy of the group and connect with it. Don't let the actual *mood* of the room influence you; just pick up its *energy*. After you connect emotionally by sensitively tuning in to what is actually going on, then you can start to take people where you want by shifting the energy. Read more about tuning in in Chapter 15.

Your tone of voice is an invitation to your students to enter a particular state. The influence of your tone happens on a level beneath consciousness so there is nothing specific for students to resist against. For example, if your tone is friendly, the suggestion is one of friendship, and the path of least resistance is to accept your suggestion. Your own energy, expressed in your tone of voice, becomes a catalyst for students' energy and is one of the unspoken secrets of successful teachers.

Voice impacts education

Jemma Rogerson, a senior speech therapist, conducted a study into the impact of a damaged voice on teachers' effectiveness in the classroom, involving 107 children of similar ages and backgrounds. Each child listened and watched a video recording of a teacher speaking in a normal voice, a slightly hoarse voice and a severely hoarse voice. The children were given tests after each recording to see how much of the information they registered. The children's performance on tasks was significantly better when the teacher spoke in the normal voice than in the mildly or severely hoarse voices, regardless of age, gender and IQ.

Speaking as an authority

Having an authentic voice that expresses who you are is a wonderful thing. However, some professions, such as law enforcement or the judiciary, require you to represent a role in society rather than express your individuality. When passengers listen to their airline pilot, for example, they want to have confidence in his professional expertise, not get to know his personal idiosyncrasies.

People understand *what* you say by *how* you say it. For this reason, airline pilots are typically trained to making announcements in calm, bland and reassuringly boring voices. If an pilot attempts a joke or speaks in a spontaneous informal way, his passengers experience subconscious unease. They feel that they're flying with a risk taker, a spontaneous 'spur of the moment' kind of person. Danger alert!

Maintaining law and order

People appreciate a non-personal tone when dealing with the law. If you're up in front of a judge, you don't want to hear a voice that reflects personality, temperament, life style, attitude and personal values. Everything in a court stresses the opposite: this is a place of formality and officialdom, and every judge is a symbol of justice. A ceremonial tone of voice gives everyone in court confidence in the system and respect for its representatives.

Like judges, most of the uniformed professions work best when their representatives put personality aside. As a police officer, for example, you're offering official support that is consistent, reliable and reassuring. You engage with the public in various situations – supporting victims, giving evidence, interviewing suspected criminals and dealing with drunk or violent members of the public. In such potentially intense situations, you want to keep conversations practical and away from emotion. The current style for police officer on the street in the UK is a low-key non-emotional practical bonhomie, which defuses tension and is more likely to get a positive response from the public.

And what about lawyers? If you're a fan of legal dramas, you've seen all manner of dramatic and emotional diatribes. However, working lawyers have discovered that high-flown drama isn't as effective with a jury as more direct traditional approaches.

Speaking impartially

In many public-speaking situations, your ability to convey emotion is your strongest weapon, but you'll find times when you need the opposite. This skill is particularly useful in formal settings such as law courts, tribunals or negotiations.

If you wish to cultivate a tone that emphasises your role rather than your personality, develop the ability to remove emotion from your voice. In Track 39 I demonstrate stepping in and out of the moment. The following gives you practice:

1. **Stand and deliver the start of a short speech on a subject you can get passionate about.**

   Feel the energy and emotion of your words as you say them. Are you feeling determined, encouraging, motivational, reassuring?

2. **After speaking a few sentences, pause and move backwards.**

   Continue delivering the same speech but imagine that you left all the emotion in the place where you were standing before. You literally stepped back away from it.

3. **Stand tall with your head up and maintain a sense of detachment as you continue to speak.**

   Notice the characteristics of impersonal speech:

   - Your voice has less variation of pitch, speed and rhythm.

   - Your language may become more impersonal. You may find yourself saying, 'It has been established that . . . ' instead of, 'I decided to . . . '

   - You may choose more formal words – 'conclusion' instead of 'end' or 'competence' instead of 'skill'.

You sound objective, so this way of speaking serves well for facts and figures and other material where you want to give an impression of neutrality and factual accuracy.

4. **After speaking a while from your impartial position, move forward to the place where you expressed emotion.**

   Restore the emotional energy and passion to your words. Realise that you choose, moment by moment, to have a voice that is passionate or impartial, depending on the needs of the situation.

If you find impersonal detached speaking easier than personal passionate speaking, begin with stages 2 and 3, and then afterwards 'step into' the passion of stages 1 or 4.

Influencing in the helping professions

You may be one of many professionals who depends heavily on your voice to deal with clients face-to-face or over the phone. The helping professions include doctors, nurses and those in associated health professions, religious leaders and many in social care or connected with education.

Emotional labour

Some medical education centres still train doctors, nurses and other health professionals based on Arlie Hochschild's 1979 definition of *emotional labour*. Hochschild, professor of sociology at Berkeley, suggested that in order to do their emotional jobs day by day, health professionals need to manage their own emotions to make clients feel safe and cared for, by suppressing personal feelings and faking more 'useful' responses. The core idea of emotional labour is that facial and bodily display – regardless of what you feel in reality – gives clients what they need emotionally. Think of an airline steward smiling at clients and saying, 'Have a nice day', regardless of what the steward is actually feeling, and trusting that the smile makes each passenger feel acknowledged and cared for. ('Have a nice day' actually came to prominence as the ultimate vacuous phrase, which suggests that the approach isn't entirely successful.)

Emotional labour is a fine theory and a genuine attempt to tackle the problem of emotional burn-out in the caring professions, but it doesn't acknowledge the fact that clients can recognise the difference between a stock 'uninvolved' emotional response and genuine feeling, if not consciously, certainly at a deeper level.

Popular researcher Malcolm Gladwell tells a story in his book *Blink* (Back Bay Books, 2007) that highlights the importance of the voice in the helping professions. Medical researcher Wendy Levinson recorded hundreds of doctor/patient conversations to investigate whether the tone of a doctor's voice had any connection with their being sued or not. Half the doctors had never been sued, and the other half had been sued twice or more. The psychologist Nalini Ambady continued the study by taking four ten-second clips from each doctor's conversation and electronically filtering them into sound tone without discernible words. Then she asked people to rate these short wordless clips in terms of warmth, hostility, dominance and anxiety. From those sounds alone, they were able to predict accurately which doctors had been sued and which not.

The part played by the voice in the helping professions – particularly the role of emotion –is surprisingly under-researched. Old ideas about appropriate and effective communication persist in many places (see the sidebar 'Emotional labour').

If you work in a helping profession, you do not need to suppress your emotions. In fact, positive emotions and their effects are the very thing that can give you energy and satisfaction. Suppressing your emotional responses or putting on a blandly happy face can drain your personal energy. Instead, model the attitudes and behaviours of caring professionals who do cope emotionally, as I discuss in the following section, and you can find ways to use positive emotions genuinely to energise your work.

Of course, as a helping professional, you also need support yourself for times when you're assailed by negative emotions in your work, but cutting out *all* genuine emotion deprives you of the positive emotional rewards of your work, without providing a safe outlet for negative emotion.

Caring with your voice

You sometimes hear people talk about a doctor or nurse's 'bedside manner', as if it were something that you can paste on. The ability to use your voice influentially isn't merely a 'nice to have' in medicine; it can be an integral part of healing.

Your tone of voice is an integral part of your caring. Appropriately deployed, your tone can achieve wonders. In caring situations, you're most influential if you're able to express in your voice the full range of human emotions, including sympathy, rigour, energy, enthusiasm, intuition and whatever else you feel that your client needs.

You can use the emotion in your voice to contribute positively to clients' internal resources by:

- ✔ Building emotional confidence in clients so they trust you.
- ✔ Creating an ambiance in which professionals can work best and clients feel most comfortable.
- ✔ Promoting courage to help clients overcome various challenges.
- ✔ Offering the genuine warmth of human connection so that clients know that they're cared for.
- ✔ Reassuring and calming clients.

Using emotion in your voice starts with careful listening, which means hearing not only what a person is saying, but also what is going on underneath the words in the voice tone. This skill requires an openness in you, and an ability to listen at various different levels. See Chapter 15 for more on tuning in.

Practise your listening skills on an occasion where the other person is needy in some way – in a professional situation or in your private life. Become aware of different levels of listening:

1. **Whatever the person is saying, feel your feet in contact with the floor, centre yourself and be aware of breathing calmly into your centre.**

2. **Hear and understand the words the other person uses, but don't make them the focus of your attention.** If the person uses a stream of emotional words, you can allow them to wash over you and focus more on the deeper emotions behind the words.

3. **Eliminate as much tension from your body and mind as you can and then scan your body to discover the place where the sound of the person's voice affects you.** Often the voice affects the area of your heart, stomach or gut.

4. **Tune in gently to this place in your body.**

5. **When you speak, keep a connection with this part of your body and speak from this place.**

Lisa was having a difficult day as a visiting carer, and due to various crises beyond her control arrived late at Mary's flat. When 80 year-old Mary opened the door, she greeted Lisa with a shrill, 'You're late!' and proceeded to unleash a stream of loud invective. Lisa's first instinct was to launch into rational explanations of the various difficulties she had met on her way in order to counteract the attack, but she resisted the temptation. Instead, she took a deep breath, calmed herself and became centred. Listening, Lisa became aware of a hole in her own stomach, a feeling that she could only describe as an emptiness or a yearning. She suddenly became aware of Mary's sadness and anxiety, hidden beneath the angry words. Lisa's own words then came from that deeper intuitive place: 'I'm sorry I'm late,' she said, 'You must have been worried.' Immediately, as she connected accurately with what was really going on for her client, Mary's anger dissolved.

Coaching others

Excellent listening is also key if you're a coach, trainer, counsellor or therapist. You want to have an open awareness, which the International Coaching Federation calls *coaching presence,* or the ability to be fully conscious and create spontaneous relationship with a client.

Presence is the ability to *be* in the moment, without judging or assessing what you hear – and without thinking about what tools you're going to employ or what you're going to say next. You just listen and meet everything with openness and intelligence in a state of not-knowing, and out of that not-knowing come the words that you speak. When you're fully present, your voice finds its tone from that state of being, and you connect easily with your client. Your presence allows your client to be present fully to his or her own experience, as well.

You know when you're speaking from that place of presence because you find no effort in speaking. The words emerge from the energy you share between you.

Inducing trance

When you share a fully present space with clients, you're able to invite them to go to places that are helpful to them. This skill is particularly noticeable in hypnotherapy but belongs too to the fields of coaching, teaching and therapy. Your voice tone connects with the voice of your client or with their general energy, and then gradually transforms the energy into something more generative, where the client can become more creative and resourceful in finding his or her own solutions.

The hypnotherapist Milton Erickson had an extraordinary ability to cure people through semi-trance. He would follow the lead of his client in innumerable subtle ways, and then into that meeting place he would introduce with his voice a little lightness, a calm centredness, the deeper voice of the subconscious or the warm voice of reassurance – whatever was needed for the client at that time. The work was beautifully nuanced, deeply respectful – in turns playful, challenging or comforting – and led his clients to find lasting resolution to their problems.

Trance and semi-trance are powerful tools that build on your voice skills. Find more on these helpful techniques in *Self-Hypnosis For Dummies* by Mike Bryant and Peter Mabbutt (Wiley).

Part VI
The Part of Tens

"Could you drop the 'blood, toil, tears and sweat' voice for a more 'bunnies, rainbows, fairies and dreams' one, Uncle Winston?"

In this part . . .

Dip into the famous *For Dummies* Part of Tens for some instant ways to sound good. Discover the secrets of sounding more authoritative and how to use charisma to move and influence your audience. Check out valuable tips for looking after your voice. Finally, I give you my top ten favourite examples of great voices to inspire you. Enjoy!

Chapter 17

Ten Ways to Sound More Authoritative

*W*hen someone comes to me for voice coaching, the most frequent question is how to sound more authoritative. When you sound more authoritative, people listen to what you have to say and find you more powerful and influential. When you hear someone speak with authority, the power of that person's delivery may give you the impression that only someone exceptional can achieve such an impact. Yet cultivating an authoritative voice is easier than you may think.

Stand Confidently

If you *look* confident, you instantly seem like someone to be reckoned with, and people pay heed. You look confident when you stand well. You also create the best conditions for producing a good sound.

Watch Shakespearean actors playing heroic roles on stage and notice how they hold themselves. Their positioning and posture is the very combination of characteristics that you need for an authoritative voice:

> ✔ **Find your balance with your weight evenly distributed between both feet.** Notice your centre of gravity in the lower part of your body just below your navel, not up in your chest and shoulders.
>
> ✔ **Stand tall.** Allow your head to lead your body up towards the sky. Doing so adds a couple of centimetres to your height without effort.

✔ **At the same time, *relax*.** Release your face and jaw, your neck and shoulders. Let go of tension all down your spine through soft knees to your feet and toes.

✔ **Take a breath and feel the air expand your whole body.** Scan your body to see that nothing is rigid. Everything is flexible, mobile and expanding. Breathe out and feel confidently at ease.

Chapter 5 is brimming with techniques for relaxing so you can present yourself confidently.

Speak Clearly

If you're clear and audible, you sound as if you mean what you say; and nothing is as self-affirming as knowing that people are really listening to you. This knowledge does wonders for both your self-esteem and confidence. Mumbling makes you sound as if you yourself don't feel you have the authority to speak – so why on earth should anyone else be interested? As I outline in Chapter 6, the keys to speaking clearly are simple:

✔ **Open your mouth when you speak.** Even if doing so feels a bit unnatural to you at first, opening your mouth actually comes across as *more* natural to other people.

✔ **Make your vowel sounds easily distinguishable.** Again, opening your mouth helps! People who mumble reduce every vowel to a version of 'er'.

✔ **Make your consonants clearer.** Pay special attention to consonants that sound rather like each other, like 'cut' and 'gut', 'pet' and 'bet', and 'zip' and 'sip'.

Your mouth movements feel bigger to you than they really are. Watch how much people's mouths move when they speak on television – much more than you may think. So exaggerate a little; be clearer than you think you need to be. Other people won't find your speech exaggerated at all.

Project Your Voice

People are most likely to take you seriously if your voice is sufficiently loud to create an impact. Your audience, not you, is the judge of that. You don't need to force your voice in order for others to hear you – simply pay attention to two crucial factors:

- ✔ **Loosen up.** Release your shoulders, neck and jaw. Shake your whole body out.

- ✔ **Take a good breath.** Imagine the kind of energetic breath you take to shout 'goal!' to cheer your favourite footballer for instance – and launch yourself straight from that dynamic breath into speaking (see Chapter 5).

Provided your vocal cords are in normal good order and you use a good breath with your body free of tension, your voice will ring out. If you *really let go,* you sound loud. The secret is releasing, not pushing – the more you strain with physical effort, the less effective you are.

You also need to *want* to be heard. Think big! Have a mental picture in your mind of sound waves radiating out strongly from you in all directions. If you really intend people to hear every word you say, they will. See Chapter 10 for more about the power of intention.

Give Your Voice Gravitas

A deeper voice always sounds more convincing. The secret of bringing out your lower tones is to allow your voice to resonate in your body. A voice that resonates in the chest and solar plexus sounds purposeful; people trust it. Do all the following to help you to speak more from your chest:

- ✔ **Find your natural low pitch.** Just hum 'Happy Birthday' quietly; now speak at the same pitch. Use that pitch for your normal speaking.

- ✔ **Breathe low down.** As you breathe in, fill yourself with confident energy. As you speak, allow your breath to flow out smoothly.

- ✔ **Focus on your chest.** Imagine that you're speaking from your body rather than from your head. Relax, and allow your whole body to be part of the action.

- ✔ **Imagine yawning before you speak.** The feeling of yawning opens up your deeper resonances.

Don't *force* your voice lower by pushing down – you sound most commanding if you speak within your own natural pitch range. And don't take all the natural high inflections out of your voice in order to sound more authoritative . . . you just end up sounding boring!

Emphasise Strongly

One of the best ways to demonstrate that you mean what you say is to use emphasis to make your point. Many people sound dreary because they put equal weight on each word, and the flatness in their tone soon sends listeners to sleep. Authoritative speakers emphasise strongly, more than you may be aware of until you listen out for it.

Copy the way that commentators in the media lay stress on particular words. You may be surprised by how strong the emphasis feels and sounds when you do it yourself. The words to stress are those that matter for the meaning of your communication. If a newsreader reports: 'News is coming in that the town has been devastated by a tornado', the crucial words that give meaning to the announcement are 'devastated' and 'tornado'. If the newsreader emphasises those words strongly, the communication has a powerful impact.

You probably need to stress your most important content words much stronger than you're currently doing if you want to be authoritative. You need plenty of breath to be able to emphasise words as strongly at the end as at the beginning of a sentence. Record and listen to yourself in order to judge how strongly you come across.

Take Your Time

Speed has a major effect on the impression you make. In films, a scene is sometimes speeded up for comic effect or slowed down to create a powerful impact. You sense the epic triumph of a film hero as his best moment unfurls in slow motion. Slowing your words has a similar effect. Think of Winston Churchill saying to the British Parliament: 'Never in the field of human conflict was so much owed by so many to so few.'

So, to sound authoritative, slow down. But don't grind to a halt! Your speech still needs to flow with a sense of rhythm. It's a matter of thinking big: big breath, big sense of space and glorious spacious resonant speech!

Your audience isn't waiting impatiently for your next word. On the contrary, people have respect for speakers who take their time and who allow their listeners processing time.

Finish Strongly

If you want to sound authoritative, end each complete statement firmly on a low pitch. What you may be doing instead is either letting your voice tail off or raising your intonation at the end of a sentence, so your statements sounds like questions. In either case, you sound uncertain of yourself or as if you're seeking reassurance.

This technique of finishing strongly is so simple yet makes an enormous difference to your impact. Of course, questions do end high, and you need a variety of pitch elsewhere, so that you remain interesting. But the low note at the end stands out with statesmanlike finality. The truth is that people respond more to intonation patterns than to the actual meaning of words.

Always take a good breath first so that you have sufficient air to finish your statement strongly.

Avoid Verbal Tags and Qualifiers

Yeah, look, you know how some of us, frankly – like – add stuff to our sentences okay? – you know what I mean? – that actually – you know? – kind of get in the, like, way of what you're trying to – you know – say?

If you add weak tags to what you say, you sound ineffectual and sacrifice your authority. So avoid all those insidious little phrases that break up sentences, such as 'you know', 'actually', 'okay?' or 'like'.

Avoid too those short questions and modifications that are meaningless and reduce the power of your statement:

Let's go with that plan, *shall we?*

I guess it'll work out, *won't it?*

I just thought it was a good idea.

It's good, *if you know what I mean.*

One way to avoid verbal tags is to slow down and give yourself more thinking time. You mostly only need the extra words if you breathe and speak too fast and therefore can't think quickly enough. Many of the little separators, the 'ers' and 'ums' and extra words, are caused by shortness of breath. They allow you moments to snatch extra little bits of air, but using them becomes a habit. Take time to breathe (see Chapter 4) and decide what you want to say.

Employ Silence

Silence is one of the powerful tools employed by authoritative speakers –yet many people don't use it and are indeed scared of it. When you speak in public, time can play strange tricks on you. A couple of seconds of silence can seem like a few minutes – or even an hour or two! You may feel a compulsion to plunge into words before you've even formulated an idea, and then keep rushing headlong to the end – anything to avoid a silence.

You don't have to fill every pause with sound. In fact, you appear more in command of yourself if you employ silence from time to time. The actor Ralph Richardson, master of the pregnant pause, asserted that acting lay in pauses.

Take a good breath before you begin. Speak slower, so that your breathing pauses can be longer without seeming awkward. And, during the pauses take the time to think about what you're going to say next so that you appear confident and natural. If you find silence difficult at first, try moving between points – for example, take a couple of steps from your starting position – to give yourself something to do.

Silence is an effective highlighter too. If you're silent just before or just after a phrase, you're essentially saying, 'Listen to this. This next phrase is important' or 'Wait for this. Something good's coming.' And people pay special attention to that point. Think of 'And the winner is . . . '

Speak Fluently

The speech of people who sound authoritative flows. You hear a steady stream of sound, not short bursts interspersed with hesitations. This rhythm makes them sound clear-thinking and confident. As I examine in greater detail in Chapter 13, speaking fluently is partly about breathing and partly about thinking – the two go together.

Take time to think of what you want to say before you utter your first word. Then take a good breath before you begin.

If you want to sound authoritative, you need to be able to speak long phrases as well as short ones. Speak at a measured pace. You may find some breaths long at first but with practice it gets easier. When you can speak long sentences smoothly right to the end, you are equipped for all occasions.

Chapter 18

Ten Ways to Speak with Charisma

*W*hich speakers give you goose bumps? Someone with charisma can make you feel as if you're the most important person in the world and truly inspire you.

Charismatic speakers are all of a piece (see Chapter 16), happy in their own skin, and know how to connect with people (Chapter 15) so that others feel at one with them. You also sense their vibrant internal energy – their 'life force' – which affects you as they speak, whether they're dynamic or calm. By the way, the word charisma actually means 'grace' – a good reminder that real charisma inspires but never overwhelms. Following are ten ways to find your charisma, and use it to engage your listeners and communicate on a deeper level.

Find Your Calm Centre

The sense of ease that you admire in people with charisma has its root in their calm centre. You can find this space for yourself.

1. **Quieten all the chaos in your mind and body.** Acknowledge and then let go of all feelings of fear or vulnerability, or any inner criticism that makes you self-conscious and ill at ease. Find that quiet place inside you where you can nurture peace and calm.

2. **Focus on your breathing, by simply breathing gently in and out.** As you breathe in, feel the air fill every part of your body, and be aware of your calm centred self and your powerhouse of energy, like a bright light inside you. Each time you breathe out, be aware of relaxing more and more. Tune into a sense of stillness and aliveness.

3. **Keep focusing on your breathing in the present moment.** Let any thoughts of past disasters or successes float away; do the same for thoughts about future triumphs or potential failures. Stay in the present, moment by moment by moment.

This calm centre is the solid base for everything you do. Whatever happens, know that you can come back to steady breathing in the moment and find a point of stillness inside you. You can find numerous other ideas for relaxing in Chapter 5. Read Chapter 4 for lots more about breathing.

Breathe with Intention

Breath is the very life behind your communication – and a vital secret of charisma. If you're delighted to see someone, you feel it in your body. That emotion provides the vital energy you need to turn thought waves into sound waves.

Each emotion creates its own special vibrations, which resonate with particular vitality. Each energy produces a different breath and different sound, whether it's joy, anger, enthusiasm, determination or calm. Delight creates a delighted breath – and you *sound* delighted.

Allow the connection between your emotional energy and sound, and your voice tone matches your intention and the life in you touches your listeners:

1. **Feel the spark of desire to speak, the emotional energy that arises with the breath.** That particular breath create its own unique vibrations, which find their special places of resonance in your body. See Chapter 9 for much more on resonance.

2. **Allow the energy and vibrations to create their unique sound, which accurately conveys the meaning of your emotional energy.** Your voice expresses *you*, and people hear you directly. When you speak from this place, others find you attractive and charismatic.

You can make attempts to *sound* delighted, friendly, firm or any other emotion when you speak, but unless you *feel* the specific emotion and breathe it, the connection with your audience can lack genuine spark.

Use Your Whole Instrument

If you connect to the emotional energy inside you, your voice is naturally full of variety, at moments high with enthusiasm, deep for reflection, fast for energy, slow to make a special point, warm to show caring and so on. Allow your whole voice to come into play. You have many variables at your disposal; have fun with them all!

- ✔ **Tone:** Make yours rough or smooth, harsh or velvety.

- ✔ **Vowels:** Elongate or shorten these sounds, use them to express feelings.

- ✔ **Consonants:** Hit them sharply or caressingly; add clarity to your speech.

- ✔ **Pitch:** Take your voice high or deep – or anywhere in between.

- ✔ **Volume:** Speak loudly or softly; let the sound grow or diminish within a phrase or sentence.

- ✔ **Tempo:** Take a sentence fast and slow; get faster or slower.

- ✔ **Emphasis:** Stress a specific word or phrase; now, hear *this*, it's important.

- ✔ **Resonance:** Let your sound vibrate in your head, chest, heart and gut; convey excitement, confidence, warmth and deep instinct.

Use Rhythm and Rhetoric

Great speakers vary rhythm and emphasis to influence their listeners and lead them towards significant portions of their speech. Think of a fine speech as poetry, and have fun creating your own rhythms. Look at Chapter 8 for a host of ideas, or get going with the following easy and highly effective techniques:

- ✔ **Alliteration (repeated consonants):** 'Lead the land we love'.

- ✔ **Repeated motif:** Luther King's repeated 'I have a dream' or Barack Obama's 'Yes, we can.'

- ✔ **Repetition of an idea, just in different words:** Think of Monty Python's parrot: 'He's passed on! This parrot is no more! He has ceased to be! He's expired and gone to meet his maker!'

- ✔ **Rhetorical questions that don't require an answer:** Shakespeare's Shylock – 'If you prick us, do we not bleed, if you tickle us, do we not laugh? If you poison us, do we not die?'

- ✔ **Contrast (not this but that):** JF Kennedy's 'Ask not what your country can do for you; ask what you can do for your country.'

- ✔ **Silence:** That amazing pause after a significant phrase, or the pause before uttering your most important words.

Fill the Space Mentally

When you have charisma, you fill your space – however large – with warmth and energy. Do the following to expand your sense of self:

1. **Stand tall and breathe calmly.** With each steady in-breath, imagine a light inside you, getting brighter and brighter. Breathe out and imagine the light expanding beyond your body and filling the room like an aura.

2. **Smile to yourself inside and feel the smile in your body grow and spread right across your chest.** Enjoy the sensation of being fully alive and ready for anything.

3. **Raise your arms and imagine that powerful beams of light are shooting out from each hand.** Imagine your beams of light can touch the walls of your space on each side. As each arm moves, sense that you can touch the boundaries of your space. Feel that you own the space.

4. **Without pretending to be something you're not, get the sense of stepping into a larger you.** The bigger the space, the more inner energy you need, so remember yourself at your most intensely alive, happy and relaxed – that's the you I'm talking about! Be that person right now. You're bigger than you think.

Use this practice at any time to build the sense of a larger, more dynamic you. Step into this larger you before you give a speech, or before any challenging encounter. Chapter 14 has more helpful things to do before you give a speech.

Connect with Your Purpose

Charisma is like an iceberg; much more is going on beneath the surface than people are aware of. People with charisma know underneath *why* they're speaking. Their sense of ease and confidence is the result of their complete confidence in their beliefs, values and attitudes inside. They connect to their deeper purpose when they speak. This inner confidence doesn't have to be solemn at all – it's certainly empowering.

Go inside yourself for a moment and connect with your deeper purpose. Ask yourself:

- ✔ What is my purpose in this talk, this presentation, this discussion? Why am I speaking?
- ✔ What is most valuable to me in this context? What matters to me?
- ✔ What do I want for my listeners? What is my gift to them?
- ✔ What is my mission? Why am I here? What do I believe in?

You don't need to have answers straightaway. As you ask these questions, just be aware of any words that float up to you. Trust your instinct. As you go deep inside yourself for answers to these questions, you begin to clarify your purpose and build your energy around your purpose. When you release this purposeful energy into your words, other people connect to your energy and are moved by what you say.

Enter the Zone

Have you ever listened to a speaker who seemed to glow with inner energy? When you possess this 'switched-on' energy, people become completely captivated by you. You're in a state of *flow*. People in flow often can't describe how they got there, but certain factors help you reach this state:

- **Practice!** You enter the zone after you've gained complete familiarity and competence with your material, when you're free to focus fully on the task in hand without conscious effort. You're *relaxed* and *energised* at the same time.

- **Let go of compulsion or insistence.** Stop trying hard to perform well. Let go of your attachment to a particular outcome.

- **Enjoy yourself.** Speaking to people is more like play than hard work.

- **Use your imagination.** Create how you'd like things to be. Act as if it has already come true. Have fun with it.

- **Use the whole of you.** Engage your mind, voice, body, heart and soul – your whole life force.

When you let go and allow yourself to flow, your inner creativity and outer expression become aligned and your concentration becomes focused. The increase in vitality and influence is phenomenal.

Lead with Your Feelings

Some professionals with presenting experience say that feelings have no place in business presentations or are too dangerous to reveal in public. Don't believe this. Emotion is what people remember and what influences them. So find your passion. If your subject excites you, get excited; if you're moved, let people hear that you're moved. Listeners notice an immediate difference in how alive you are when your feelings and passions show. They see light in your eyes, they hear energy in your voice and they become entranced by you.

Practise speaking with passion in safe situations with friends. Allow them more access than usual to what you really feel. Notice the positive responses you get when you do this. You may feel vulnerable, but the risk you're taking produces pure gold.

Create Rapport with Your Voice

Charismatic speakers make you feel specially connected to them. How do you tune into other people and connect with them? You do it by finding similarities. Here's how:

1. **Really notice your audience.** Take time to see them, listen to their voices and the sound of their silence, and sense their mood and energy. Step metaphorically into their shoes and get the feeling of how things look from their point of view.

2. **Adjust your communication to fit in empathetically with what you find.** If your audience's energy is low, start by speaking quietly and slowly. If you sense a general excitement, start with a bright, energetic voice. When you start where your audience already is emotionally, people feel harmony with you and engage willingly with you.

3. **After matching their energy, move gradually towards a different emotional energy.** Shift the energy towards enthusiasm or determination, for instance, and watch your audience follow your lead. You become like the charismatic Pied Piper of Hamelin and your audience willingly follows you anywhere!

See Chapter 15 for more about creating connection.

Speak Congruently

Most people act a bit at times. Perhaps you feel angry but put on a pleasant voice, or you speak enthusiastically when you're actually feeling upset inside.

Charismatic speakers are neither self-conscious nor acting a role. Their tone of voice matches their inner thoughts and emotions. They're just happy to be themselves, and this happiness communicates itself in their voice and body language and makes listeners feel comfortable too.

If you don't feel confident, your first instinct when you speak may be to hide your insecurity by acting up. However, if you hide away your real self too much, you haven't anything *of you* to give your listeners. Instead, permit yourself to feel a bit vulnerable, and as far as possible act naturally. You may think that's letting yourself down; but other people will feel more able to connect with you, and find you more engaging – they'll catch your charisma.

Chapter 19

Ten Ways to Take Care of Your Voice

Most people I ask confess that they spend more time and money on hair lotions, skin potions or shaving accessories than they spend on their voices. Is it the same for you? Only when something goes wrong with your voice do you realise just how much you value it. Imagine life without your voice!

Looking after your voice is truly worthwhile. Not just because you don't want to lose it, but because a healthy voice is your amazing gift for communicating, influencing and connecting with others. Following are ten top strategies to point you in the right direction.

Take It Easy

When your body is relaxed, your voice can happily vibrate and work well. So chill out! If you use your voice a lot or frequently speak in public, do the following:

- **Scan your body every now and then for physical tension.** Check your neck, shoulders, jaw and tongue, and your spine and knees. Allow any tension to melt away. See Chapter 5 for more on relaxation.

- **Do a bit of gentle physical stretching to warm up your muscles.** Ease out your shoulders, move your neck, stretch and bend your spine, and loosen your knees.

- **Warm up your voice easily.** Glide gently from low to high sounds on different vowels and trill with your lips or tongue. See Chapter 6 for more vocal warm-up activities.

Your mind and body work together, so all the preceding activities are more effective when your mind is at ease as well. If you're feeling stressed, that is the very time to check for tension and ease out your body.

Be kind to your voice if you're feeling a bit stiff after a night out or a strenuous sporting session, or if you're feeling under par. Allow yourself an easier day (see the later section 'Enjoy Silence Sometimes') and avoid putting your voice under too much pressure.

Support Your Voice with the Breath

Breath is a crucial element in looking after your voice. As I discuss in Chapter 4, use your breath to power your voice instead of pushing from your throat. This approach allows your voice to sound great and stay strong.

Breathing well means taking the time to fill your lungs *before* you say something and then using the energy of that breath to make sound. You may find that you don't normally pay any attention to your breath when you speak, and if so you may take in scarcely any air. Start remedying this situation now: for a while each day, think about taking a breath before you say something and using the air as you speak. Your vocal folds benefit, you sound much more definite and your voice becomes fuller.

Don't forget how to fill your lungs with air: breathe out strongly as far as you possibly can and keep breathing out until you absolutely have to take in air. Then release any tension in your body and notice how the air rushes in. You feel the rush of air low in your body. That's a good breath!

Start Your Voice Smoothly

One vocal habit is worse for your voice than anything – and that's banging against the vocal folds. You sometimes hear the hard glottal sound of someone attacking words in this way. Poor folds!

Your vocal folds are tiny, and yet they serve you to make robust sounds and to keep going all day, every day. If your breath is lazy and you persist in speaking loudly, all the muscles around you throat and jaw push the sound out with too much pressure instead of your strong lower body muscles providing support – a sure-fire way to give your vocal folds a hard time.

Take a good breath and imagine that you launch into sound without your breath really stopping, like a ski jumper using the downwards slope to launch into the air. Think of how you launch into sound when you sing – you generally use a smoother and easier onset than when you speak. Use the feeling of that onset when you speak. Your vocal cords will love you!

Speak at a Comfortable Pitch Level

Everyone wants a rich low voice, like Sean Connery or Lauren Bacall. Lower voices sound more authoritative and confident and are favoured in the media.

The deepness of your voice depends mainly on the length and thickness of your vocal cords, and you can't easily do anything about that. If you force your voice from the lower part of your throat, you may feel authoritative and powerful to you, but producing low sounds this way has no power, and frequently people can't understand you. Moreover, speaking this way inflicts serious strain on your vocal cords and can damage your voice.

Instead, if you want gravitas in your voice:

- **Find the pitch that is comfortable for you.** When you agree with someone with the sound 'mmm' or 'aha,' you're usually using your natural pitch. The next time you use such sounds to agree with someone, follow up with words spoken at the same pitch.

- **Imagine that your voice sounds low.** Breathe low and allow your voice to resonate in your body where it sounds strong and confident. Chapter 9 has all the details on resonance.

- **Vary your pitch so that people hear the contrasts in your voice.** Don't stick relentlessly to the same low pitch. Gravitas doesn't have to be dull! Look for ways to vary your voice in Chapter 8.

Follow these guidelines and you'll sound authoritative – plus you'll protect your voice.

Raise Your Volume – Without Strain

When in doubt, don't shout. Yelling at the top of your voice on the football pitch, shouting in a noisy nightclub, screaming at a live concert – these things just aren't good for your voice. You realise this fact when you wake up next morning hoarse or with a sore throat! Yes, these things happen occasionally, but when they do, give your voice a good rest the next day.

When you want to raise your volume, think about all the following so you protect your voice in the process:

- Take a big energetic breath low down when you raise your voice, so that you don't have to push from your throat.
- Relax! The more you release your neck, shoulders, jaw and tongue, the freer and fuller your sound.

- Realise that being heard is largely about being understood, so articulate your words clearly (see Chapter 6).
- Use strong mental energy to communicate; your desire to be heard is the power behind your physical sound (see Chapter 10).
- Vary the pitch of your voice. You strain your voice by producing the sound from the same place the whole time.

Take Your Time

Something that really tires out your voice is pounding out the words without pause, especially if you talk with the same pitch and tone all the time, which puts strain on the same part of your voice. The most tiring kind of speaking is continuous, like the report of a horse racing radio commentator during the race or the calling of an auctioneer during a long bidding period.

Give your voice a break! Even a pause of a second or two allows vocal cords to return to rest position and can make all the difference. Think of a physical pursuit such as tennis; you have periods of high activity followed by pauses between shots and between sets and games. Most sports work in this way.

When you give a presentation, take time to breathe between each statement. Give your audience the odd pause for them to reflect on what you said. Move to a different spot on the platform in silence between sections of your presentation in order to allow yourself (and your audience) to rest for a moment. As well as keeping your voice fresh, you make the presentation easier to listen to. You also feel calmer and more relaxed.

Look After Your General Health

Your voice is affected by your health. When you feel good, your voice generally feels good too. Look out for signs that all isn't well with your voice, including hoarseness, a raw throat, feelings of strain and effort when you talk, loss of higher sounds and people asking whether you have a cold.

You can easily look after the health of your voice by following these basic 'do's' and 'don'ts':

- Don't talk too much if you have a cough, a cold or a sore throat; and give yourself time to get well again before you use your voice to any extent.
- Don't push your voice when you're tired or unwell, or feeling emotionally stressed.

- Do make allowances for changes in your life, such as changing your diet, losing weight, changing house or job or any personal trauma. Recognise that your voice is as affected as the rest of you.

- Do try talking gently through any discomfort, instead of coughing or clearing your throat, when you want to get rid of mucous. You may want to avoid milky foods that create mucus too.

Enjoy Silence Sometimes

If you love your voice, beware of noise! Keeping up a conversation when background sounds are really loud is hard on your voice. Yes, this does include various venues that may be your favourites! But you don't need to avoid them entirely, just think a bit about your voice when you're there:

- If you speak in an over-large venue or noisy environment, insist on a microphone.

- If you must speak in noisy situations or for prolonged periods, make sure that you know how to produce your voice efficiently (see Chapters 4 and 5).

- Find somewhere quieter to converse one-to-one; if you must talk in a noisy space, face each other, articulate well and watch his or her lips.

- Find times for silence – even a few hours or a whole day occasionally. Everyone enjoys a rest from time to time – and so does your voice.

- If your job involves a lot of talking, make sure that you receive professional training and support for your voice. See the Appendix for more on finding a voice coach.

Stay Well-Lubricated

Your voice needs good lubrication to avoid irritation or real damage and modern life contains many hazards that dry out your voice. Staying properly hydrated, however, is about more than drinking lots of water. Look at the following list and see what factors you can mitigate. All the following can dry out your throat:

- **Medicines:** Penicillin as well as most allergy, anti-anxiety and cholesterol medications; medications for coughs and colds that contain menthol or eucalyptus designed to dry up mucus; some vitamin supplements that include vitamin C.

- **Atmosphere:** The drying effects of central heating or air conditioning, in your home or your car; recirculated air during air travel.

- ✔ **Environments:** Spaces polluted by dust, smoke or fumes or even deodorants and strong household cleaners.

- ✔ **Caffeinated beverages:** Speed up mucous production and give you too much phlegm.

- ✔ **Smoking, alcohol and drugs:** Dry and damage the quality of your voice, and also irritate and damage the linings of your nose and throat.

- ✔ **Chronic tension:** Releases adrenalin, which further dries your throat!

The best response to these drying conditions is to drink water at room temperature. When your voice feels dry and your first instinct is to cough or to push your voice more, stop! Take a drink.

Get Help When You Need It

Your voice is pretty tough, and you can recover from most over-use by acting sensibly to look after your voice as I highlight in this chapter.

Sometimes, however, the best course of action is to consult a doctor or a laryngologist or an ear, nose and throat consultant. Following are the crucial times to seek further help:

- ✔ If you lose your voice, especially if it happens regularly.

- ✔ If your voice becomes hoarse or croaky, especially over several days.

- ✔ If your voice sounds weak and you're unable to project it.

- ✔ If your voice is getting tired more quickly than before.

- ✔ If your voice or throat feels constantly painful, if you've a lump in your throat, or if you find speaking or swallowing painful.

- ✔ If you constantly and regularly need to clear your throat.

- ✔ If your voice becomes unreliable – changing pitch, swooping unexpectedly or getting stuck in one tone.

Getting help in time is often the way to save your voice and is well worth it!

Chapter 20

Ten Inspiring Voices

In This Chapter

▶ Discovering the vocal qualities that listeners prefer

▶ Looking at what makes a great speaker

▶ Appreciating key moments that capture attention

*W*hose voices are the best loved? Surveys investigating preferred voices in different parts of the English-speaking world arrived at certain common factors. They agree that the best voices all share characteristics associated with confidence and trust, including:

✓ **A fairly low pitch** for both men and women

✓ **A melodious and full quality;** in other words, a *rich* sound

✓ **An absence of high frequency noise** such as screechy sounds

✓ **A measured pace** with brief pauses now and then

✓ **Sentences that fall at the end, rather than rise,** which make the speaker sound confident

This list is a good start but isn't sufficient. A melodious low voice on its own doesn't make the hairs on the back of your neck stand up. For that, you need a voice that communicates to every cell of your body – by its energy and the power of its feeling, imagination or intellect. Then a voice becomes truly exciting.

A Voice That Stirred a Nation – Winston Churchill

Winston Churchill's voice emerged at a critical time in world history. He encouraged his generation and has gone on to inspire people ever since.

What is it about Churchill's voice that just sends shivers down your spine? In some ways, he's an unusual choice because he didn't love public speaking. But he understood the secrets of powerful delivery:

- ✔ **His sense of solemnity and grandeur gave depth and pace to his voice.** His low endings (see Chapter 16) are so low, so final, that you *know* he's going to get his nation through the worst that can be thrown at it. His pace is slow, but he carries the sense through each long sentence with the intensity of his tone.

- ✔ **He crafted his speeches beautifully.** He was the master of language and rhetoric, and you hear fine music in his words. No one quite matched Churchill for the heroic cadence.

- ✔ **He wrote his speeches with passion and read them with passion too.** Many leaders have had fine words, but Churchill brought his language to life. Listen to his speech to Parliament in June 1940. His phrasing and passion at the end – 'If the British Empire and its Commonwealth last for a thousand years, men will still say, This was their finest hour' – are a perfect match of words and voice.

A Voice to Launch a Thousand Ships – Lauren Bacall

Every so often, a particular woman's voice has that certain something that thrills listeners to the core. Often such a voice is inextricably linked with a beautiful image, but sometimes the voice on its own is enough. Rather than sweet or cute, this voice is typically low, with just a suggestion of huskiness and a beautiful sense of timing. Some of the best actors have had this 'X factor': Kathleen Turner, Whoopi Goldberg and Barbra Streisand for example; Julia Roberts and Helen Mirren have it too.

My choice is Lauren Bacall, whose voice has depth and huskiness, and a commanding intensity even when she speaks softly. Her voice is there from the beginning of her career; listen to its riveting quality in her very first film, *To Have and Have Not*.

A Rich Voice that Thrills Audiences – Alan Rickman

When you ask people to think of a great voice, they often describe the mature voice of a male actor. People said of Richard Burton that he had a 'rich brown voice'. Everyone has their favourite, be it Sean Connery as James Bond, the wonderful gravelly tones of Jeremy Irons or the distinctive bass of James Earl Jones. These actors all share depth of tone, a slightly rough quality and a measured pace that makes them sound manly and trustworthy.

Alan Rickman possesses all these qualities in abundance and has one of the most admired voices in the profession. Whether he is playing a villain or a hero, his voice mesmerises you with its beautiful deep tone and the suspense of his timing. Most people recognise his voice as the complex character Snape in the *Harry Potter* films, but look out for a recording of him reading Shakespeare for a different kind of magic. As he speaks, you step into his private world, where he speaks the words with deep intensity as if for himself alone.

A Voice to Warm People's Hearts – Diane Sawyer

Some voices seem as comfortable as a warm sofa and a glass of red wine by a blazing fire; you hear a wonderful warmth in such a voice that draws you in. It's not just a matter of the depth and quality of the voice; the tone speaks of experience and sensibility and makes you trust the speaker like a personal friend, even when addressing an audience of millions. I selected American broadcaster Diane Sawyer of ABC to exemplify these qualities, though I could have chosen Katie Couric, also of ABC, or Sue McGregor of the BBC.

Diane Sawyer has a rounded mature voice. She speaks with genuine feeling, which connects powerfully with listeners. In this age of the sound-bite and clever repartee, her voice attracts you into her world and promotes trust and friendship.

A Voice that Gave Courage – Martin Luther King Jr

Martin Luther King Jr had an oratorical style that owed much to the church preaching tradition. When King spoke on issues that mattered to him, he dug deep into himself and out came a voice of pure heart and soul. His manner of speaking was nearer to music than anyone I can think of. No one had longer vowels or smoother phrases. Indeed, when he spoke, singing and speaking became one.

Listen again to his most famous speech, 'I have a dream' from August 1963. Hear how long he stretches out that signature phrase in its various repetitions. His audience catches his fervour and cannot resist joining in with its own musical affirmations. His sense of timing is impeccable too. He chooses a slow pace, but builds up to an exhilarating climax. To hear his passion at its strongest, listen to his last speech in April 1968 in which he prophetically talks about death.

The Voice of an Excellent Storyteller – Stephen Fry

Stephen Fry's English accent is well known far beyond the shores of the United Kingdom. He appears as himself on wordy quiz shows such as QI, but his voice is equally well known by children listening to his array of characters in audio books. He clearly loves words and loves language and is eager for you to share his enthusiasm for both.

Fry's voice with its educated English accent is rich and deep, and his timing exquisite. His vocabulary is enormous, his choice of words precise. When Stephen says a word like 'preposterous', it sounds utterly *preposterous*, and you can tell that he adores the very sound of the word. Fry can create similar experiences with a seemingly unlimited palette of words and phrases. Moreover, his ability to take on any voice he wishes is seemingly inexhaustible.

Critics have sometimes called him facile and too 'urbane', but I also hear a subtlety in his expression and language that belongs to the best British speaking tradition of Alistair Cooke, David Attenborough and other intelligent raconteurs.

A Voice of Hope – Wangari Maathai

In 2004, the Kenyan environmental and political activist Wangari Maathai won the Nobel Peace Prize for her contribution to sustainable development, democracy and peace. It is always tempting for a woman in a position of responsibility to assume male attributes in the way she communicates. Wangari Maathai didn't do that; she was a woman who found her own authentic way to communicate, and her voice is a mix of powerful intelligence, strong belief and fun.

She has a voice that connects. All her commitment and depth of feeling, her passion, determination, joy and lightness are in her voice – and give it a great range. She experienced the ups and downs of life and wasn't afraid to be herself. Hers is an wonderful example of a transparent voice – one that faithfully portrays who she is as she speaks her truth without being afraid to show strong emotion.

A generation of women are finding their own individual ways to show their strength as speakers on the world stage. Listen to Christine Lagarde, the managing director of the IMF, Noeleen Heyzer, Executive Secretary of the United Nations Economic and Social Commission for Asia and the Pacific (ESCAP) and Arundhati Roy, author and campaigning activist, to hear other women who have found styles both powerful and empathetic.

A Voice that Connects – Bill Clinton

Many politicians have fine voices and speak with power and authority. Bill Clinton has something more than that. Clinton's power isn't the quality of tone – his voice gets rougher by the year.

What Clinton has that many other politicians lack is the ability to connect with people in a surprisingly personal way. When he speaks, you don't have the impression of someone giving a speech; you get the sense that he is talking directly to you, simply and powerfully in normal colloquial language with the strong emphasis of everyday speech. You feel that he is there in the present moment and that he is thinking about what he is saying there and then – his words never sound scripted. His speeches to thousands feel like one-to-one conversation. Listen to his 1992 presidential debate against George Bush to hear the difference in approach between the two men.

An audience is never any old audience; you're always engaging with a group of people with whom you can, like Clinton, have a relationship. Audiences feel that Bill Clinton cares, and this feeling is an important part of his charisma (see Chapter 18 for more on charisma).

The Voice of a National Treasure – Judi Dench

Unlike Meryl Streep, with her amazing ability to speak in different tones and accents, whatever role Dame Judi Dench plays, audiences recognise her voice. But that voice! Her ability to express in sound the most difficult emotions and move you to the deepest level is shared by few actors.

Her secret is sensibility (see Chapter 15). She feels her way into each character and then the character's emotions are like a light shining within her, utterly genuine and convincing. The emotions are transparent in her voice, and as a result audiences feel them directly.

Dench is a magnificent example of how a great voice is always much more than a beautiful sound. Her voice is quite husky (her biography is called *With a Crack in Her Voice),* yet capable of the most subtle nuances of expression.

The actor Leonardo Di Caprio, working with her, said, 'You hear that voice, it's powerful . . . She has a way of commanding a scene in a room, and it's just astounding.' Other actors love her – and so does her public.

The Voice of a Creative Speaker – Ken Robinson

Certain speakers from every profession have the power to rivet listeners in different ways. I've taken Ken Robinson as an example of the many speakers who have freshness, originality and authenticity and combine these qualities with humour, surprise and variety.

Sir Ken Robinson is a university professor of education who has won international recognition for his work in education and creativity. He works with governments, international agencies and the world's largest companies and organisations, speaking to worldwide audiences about today's creative challenges.

The all-important quality in Ken Robinson's voice is its freshness. How he feels and thinks is how he sounds. You forget the voice and hear the person. Listen, for example, to Ken's talk on creativity in schools at www.ted.com. His delivery varies constantly, from solemn statement of belief to humorous aside to surprise revelation. His voice isn't the deepest, most sexy or most authoritative, but it is wonderfully transparent – it expresses the person he is. Just as your voice can be fresh and authentic – and be you!

Appendix A

Resources for Further Developing Your Voice

· ·

*H*ere are some suggestions of additional areas and ideas for voice development. The list is far from exhaustive, but I hope it gives you useful avenues of exploration for more information on voice coaching, looking after your voice and other topics.

Contacting the Author

Judy Apps: Voice of Influence, www.voiceofinfluence.co.uk

My website has current information and booking details for my regular voice, presentation, and neuro-linguistic programming (NLP) workshops in London; plus a host of goodies to freely download including my newsletter, articles and e-courses on voice, dealing with performance anxiety, raising your profile and related topics. Contact me by email at info@voiceofinfluence.co.uk for one-to-one coaching with me in person or via Skype or phone.

Voice Coaching

Voice coaching includes a broad spectrum of activities, and practitioners come with a variety of qualifications and skills.

- ✔ **A good coach with an acting background** has many skills to help you develop your voice well and create an impact with an audience. If you want an influential voice, make sure that you're also discovering how to be authentic and connect strongly with people, not just how to articulate clearly and project your voice.

- ✔ **A good voice coach with a singing background** is skilful in voice control, knows healthy ways to expand the use of your voice and has good techniques for caring for your voice. Make sure that your coach understands the spoken voice as well because not everything translates from singing to speech.

- ✔ **An elocution teacher or elocution coach** can help you with speech clarity and expressiveness and reducing a regional accent if required. Pronunciation is often the main focus.

- ✔ **An experienced NLP professional** can help you to deal with vocal blocks through identifying and working through the psychological or root causes of voice difficulties. In the UK, a good place to start is the Association of NLP (www.anlp.org). If you can, find an NLP Practitioner with voice experience as well.

- ✔ **An NLP professional with experience of working with stuttering** can help you become more fluent in your speech. Contact Bob Bodenhamer at www.masteringstuttering.com. You can find other help with stuttering from:

  - **British Stammering Association (BSA):** www.stammering.org
  - **Minnesota State University, The Stuttering Home Page:** www.mnsu.edu/comdis/kuster
  - **National Stuttering Association (NSA):** www.nsastutter.org

The best way to find a voice coach or speaking coach is through personal recommendation. Think about what exactly you need and how you prefer being coached – face-to-face, Skype or phone, regular sessions or a one-off meeting to prepare for a particular speech or presentation. Then test the waters with your coach candidates. What experience do they bring? Do they walk their talk? Schedule an initial face-to-face session with a coach before going ahead with a series of sessions. You can find lists of coaches here:

- ✔ **Natural Voice Practitioners Network:** www.naturalvoice.net/index.asp
- ✔ **Voice and Speech Trainers Association (VASTA):** www.vasta.org
- ✔ **Voicesource:** www.voicesource.co.uk/teachers

Books and Audio

Here are a few of my favourite books on voice, public speaking and presentations, selected for readability and the authors' practical approach.

Voice

The Actor Speaks: Voice and the Performer by Patsy Rodenburg (Methuen)

Freeing the Natural Voice by Kristin Linklater (Drama)

The Human Voice: The Story of a Remarkable Talent by Anne Karpf (Bloomsbury)

I Have a Voice: How to Stop Stuttering by Bobby G. Bodenhamer (Crown House)

Voice of Influence: How to Get People to Love to Listen to You by Judy Apps (Crown House)

Public speaking and presentations
Butterflies and Sweaty Palms: 25 Sure-fire Ways to Speak and Present with Confidence by Judy Apps (Crown House)

Going Public: Practical Guide to Developing Personal Charisma by Hal Milton (HCI)

My Lessons With Kumi: How I Learned to Perform with Confidence in Life and Work by Michael Colgrass (Grinder DeLozier Associates)

Peak Performance Presentations: How to Present with Passion and Purpose by Richard Olivier and Nicholas Janni (Articulate Press)

Public Speaking and Presentations For Dummies by Rob Yeung and Malcolm Kushner (Wiley)

Voice-related subjects
The following list includes subjects I touch upon in the book:

Alexander Technique: *Use Of The Self* by F. M. Alexander (Orion)

Feldenkrais: *Awareness through Movement: Easy-to-Do Health Exercises to Improve Your Posture, Vision, Imagination, and Personal Awareness* by Moshe Feldenkrais (Harper Collins)

Body Language: *Body Language For Dummies* by Elizabeth Kuhnke (Wiley)

Self-Confidence: *Confidence For Dummies* by Kate Burton and Brinley Platts (Wiley)

Presence: *The Power of Now: A Guide to Spiritual Enlightenment* by Eckhart Tolle (Hodder & Stoughton)

Relaxation: *Relaxation For Dummies* by Shamash Alidina (Wiley)

Audio
YouTube is an excellent source for hearing speakers and particular speeches that I mention in this book (www.youtube.com).

Accents and dialects

British Library Sounds (sounds.bl.uk) offers a huge range of short audio clips of different accents from across the UK.

The Speech Accent Archive (http://accent.gmu.edu) offers audio clips of different accents from across North America.

Historical recordings

American Rhetoric (www.americanrhetoric.com/speechbank.htm) offers audio clips and transcripts of speeches by 100 top American politicians and public figures.

Michigan University (www.lib.msu.edu/cs/branches/vvl/presidents) archives sound recordings of more than 20 US presidents.

Miller Centre (millercenter.org) includes a large collection of American historical recordings.

Useful Mind-Body Activities for Speakers

Your voice is affected by what's going on in your mind and by the balance and freedom of your body. For this reason, many people who work on their voices also take part in activities that stretch and relax their bodies and minds. I mention these activities in this book:

Alexander Technique: www.alexandertechnique.com The Alexander Technique helps you discover your natural body balance and poise that you may have lost through habits of tension and excessive effort.

Feldenkrais: www.feldenkrais.com Through the Feldenkrais Method, you increase awareness of your body and rediscover comfort in your body movements.

Aikido: www.aikidoyuishinkai.com The martial art of Aikido, 'the way of harmony with nature', uses balance and relaxed alertness to redirect an aggressor's force with well-timed, flowing, circular movements. The practice offers you balance, confidence and flow as a speaker.

Voice Care

Here's a short list of professional voice bodies and voice associations whose websites are good sources of information on voice. I also include a list of resources for getting medical and therapeutic help for your voice – after you've first consulted your doctor.

British Voice Association: www.british-voice-association.com/archive.htm

Voice Care Network UK: www.voicecare.org.uk

The Voice Foundation: www.voicefoundation.org

Voice Care for Teachers: www.education.vic.gov.au/hr/ohs/hazards/voice.htm

The American Speech-Language-Hearing Association: www.asha.org

The Association of Speech and Language Therapists in Independent Practice: www.helpwithtalking.com

The Royal College of Speech and Language Therapists: www.rcslt.org

The British Voice Association lists voice clinics in the UK: www.british-voice-association.com/voice_clinics.htm

Appendix B

Audio Tracks

• •

*V*oice and Speaking Skills For Dummies comes with plenty of helpful audio tracks – indicated in the chapters by the 'Play This' icon.

In this appendix, I provide a complete track listing.

Discovering What's On the Audio Tracks

Table B-1 lists all the tracks along with a description, so you can quickly look up any exercise.

Table B-1 *Voice and Speaking Skills For Dummies* Audio Tracks

Track	Description
1	Introduction.
2	Meeting people in different ways (Chapter 3).
3	Breathing naturally (Chapter 4).
4	Breathing using your diaphragm (Chapter 4).
5	Whispering (Chapter 4).
6	Turning breath into sounds and words (Chapter 4).
7	Long, flowing phrases (Chapter 4).
8	The floating upwards exercise (Chapter 5).
9	Moving and speaking (Chapter 5).
10	Consonant workout (Chapter 6).
11	Speaking on the flow of air (Chapter 6).
12	Demonstrating vowel sounds (Chapter 6).
13	Descriptive vowel sounds (Chapter 6).
14	Long consonants (Chapter 6).

(continued)

Table B-1 *(continued)*

Track	Description
15	Expressive word games with consonants (Chapter 6).
16	Short consonants (Chapter 6).
17	Projecting your voice (Chapter 7).
18	Changing your meaning with volume (Chapter 7).
19	Crescendo and decrescendo (Chapter 7).
20	Speaking slowly (Chapter 7).
21	Emphasis exercise (Chapter 8).
22	Emphasis and meaning (Chapter 8).
23	Rhythm and impact (Chapter 8).
24	Varying the rhythm (Chapter 8).
25	Pitch variations (Chapter 8).
26	The rhetorical rule of three (Chapter 8).
27	Alliteration (Chapter 8).
28	Finding your high voice and your low voice (Chapter 9).
29	Chest voice (Chapter 9).
30	Head voice (Chapter 9).
31	Heart voice (Chapter 9).
32	Gut voice (Chapter 9).
33	Demonstrating different resonances (Chapter 9).
34	Speaking mechanically (Chapter 10).
35	Prima donna voices (Chapter 10).
36	Creating rapport in questions (Chapter 14).
37	The effect of different tones (Chapter 15).
38	Catching the attention of a group (Chapter 16).
39	Stepping in and out of the moment (Chapter 16).

Index

FOR DUMMIES®

Making Everything Easier!™

UK editions

BUSINESS

Bookkeeping FOR DUMMIES
978-0-470-97626-5

Persuasion & Influence FOR DUMMIES
978-0-470-74737-7

Starting & Running a Business ALL-IN-ONE FOR DUMMIES
978-1-119-97527-4

Asperger's Syndrome For Dummies
978-0-470-66087-4

Basic Maths For Dummies
978-1-119-97452-9

Body Language For Dummies,
2nd Edition
978-1-119-95351-7

Boosting Self-Esteem For Dummies
978-0-470-74193-1

British Sign Language For Dummies
978-0-470-69477-0

Cricket For Dummies
978-0-470-03454-5

Diabetes For Dummies, 3rd Edition
978-0-470-97711-8

Electronics For Dummies
978-0-470-68178-7

English Grammar For Dummies
978-0-470-05752-0

Flirting For Dummies
978-0-470-74259-4

IBS For Dummies
978-0-470-51737-6

Improving Your Relationship
For Dummies
978-0-470-68472-6

ITIL For Dummies
978-1-119-95013-4

Management For Dummies,
2nd Edition
978-0-470-97769-9

Neuro-linguistic Programming
For Dummies, 2nd Edition
978-0-470-66543-5

Nutrition For Dummies, 2nd Edition
978-0-470-97276-2

Organic Gardening For Dummies
978-1-119-97706-3

REFERENCE

British Politics FOR DUMMIES
978-0-470-68637-9

DIY FOR DUMMIES
978-0-470-97450-6

Dad's Guide to Pregnancy FOR DUMMIES
978-1-119-97660-8

HOBBIES

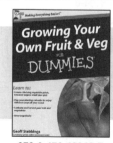

Growing Your Own Fruit & Veg FOR DUMMIES
978-0-470-69960-7

Keeping Chickens FOR DUMMIES
978-1-119-99417-6

Beekeeping FOR DUMMIES
978-1-119-97250-1

Available wherever books are sold. For more information or to order direct go to www.wiley.com or call +44 (0) 1243 843291

11-37870

FOR DUMMIES®

Making Everything Easier!™

COMPUTER BASICS

978-0-470-57829-2

978-0-470-61454-9

978-0-470-49743-2

Access 2010 For Dummies
978-0-470-49747-0

Android Application Development For Dummies
978-0-470-77018-4

AutoCAD 2011 For Dummies
978-0-470-59539-8

C++ For Dummies, 6th Edition
978-0-470-31726-6

Computers For Seniors For Dummies, 2nd Edition
978-0-470-53483-0

~~Dreamweaver CS5 For Dummies~~

DIGITAL PHOTOGRAPHY

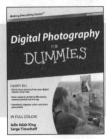

978-0-470-25074-7

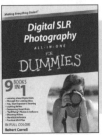

978-0-470-76878-5

978-1-118-00472-2

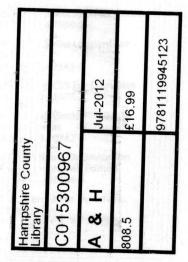
MICROSOFT OFFICE 2010

978-0-470-48998-7

978-0-470-58302-9

978-0-470-48953-6

Web Analytics For Dummies
978-0-470-09824-0

Word 2010 For Dummies
978-0-470-48772-3

WordPress For Dummies, 4th Edition
978-1-118-07342-1

Available wherever books are sold. For more information or to order direct go to
www.wiley.com or call +44 (0) 1243 843291

11-37870